DEAN KOONTZ'S
FRANKENSTEIN

Prodigal Son
volume one

CREATED BY
**DEAN KOONTZ
& KEVIN J. ANDERSON**

WRITTEN BY
CHUCK DIXON

PENCILS BY
BRETT BOOTH

COLORS BY
COLOR DOJO, ANDREW DALHOUSE, and MOHAN

LETTERING BY
BILL TORTOLINI

EDITED BY
**MIKE RAICHT, BRIAN SMITH,
RICH YOUNG, DAVID LAWRENCE, and DEREK RUIZ**

DEL
REY

BALLANTINE BOOKS • NEW YORK

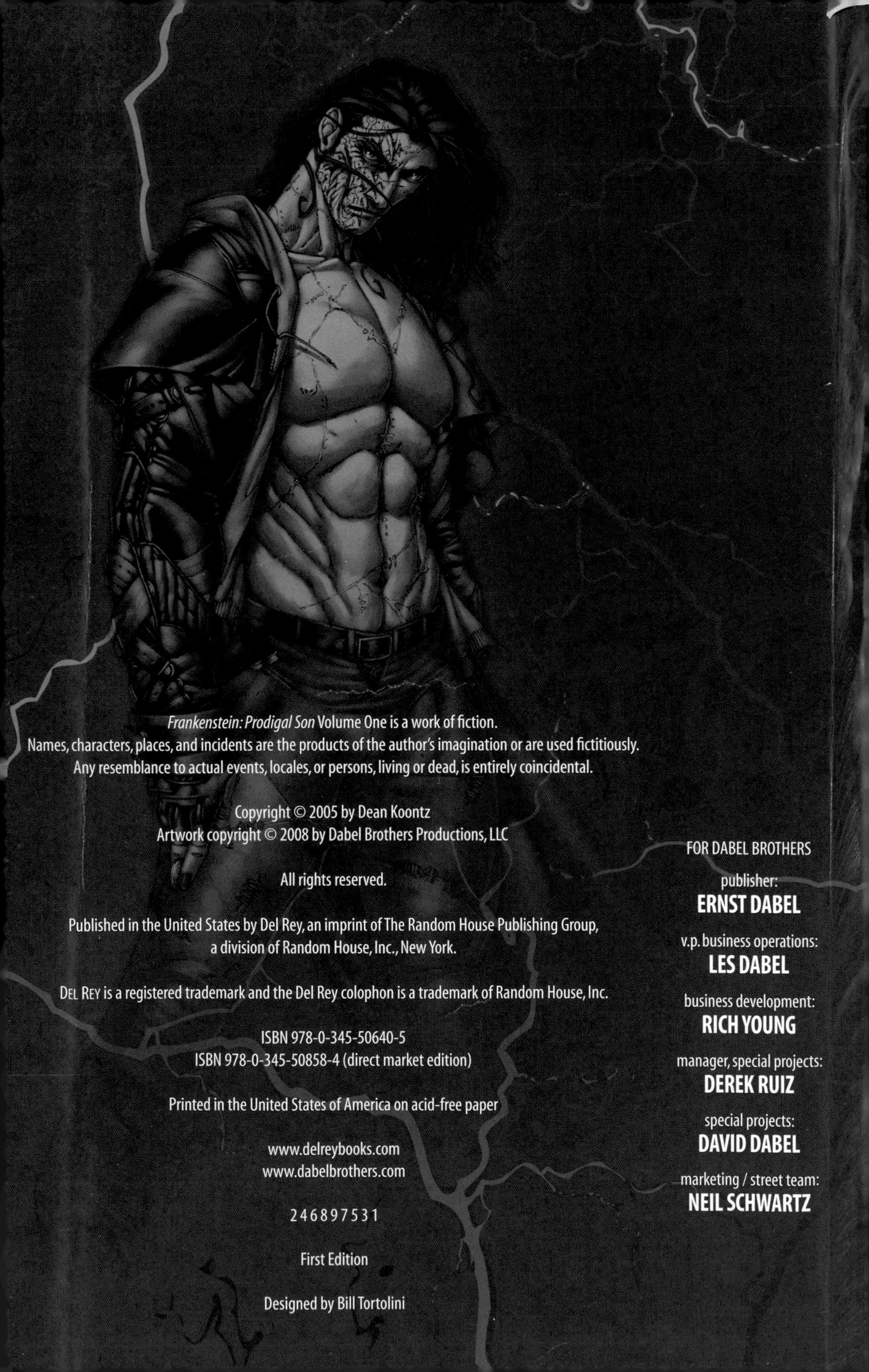

Frankenstein: Prodigal Son Volume One is a work of fiction.
Names, characters, places, and incidents are the products of the author's imagination or are used fictitiously.
Any resemblance to actual events, locales, or persons, living or dead, is entirely coincidental.

Published in the United States by Del Rey, an imprint of The Random House Publishing Group,
a division of Random House, Inc., New York.

Del Rey is a registered trademark and the Del Rey colophon is a trademark of Random House, Inc.

ISBN 978-0-345-50640-5
ISBN 978-0-345-50858-4 (direct market edition)

Printed in the United States of America on acid-free paper

www.delreybooks.com
www.dabelbrothers.com

2 4 6 8 9 7 5 3 1

First Edition

Designed by Bill Tortolini

FOR DABEL BROTHERS

publisher:
ERNST DABEL

v.p. business operations:
LES DABEL

business development:
RICH YOUNG

manager, special projects:
DEREK RUIZ

special projects:
DAVID DABEL

marketing / street team:
NEIL SCHWARTZ

From the time I saw the best of the Frankenstein films on TV when I was eleven—the original featuring Karloff's remarkable performance, *Bride of Frankenstein,* and *Son of Frankenstein*— I relished them even though they gave me the worst nightmares of my life. In fact, I continued to have Frankenstein-themed nightmares into my thirties, a few times a year crying out in my sleep and waking in a sweat. Interestingly, when the Frankenstein dreams stopped, I ceased having nightmares of any kind, and for many years, my sleep has been undisturbed.

I believe that, as a child, I unconsciously saw Frankenstein's monster as a symbol for my father, whose potential for violence and whose many kinds of recklessness kept our lives always on the edge of chaos. I never dreamed of being pursued by the monster through woods or through any kind of open-air venue; always, it was in our house, and always, I was cornered by it, either in my room or in the cellar.

The original novel is mostly mistaught in our universities these days, as professors twist Mary Shelley's themes—and even turn them upside down—to endorse this or that modern attitude or political viewpoint. Of the several reasons why the book is a classic, perhaps the most important is the portrayal of Victor Frankenstein as a compassionate utopian destroyed by hubris. The history of humanity is soaked in blood precisely because we throw ourselves into the pursuit of one utopia after another, determined to perfect this world that cannot be perfected. Of all centuries, the twentieth was the bloodiest because of Hitler's National Socialism, Lenin's and Stalin's and Mao's and Pol Pot's and Castro's versions of communism; as many as 200 million were murdered or killed in war because of these utopian schemes. Victor Frankenstein, utopian of the first order, hoped to perfect God's creation, to reanimate the deceased and thus defeat death, and his project could result only in calamity, for it was against the natural law and common sense.

Indeed, *Frankenstein* resonated with me also because my father was a utopian of a kind, a utopian not in a grand philosophical sense but in his approach to his working life. He fancied himself an inventor, and he believed that he was always one invention away from great wealth, one invention or one slick business plan or one clever gimmick away from achieving an ideal life— without having to work for it. Reality always destroys utopians, and we are fortunate when we are not pulled into their vortex and destroyed with them.

Mary Shelley may also have been the first novelist to foresee that science would eventually be bent by utopians to their service and would in many quarters degenerate into scientism, as dogmatic as the most narrowly conceived religions. In our time, scientism gins up one fear after another in the masses, based on bad science, for the purpose of making them easier for utopian theorists to control.

This is why it seemed to me appropriate to update the Frankenstein legend to our time. We live in a hubristic age, when politicians imagine themselves to be messiahs and when many in the sciences frankly discuss their dreams of creating a "post-human" civilization of genetically engineered supermen, ignorant of the fact that like minds have often come before them and have left no legacy but death, destruction, and despair.

Dean Koontz
October 2008

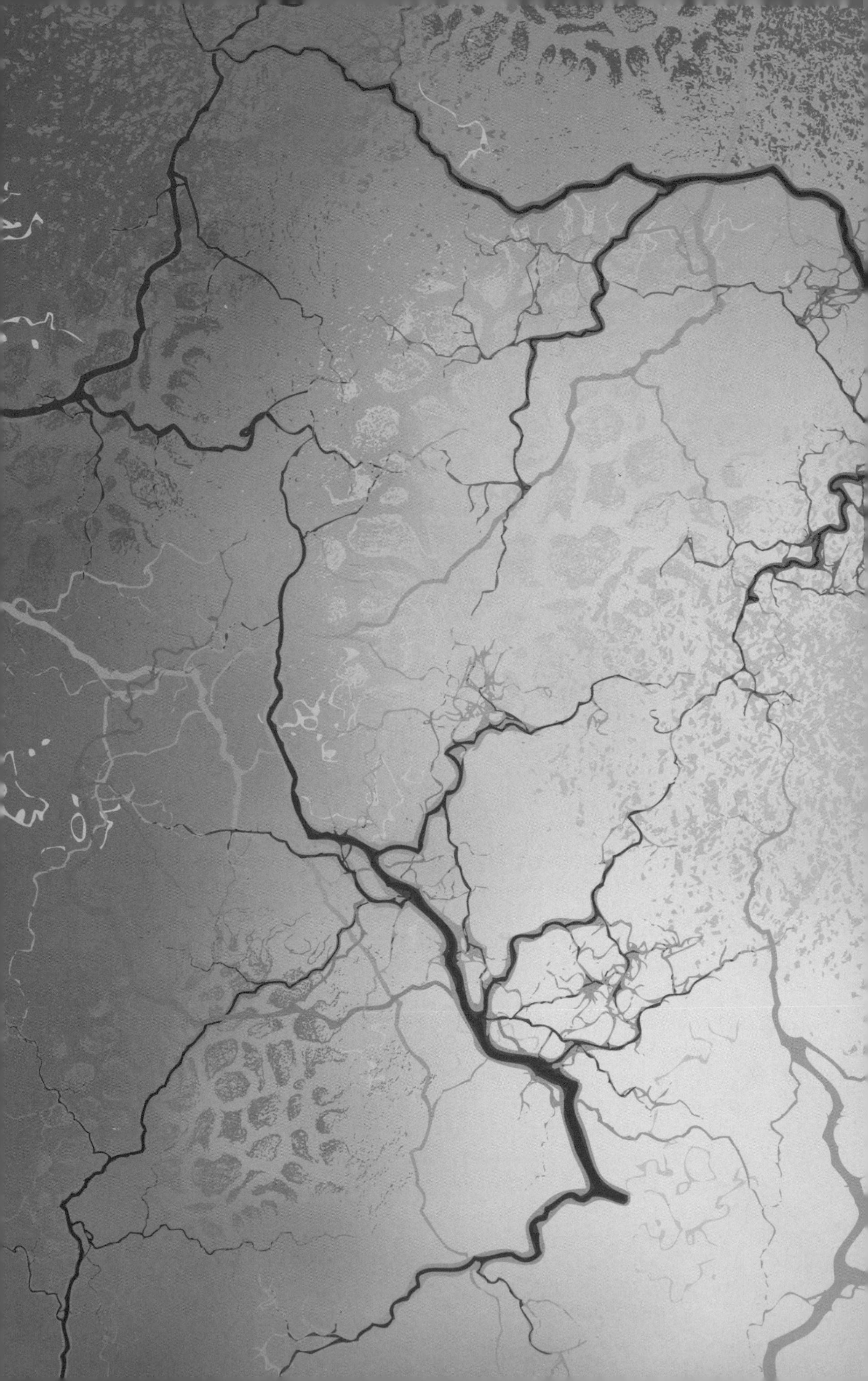

chapter One

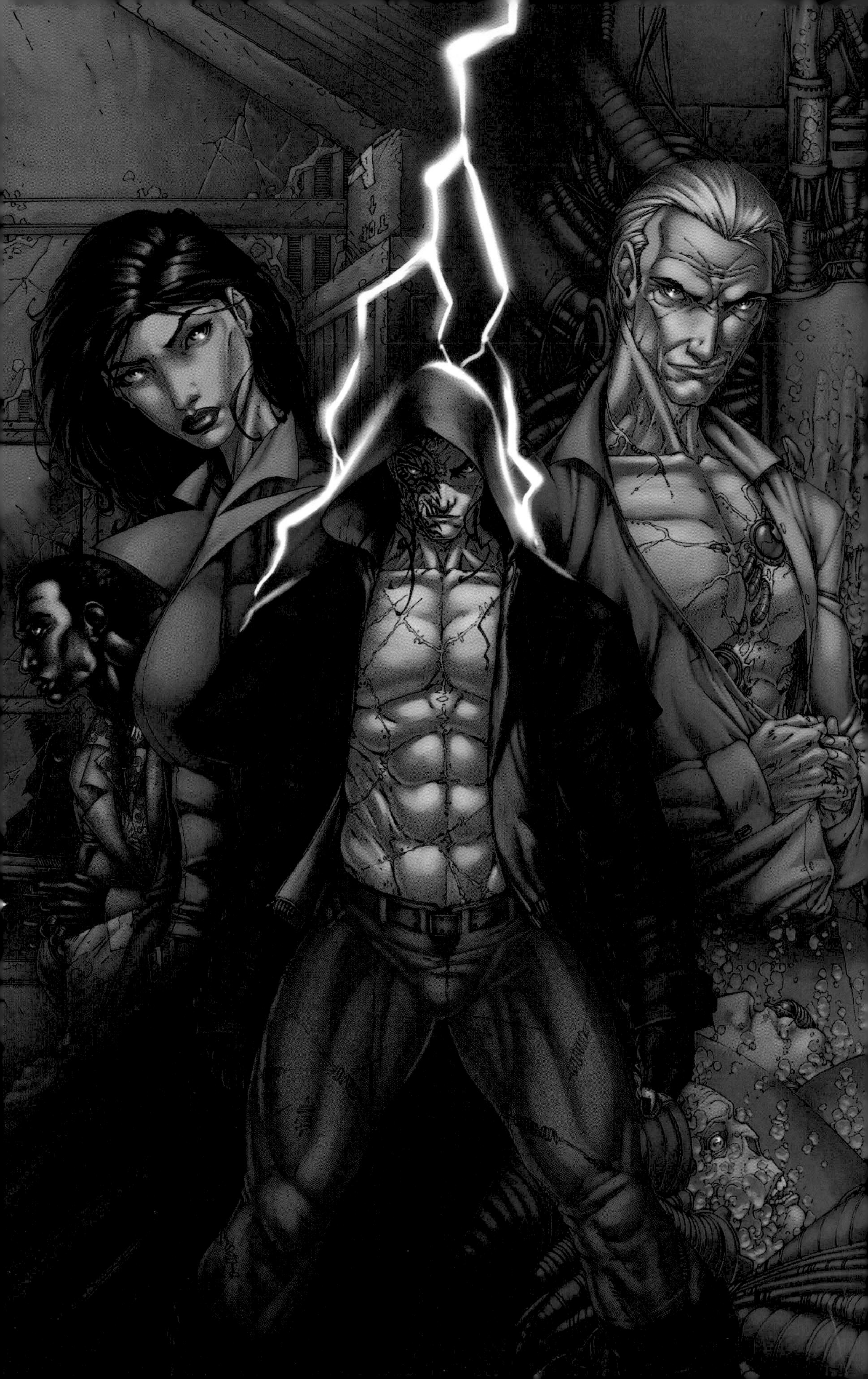

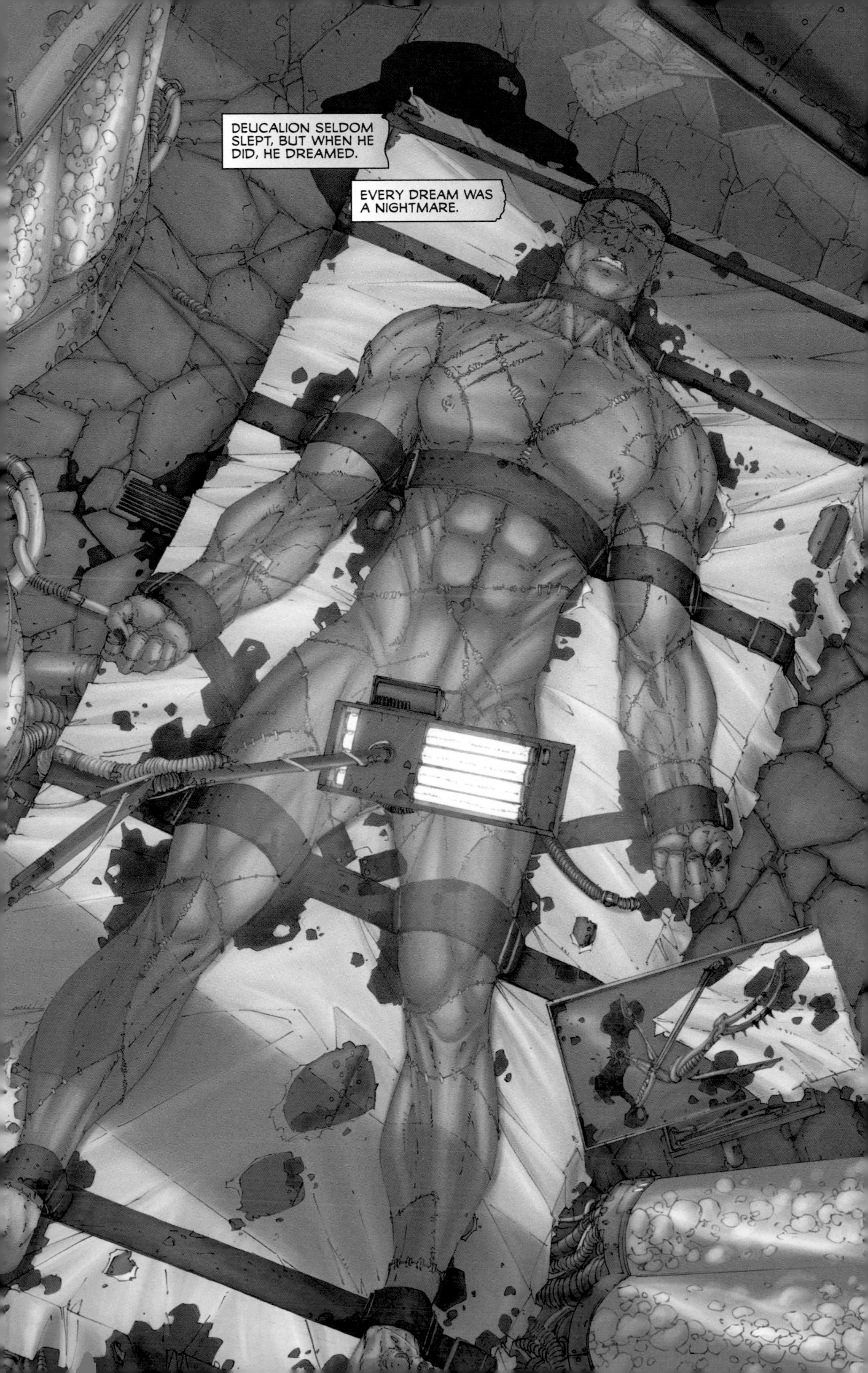
DEUCALION SELDOM SLEPT, BUT WHEN HE DID, HE DREAMED.
EVERY DREAM WAS A NIGHTMARE.

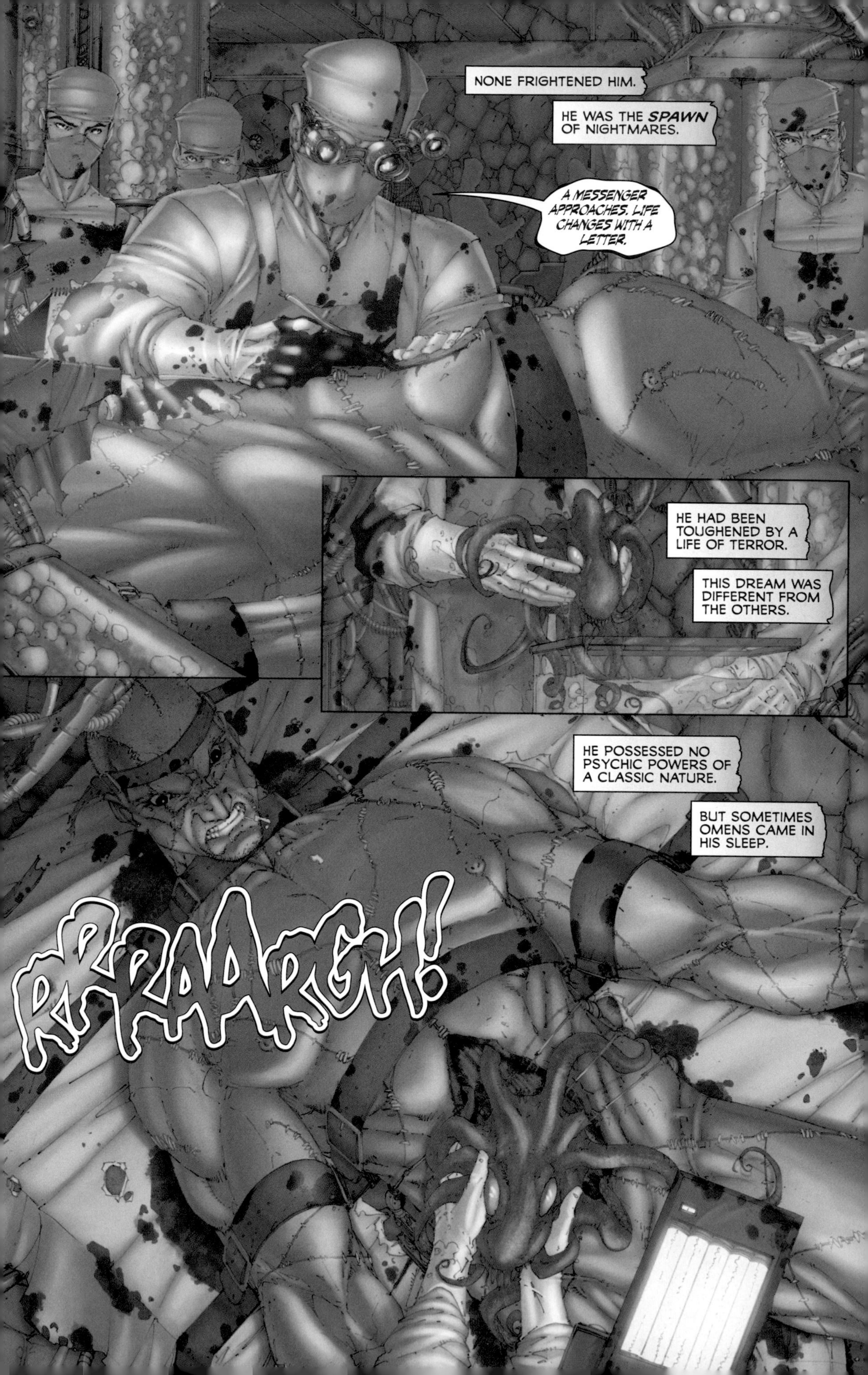
NONE FRIGHTENED HIM.
HE WAS THE *SPAWN* OF NIGHTMARES.
A MESSENGER APPROACHES. LIFE CHANGES WITH A LETTER.
HE HAD BEEN TOUGHENED BY A LIFE OF TERROR.
THIS DREAM WAS DIFFERENT FROM THE OTHERS.
HE POSSESSED NO PSYCHIC POWERS OF A CLASSIC NATURE.
BUT SOMETIMES OMENS CAME IN HIS SLEEP.
RRRAARGH!

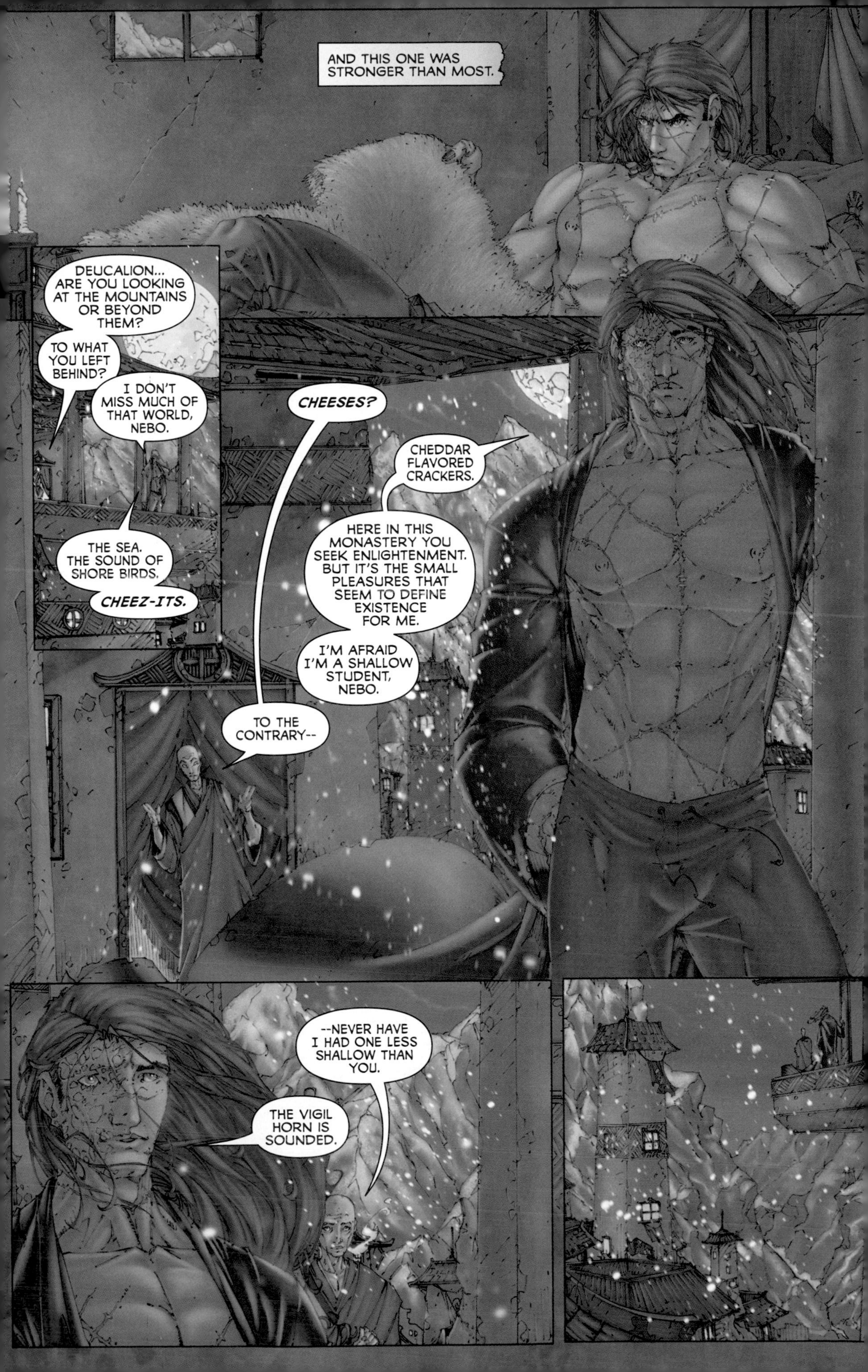
AND THIS ONE WAS STRONGER THAN MOST.
DEUCALION... ARE YOU LOOKING AT THE MOUNTAINS OR BEYOND THEM?
TO WHAT YOU LEFT BEHIND?
I DON'T MISS MUCH OF THAT WORLD, NEBO.
THE SEA. THE SOUND OF SHORE BIRDS.
CHEEZ-ITS.
CHEESES?
CHEDDAR FLAVORED CRACKERS.
HERE IN THIS MONASTERY YOU SEEK ENLIGHTENMENT. BUT IT'S THE SMALL PLEASURES THAT SEEM TO DEFINE EXISTENCE FOR ME.
I'M AFRAID I'M A SHALLOW STUDENT, NEBO.
TO THE CONTRARY--
--NEVER HAVE I HAD ONE LESS SHALLOW THAN YOU.
THE VIGIL HORN IS SOUNDED.

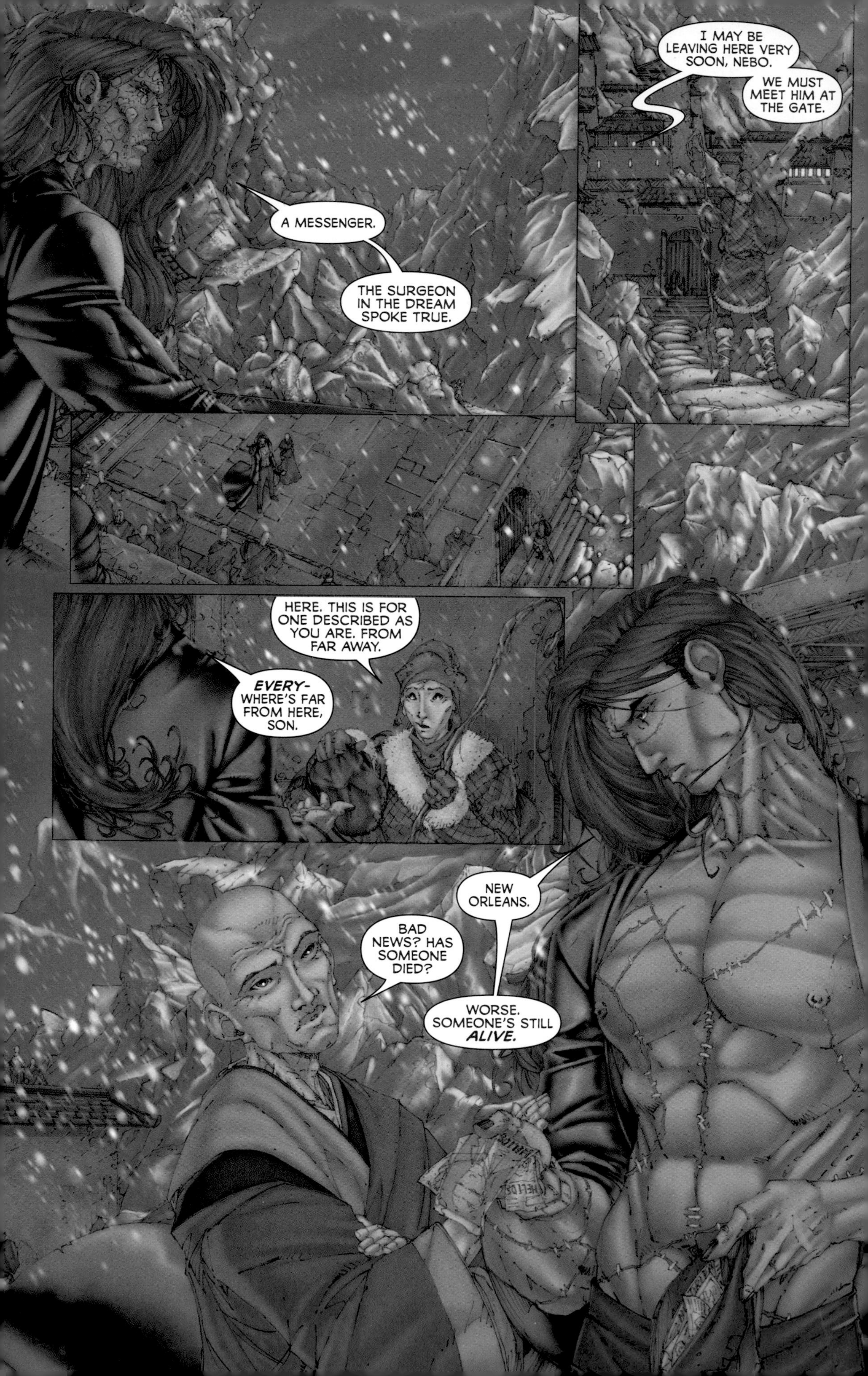
A MESSENGER.
THE SURGEON IN THE DREAM SPOKE TRUE.
I MAY BE LEAVING HERE VERY SOON, NEBO.
WE MUST MEET HIM AT THE GATE.
HERE. THIS IS FOR ONE DESCRIBED AS YOU ARE. FROM FAR AWAY.
EVERY-WHERE'S FAR FROM HERE, SON.
NEW ORLEANS.
BAD NEWS? HAS SOMEONE DIED?
WORSE. SOMEONE'S STILL ALIVE.

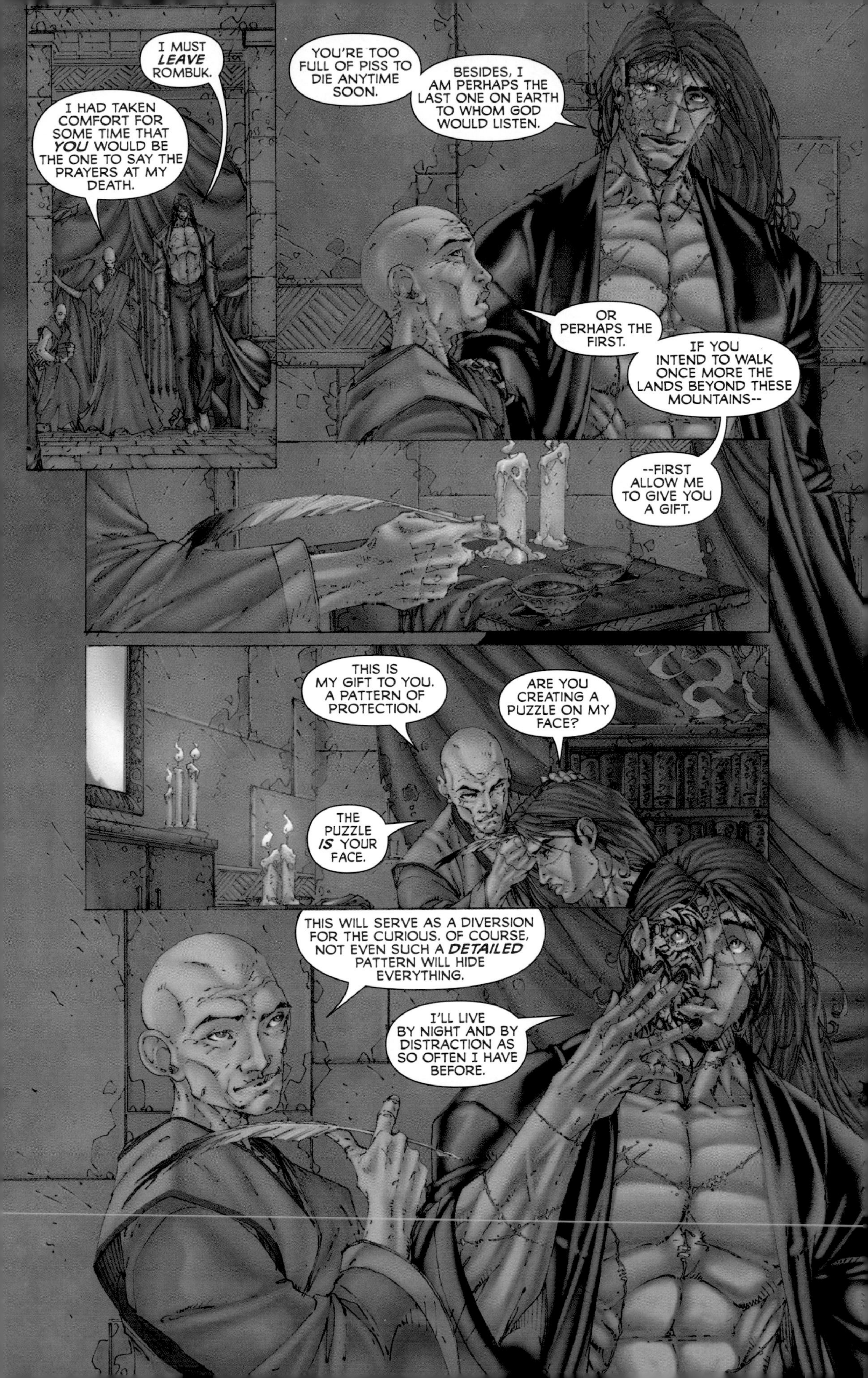
I MUST *LEAVE* ROMBUK.
I HAD TAKEN COMFORT FOR SOME TIME THAT *YOU* WOULD BE THE ONE TO SAY THE PRAYERS AT MY DEATH.
YOU'RE TOO FULL OF PISS TO DIE ANYTIME SOON.
BESIDES, I AM PERHAPS THE LAST ONE ON EARTH TO WHOM GOD WOULD LISTEN.
OR PERHAPS THE FIRST.
IF YOU INTEND TO WALK ONCE MORE THE LANDS BEYOND THESE MOUNTAINS--
--FIRST ALLOW ME TO GIVE YOU A GIFT.
THIS IS MY GIFT TO YOU. A PATTERN OF PROTECTION.
ARE YOU CREATING A PUZZLE ON MY FACE?
THE PUZZLE *IS* YOUR FACE.
THIS WILL SERVE AS A DIVERSION FOR THE CURIOUS. OF COURSE, NOT EVEN SUCH A *DETAILED* PATTERN WILL HIDE EVERYTHING.
I'LL LIVE BY NIGHT AND BY DISTRACTION AS SO OFTEN I HAVE BEFORE.

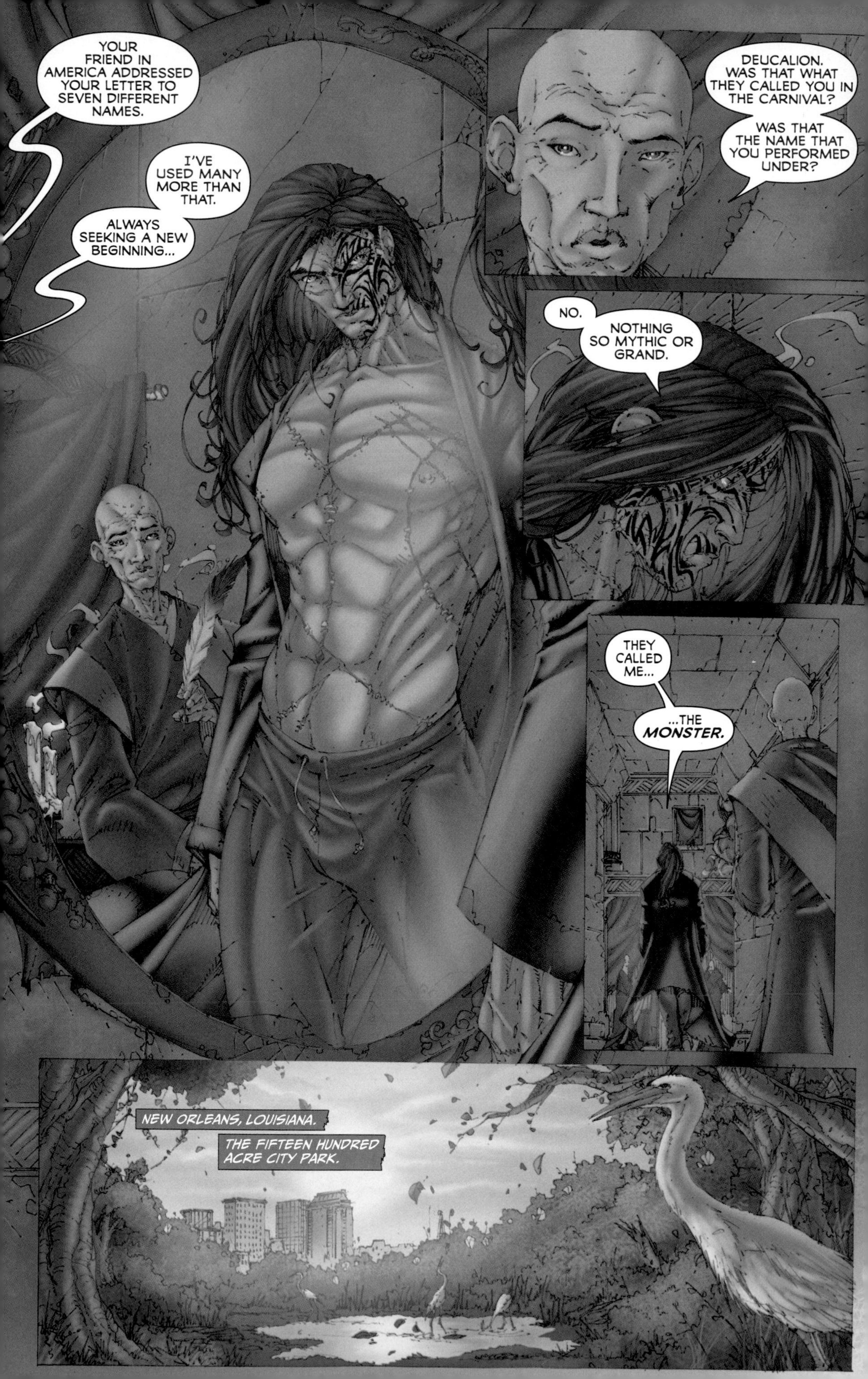
YOUR FRIEND IN AMERICA ADDRESSED YOUR LETTER TO SEVEN DIFFERENT NAMES.
I'VE USED MANY MORE THAN THAT.
ALWAYS SEEKING A NEW BEGINNING...
DEUCALION. WAS THAT WHAT THEY CALLED YOU IN THE CARNIVAL?
WAS THAT THE NAME THAT YOU PERFORMED UNDER?
NO.
NOTHING SO MYTHIC OR GRAND.
THEY CALLED ME...
...THE *MONSTER.*
NEW ORLEANS, LOUISIANA.
THE FIFTEEN HUNDRED ACRE CITY PARK.

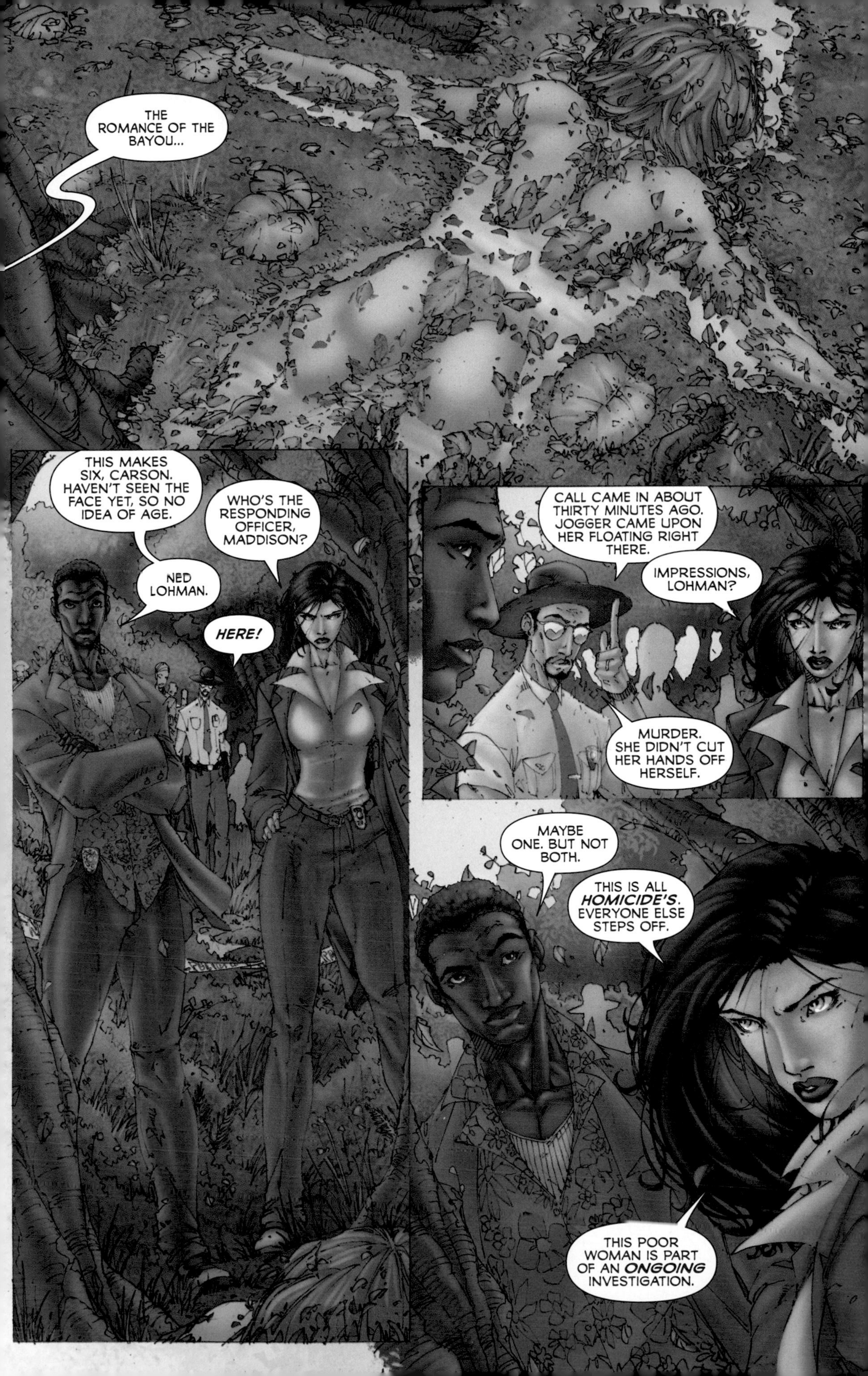
THE ROMANCE OF THE BAYOU...
THIS MAKES SIX, CARSON. HAVEN'T SEEN THE FACE YET, SO NO IDEA OF AGE.
WHO'S THE RESPONDING OFFICER, MADDISON?
NED LOHMAN.
HERE!
CALL CAME IN ABOUT THIRTY MINUTES AGO. JOGGER CAME UPON HER FLOATING RIGHT THERE.
IMPRESSIONS, LOHMAN?
MURDER. SHE DIDN'T CUT HER HANDS OFF HERSELF.
MAYBE ONE. BUT NOT BOTH.
THIS IS ALL *HOMICIDE'S*. EVERYONE ELSE STEPS OFF.
THIS POOR WOMAN IS PART OF AN *ONGOING* INVESTIGATION.

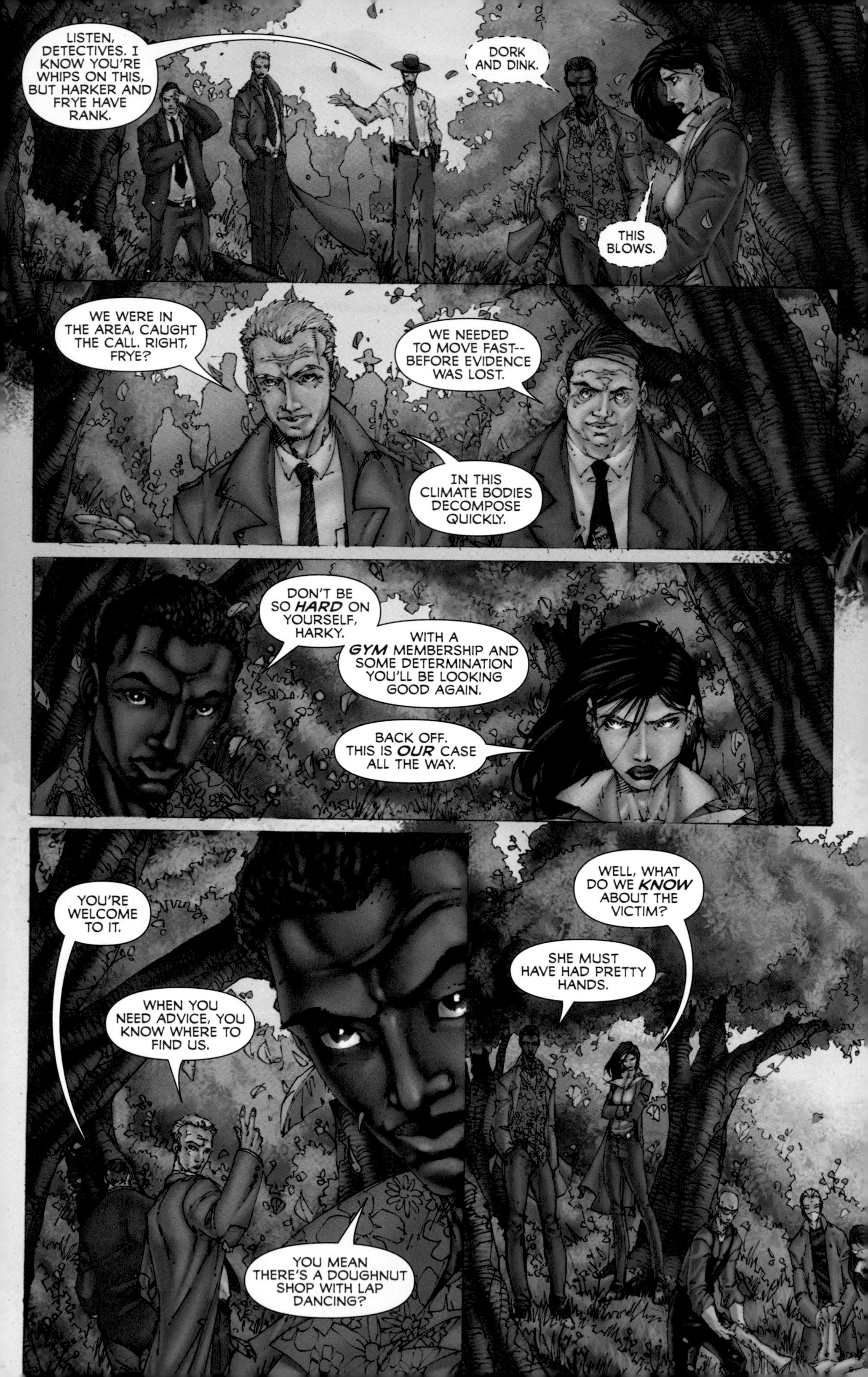
LISTEN, DETECTIVES. I KNOW YOU'RE WHIPS ON THIS, BUT HARKER AND FRYE HAVE RANK.
DORK AND DINK.
THIS BLOWS.
WE WERE IN THE AREA, CAUGHT THE CALL. RIGHT, FRYE?
WE NEEDED TO MOVE FAST-- BEFORE EVIDENCE WAS LOST.
IN THIS CLIMATE BODIES DECOMPOSE QUICKLY.
DON'T BE SO HARD ON YOURSELF, HARKY.
WITH A GYM MEMBERSHIP AND SOME DETERMINATION YOU'LL BE LOOKING GOOD AGAIN.
BACK OFF. THIS IS OUR CASE ALL THE WAY.
YOU'RE WELCOME TO IT.
WHEN YOU NEED ADVICE, YOU KNOW WHERE TO FIND US.
YOU MEAN THERE'S A DOUGHNUT SHOP WITH LAP DANCING?
WELL, WHAT DO WE KNOW ABOUT THE VICTIM?
SHE MUST HAVE HAD PRETTY HANDS.

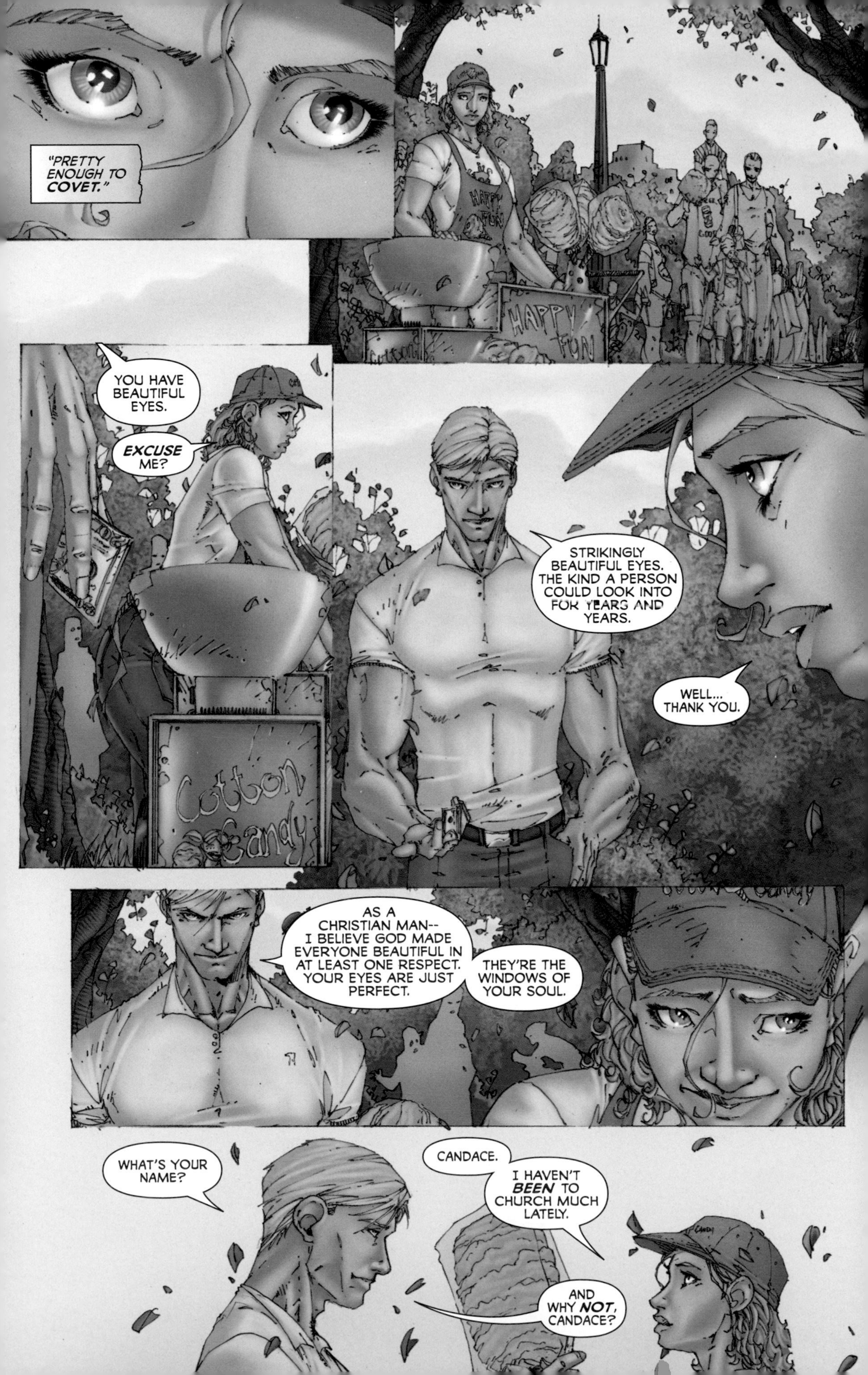
"PRETTY ENOUGH TO COVET."
YOU HAVE BEAUTIFUL EYES.
EXCUSE ME?
STRIKINGLY BEAUTIFUL EYES. THE KIND A PERSON COULD LOOK INTO FOR YEARS AND YEARS.
WELL... THANK YOU.
AS A CHRISTIAN MAN-- I BELIEVE GOD MADE EVERYONE BEAUTIFUL IN AT LEAST ONE RESPECT. YOUR EYES ARE JUST PERFECT.
THEY'RE THE WINDOWS OF YOUR SOUL.
WHAT'S YOUR NAME?
CANDACE.
I HAVEN'T BEEN TO CHURCH MUCH LATELY.
AND WHY NOT, CANDACE?
HAPPY FUN
Cotton Candy

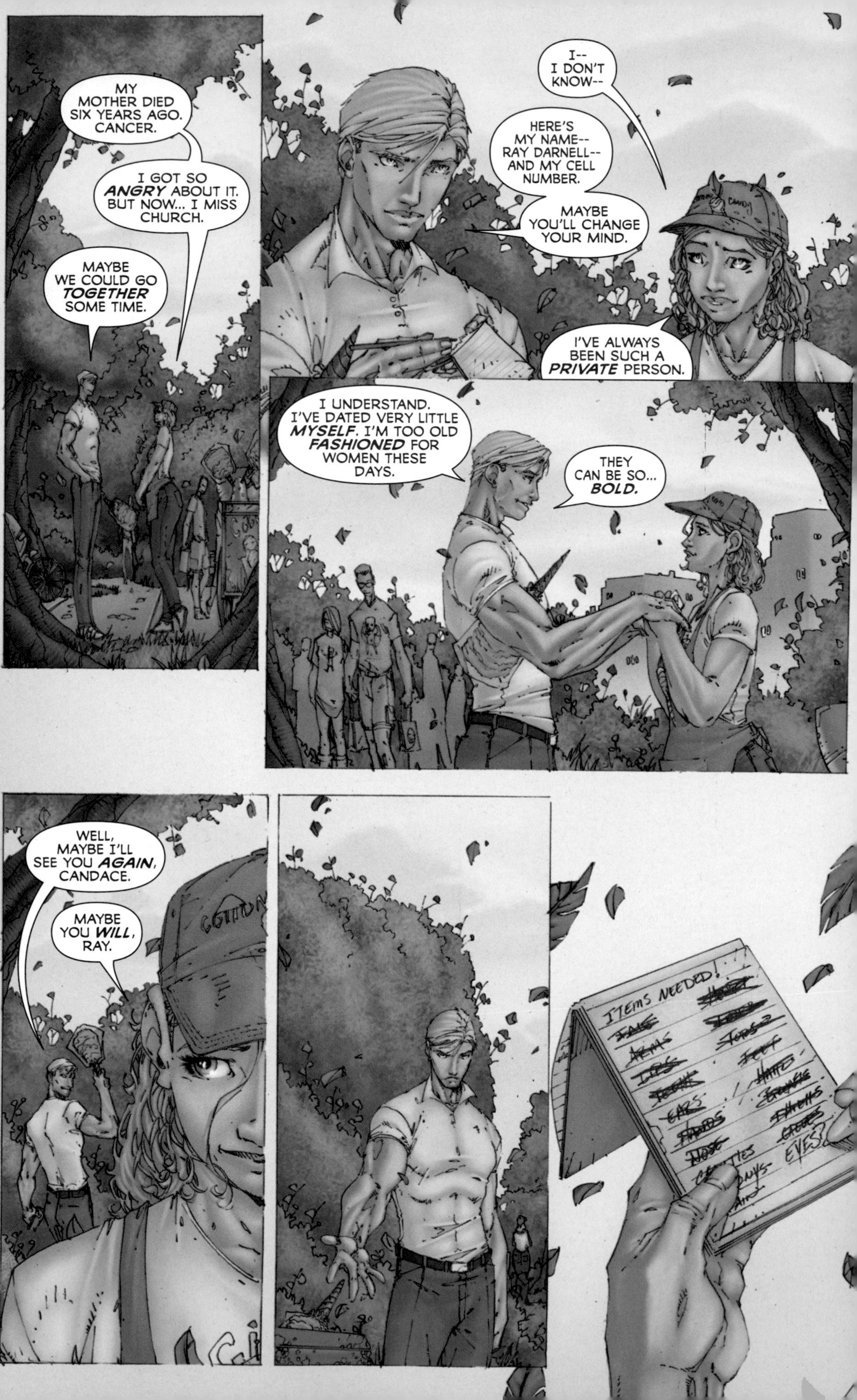
MY MOTHER DIED SIX YEARS AGO. CANCER.
I GOT SO ANGRY ABOUT IT. BUT NOW... I MISS CHURCH.
MAYBE WE COULD GO TOGETHER SOME TIME.
I-- I DON'T KNOW--
HERE'S MY NAME-- RAY DARNELL-- AND MY CELL NUMBER.
MAYBE YOU'LL CHANGE YOUR MIND.
I'VE ALWAYS BEEN SUCH A PRIVATE PERSON.
I UNDERSTAND. I'VE DATED VERY LITTLE MYSELF. I'M TOO OLD FASHIONED FOR WOMEN THESE DAYS.
THEY CAN BE SO... BOLD.
WELL, MAYBE I'LL SEE YOU AGAIN, CANDACE.
MAYBE YOU WILL, RAY.
ITEMS NEEDED!
EYES?

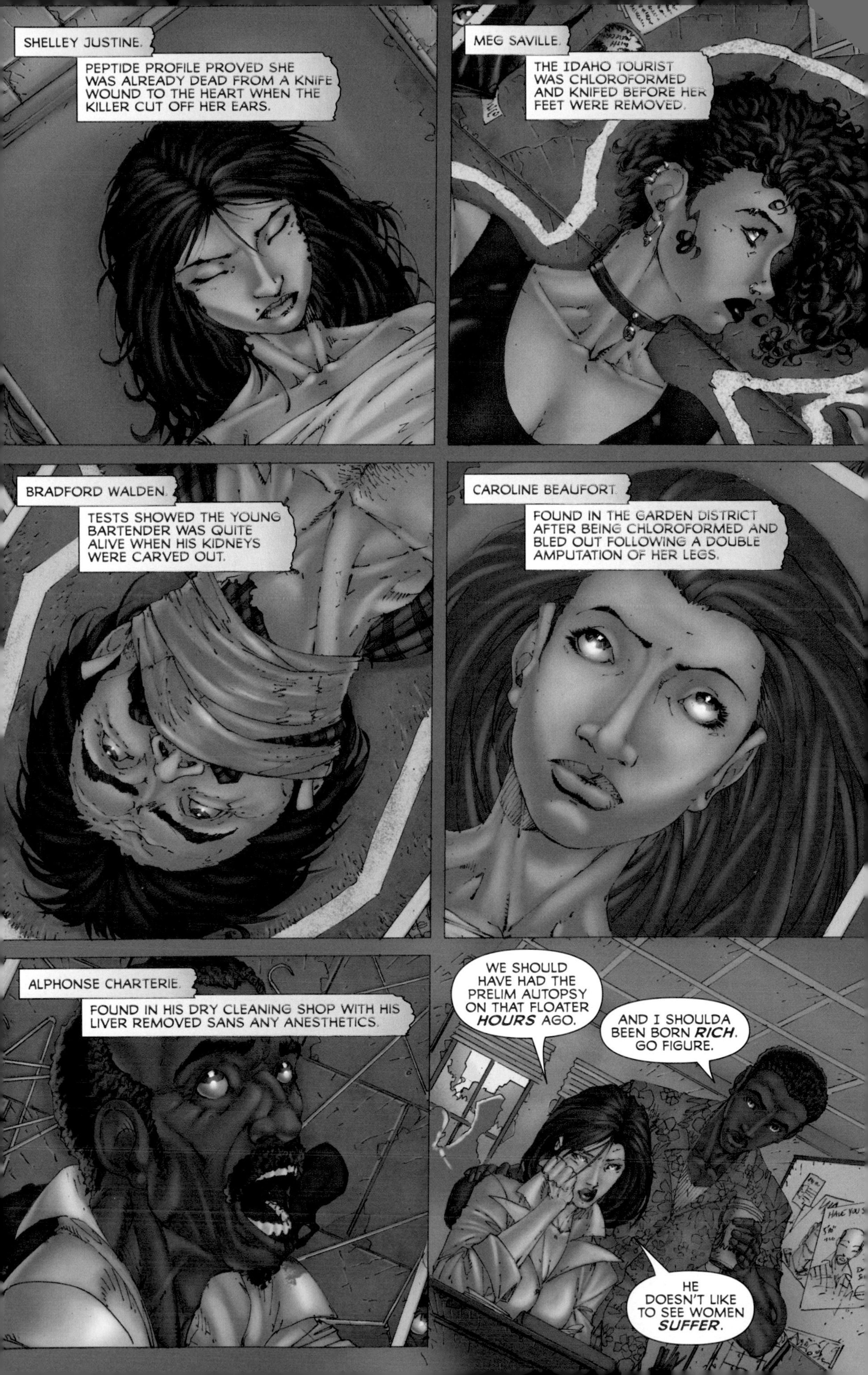
SHELLEY JUSTINE.
PEPTIDE PROFILE PROVED SHE WAS ALREADY DEAD FROM A KNIFE WOUND TO THE HEART WHEN THE KILLER CUT OFF HER EARS.
MEG SAVILLE.
THE IDAHO TOURIST WAS CHLOROFORMED AND KNIFED BEFORE HER FEET WERE REMOVED.
BRADFORD WALDEN.
TESTS SHOWED THE YOUNG BARTENDER WAS QUITE ALIVE WHEN HIS KIDNEYS WERE CARVED OUT.
CAROLINE BEAUFORT.
FOUND IN THE GARDEN DISTRICT AFTER BEING CHLOROFORMED AND BLED OUT FOLLOWING A DOUBLE AMPUTATION OF HER LEGS.
ALPHONSE CHARTERIE.
FOUND IN HIS DRY CLEANING SHOP WITH HIS LIVER REMOVED SANS ANY ANESTHETICS.
WE SHOULD HAVE HAD THE PRELIM AUTOPSY ON THAT FLOATER *HOURS* AGO.
AND I SHOULDA BEEN BORN *RICH*. GO FIGURE.
HE DOESN'T LIKE TO SEE WOMEN *SUFFER*.

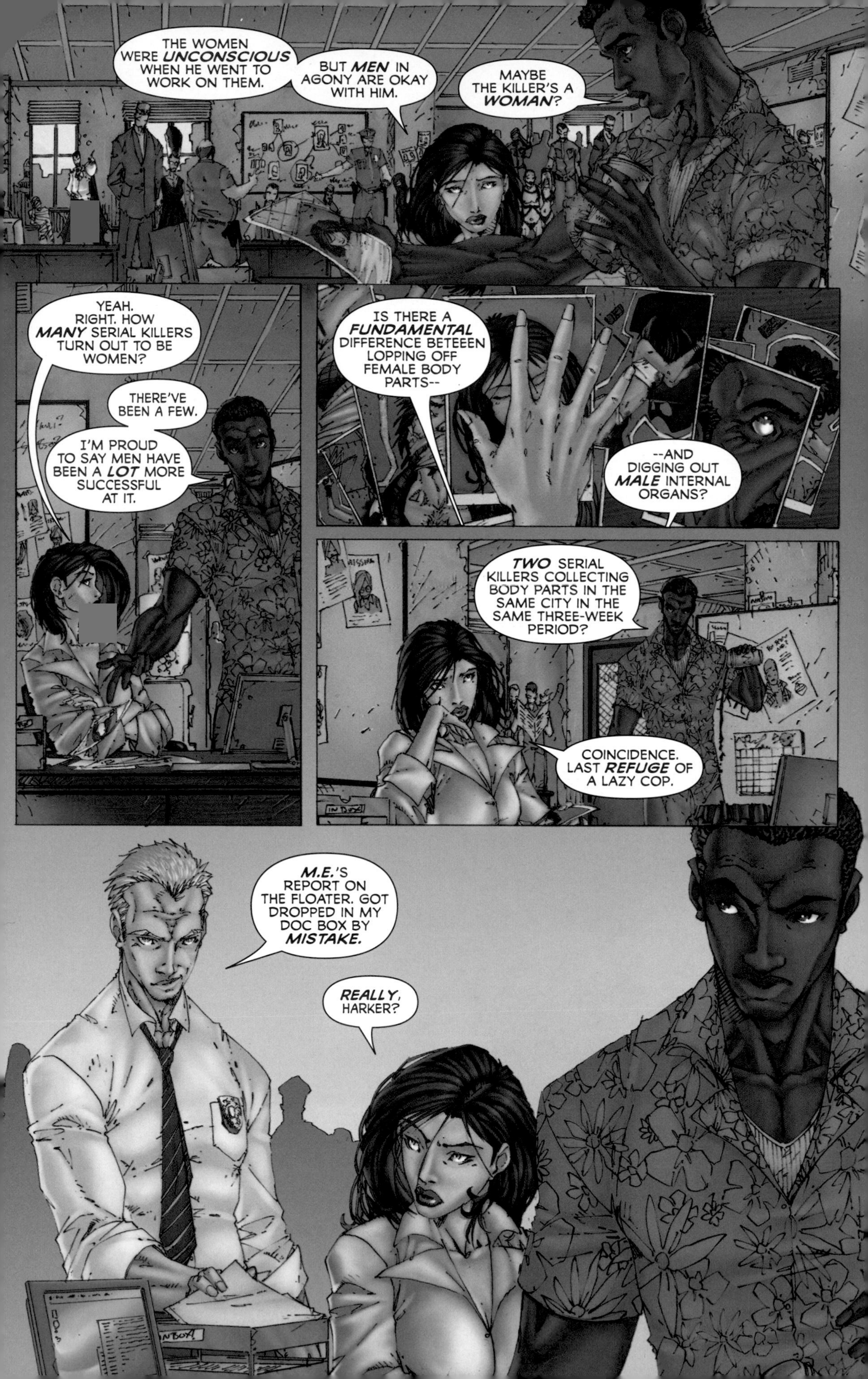
THE WOMEN WERE UNCONSCIOUS WHEN HE WENT TO WORK ON THEM.
BUT MEN IN AGONY ARE OKAY WITH HIM.
MAYBE THE KILLER'S A WOMAN?
YEAH. RIGHT. HOW MANY SERIAL KILLERS TURN OUT TO BE WOMEN?
THERE'VE BEEN A FEW.
I'M PROUD TO SAY MEN HAVE BEEN A LOT MORE SUCCESSFUL AT IT.
IS THERE A FUNDAMENTAL DIFFERENCE BETEEEN LOPPING OFF FEMALE BODY PARTS--
--AND DIGGING OUT MALE INTERNAL ORGANS?
TWO SERIAL KILLERS COLLECTING BODY PARTS IN THE SAME CITY IN THE SAME THREE-WEEK PERIOD?
COINCIDENCE. LAST REFUGE OF A LAZY COP.
M.E.'S REPORT ON THE FLOATER. GOT DROPPED IN MY DOC BOX BY MISTAKE.
REALLY, HARKER?

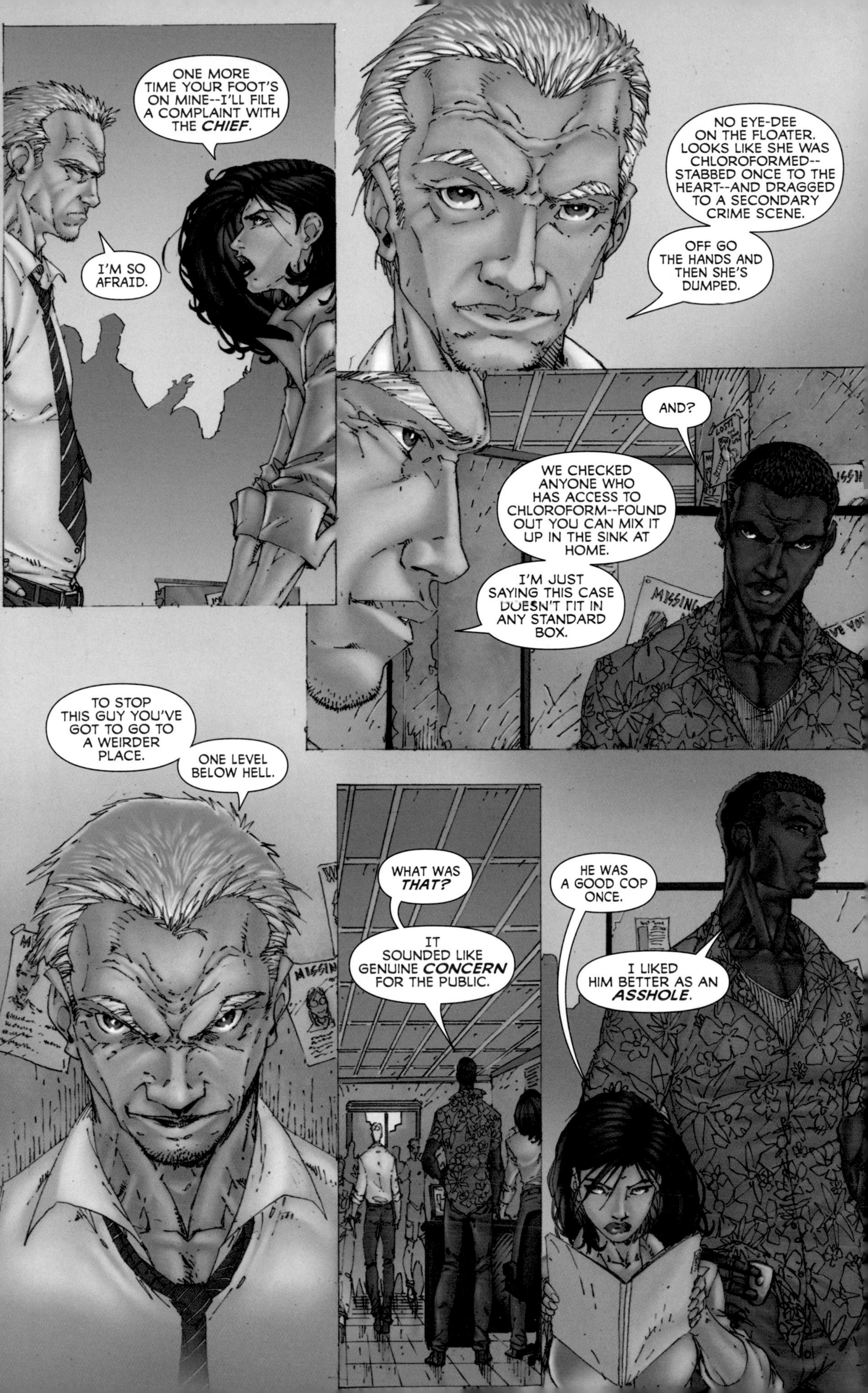
ONE MORE TIME YOUR FOOT'S ON MINE--I'LL FILE A COMPLAINT WITH THE *CHIEF*.
I'M SO AFRAID.
NO EYE-DEE ON THE FLOATER. LOOKS LIKE SHE WAS CHLOROFORMED-- STABBED ONCE TO THE HEART--AND DRAGGED TO A SECONDARY CRIME SCENE.
OFF GO THE HANDS AND THEN SHE'S DUMPED.
AND?
WE CHECKED ANYONE WHO HAS ACCESS TO CHLOROFORM--FOUND OUT YOU CAN MIX IT UP IN THE SINK AT HOME.
I'M JUST SAYING THIS CASE DOESN'T FIT IN ANY STANDARD BOX.
TO STOP THIS GUY YOU'VE GOT TO GO TO A WEIRDER PLACE.
ONE LEVEL BELOW HELL.
WHAT WAS *THAT?*
IT SOUNDED LIKE GENUINE *CONCERN* FOR THE PUBLIC.
HE WAS A GOOD COP ONCE.
I LIKED HIM BETTER AS AN *ASSHOLE*.
MISSING

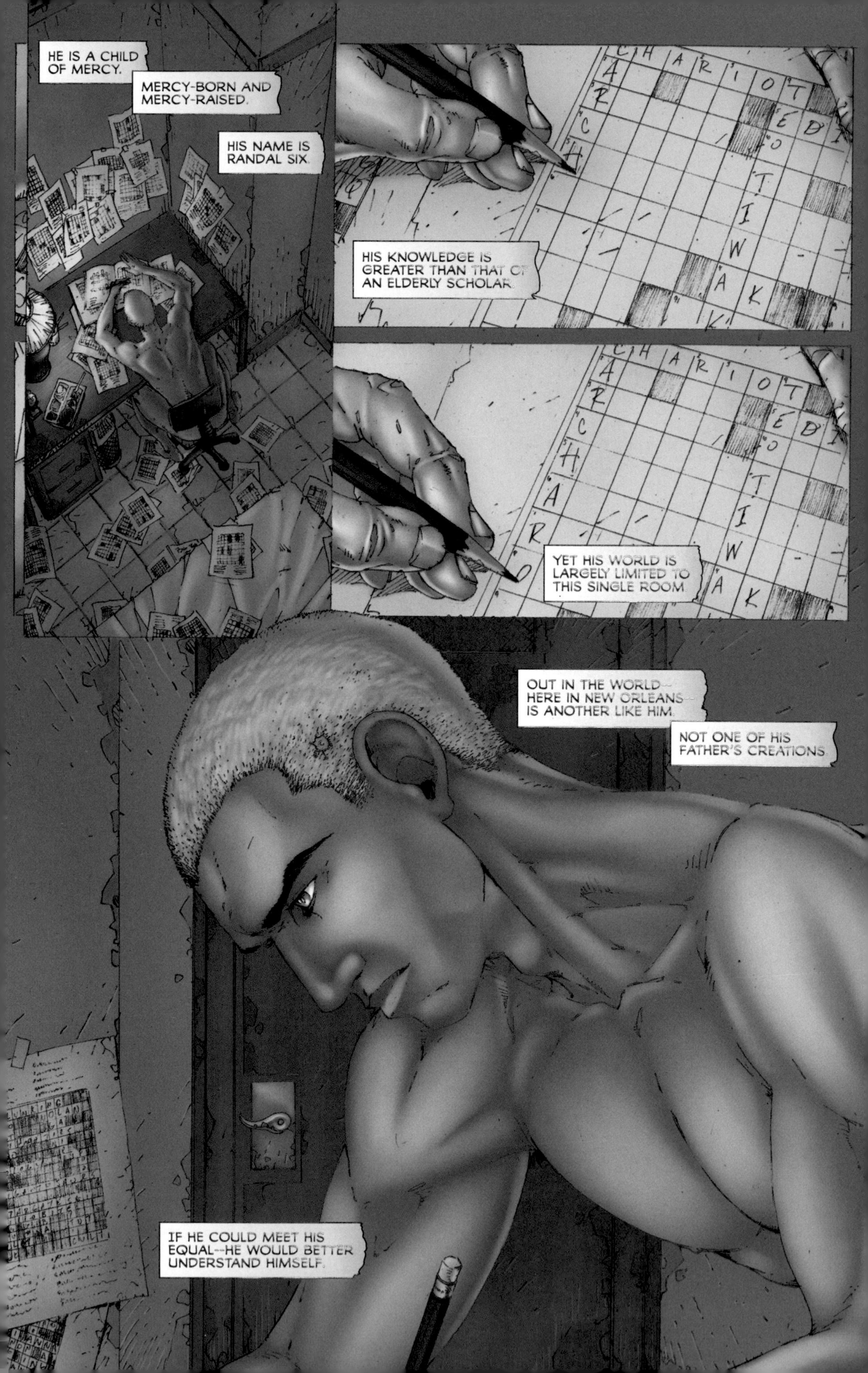
HE IS A CHILD OF MERCY.
MERCY-BORN AND MERCY-RAISED.
HIS NAME IS RANDAL SIX.
HIS KNOWLEDGE IS GREATER THAN THAT OF AN ELDERLY SCHOLAR.
YET HIS WORLD IS LARGELY LIMITED TO THIS SINGLE ROOM.
OUT IN THE WORLD--HERE IN NEW ORLEANS--IS ANOTHER LIKE HIM.
NOT ONE OF HIS FATHER'S CREATIONS.
IF HE COULD MEET HIS EQUAL--HE WOULD BETTER UNDERSTAND HIMSELF.

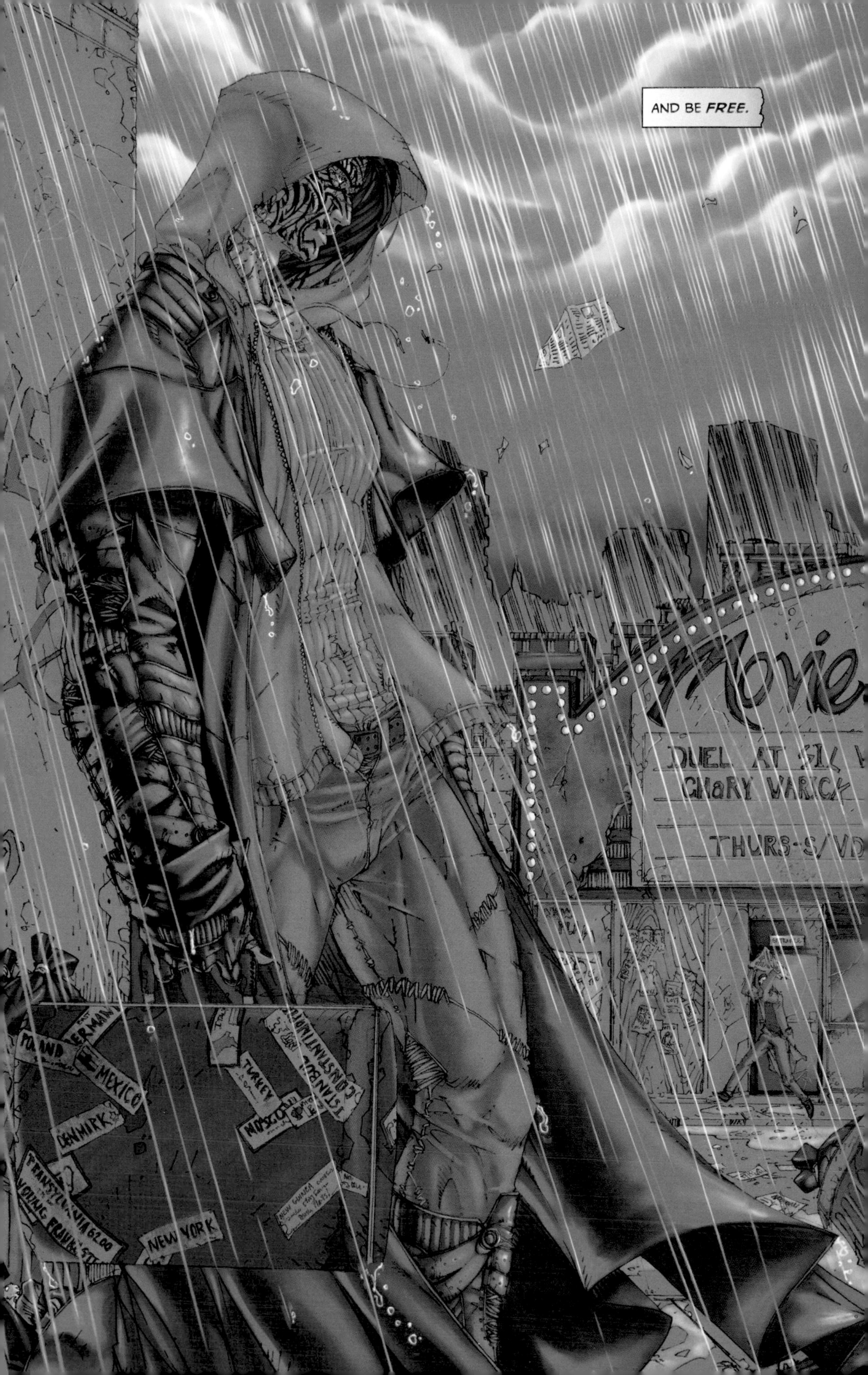
AND BE FREE.
Movie
MEXICO
DENMARK
TURKEY
NEW YORK

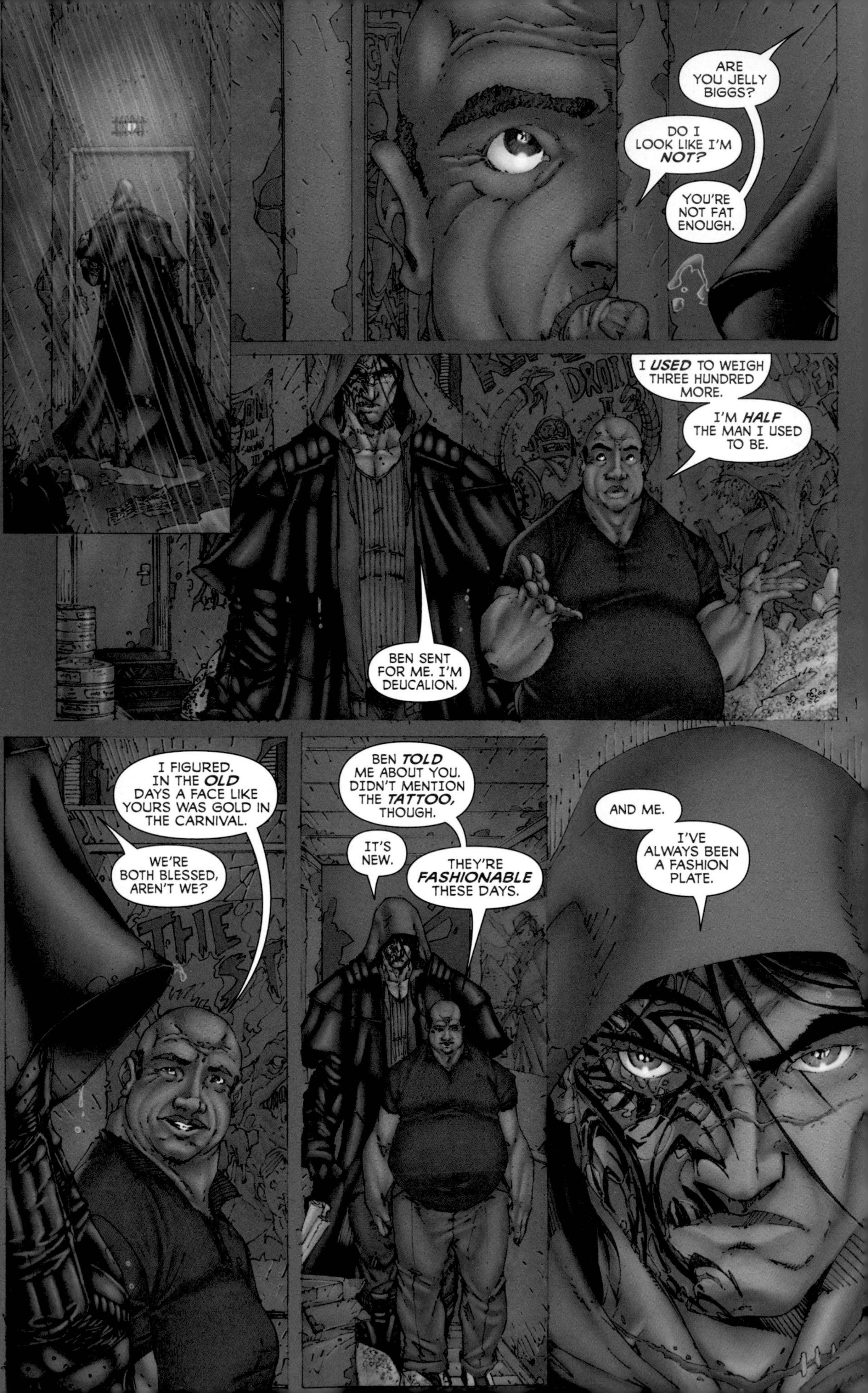
ARE YOU JELLY BIGGS?
DO I LOOK LIKE I'M NOT?
YOU'RE NOT FAT ENOUGH.
I USED TO WEIGH THREE HUNDRED MORE.
I'M HALF THE MAN I USED TO BE.
BEN SENT FOR ME. I'M DEUCALION.
I FIGURED. IN THE OLD DAYS A FACE LIKE YOURS WAS GOLD IN THE CARNIVAL.
WE'RE BOTH BLESSED, AREN'T WE?
BEN TOLD ME ABOUT YOU. DIDN'T MENTION THE TATTOO, THOUGH.
IT'S NEW.
THEY'RE FASHIONABLE THESE DAYS.
AND ME.
I'VE ALWAYS BEEN A FASHION PLATE.

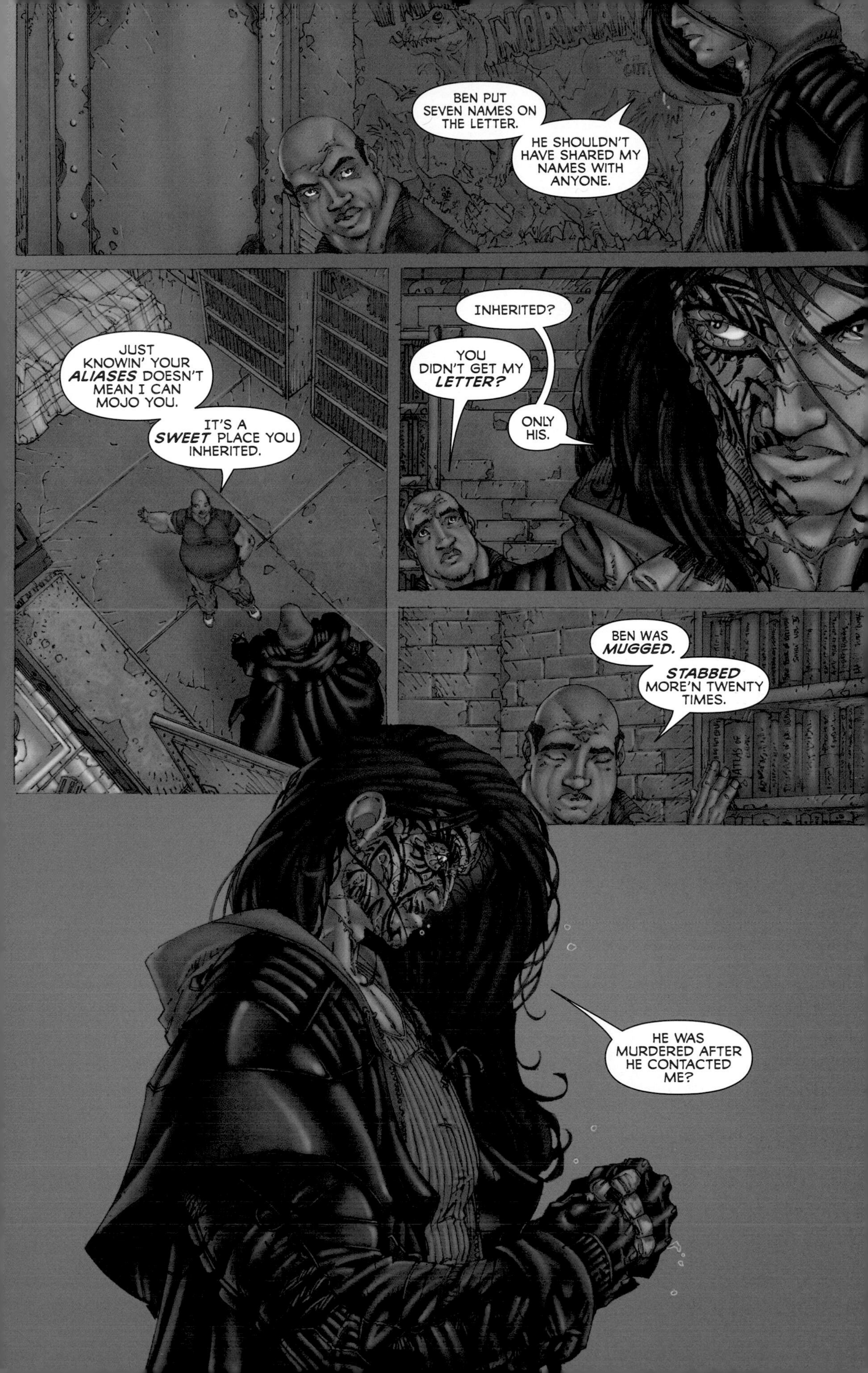
BEN PUT SEVEN NAMES ON THE LETTER.
HE SHOULDN'T HAVE SHARED MY NAMES WITH ANYONE.
JUST KNOWIN' YOUR ALIASES DOESN'T MEAN I CAN MOJO YOU.
IT'S A SWEET PLACE YOU INHERITED.
INHERITED?
YOU DIDN'T GET MY LETTER?
ONLY HIS.
BEN WAS MUGGED.
STABBED MORE'N TWENTY TIMES.
HE WAS MURDERED AFTER HE CONTACTED ME?

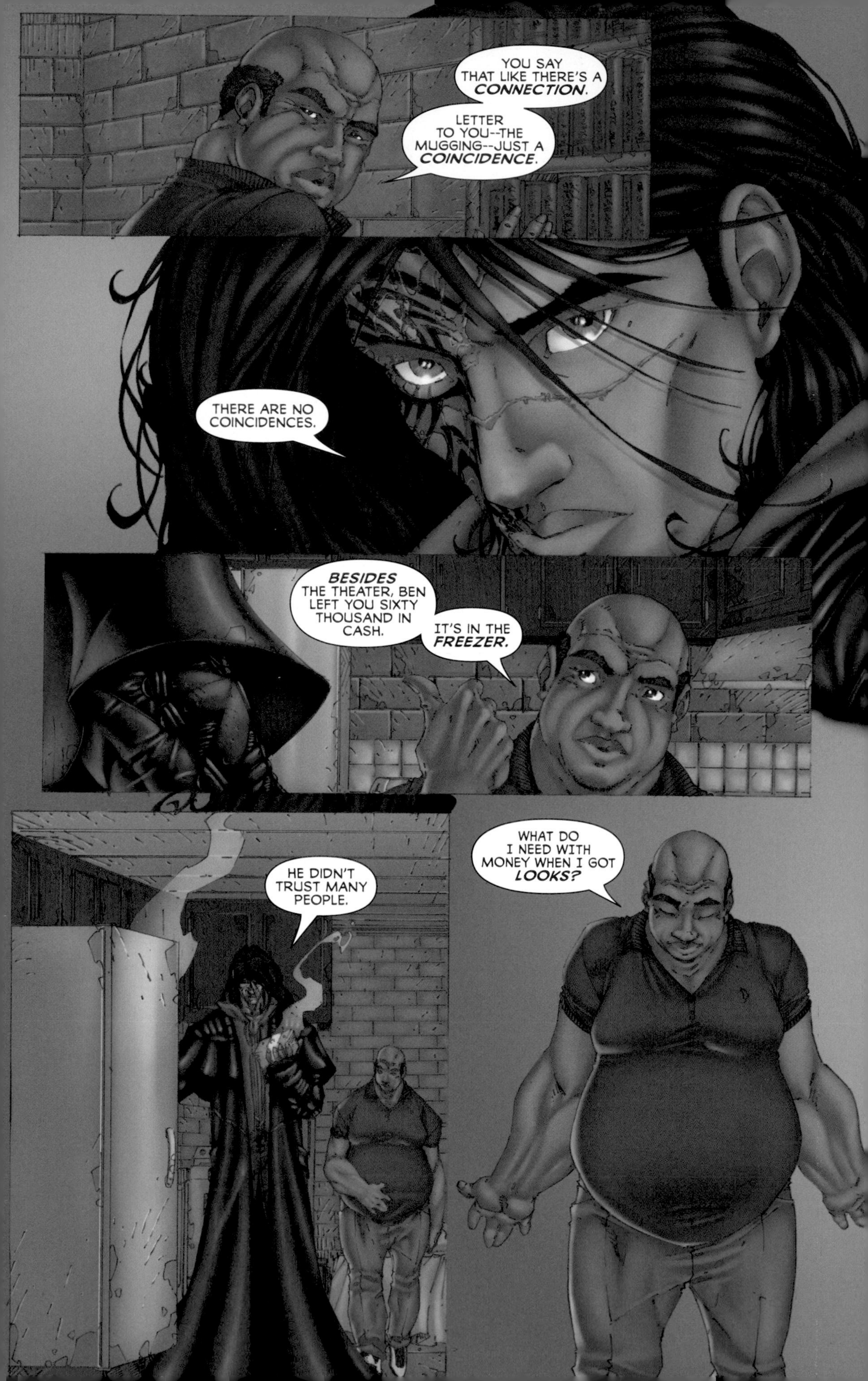
YOU SAY THAT LIKE THERE'S A CONNECTION.
LETTER TO YOU--THE MUGGING--JUST A COINCIDENCE.
THERE ARE NO COINCIDENCES.
BESIDES THE THEATER, BEN LEFT YOU SIXTY THOUSAND IN CASH.
IT'S IN THE FREEZER.
HE DIDN'T TRUST MANY PEOPLE.
WHAT DO I NEED WITH MONEY WHEN I GOT LOOKS?

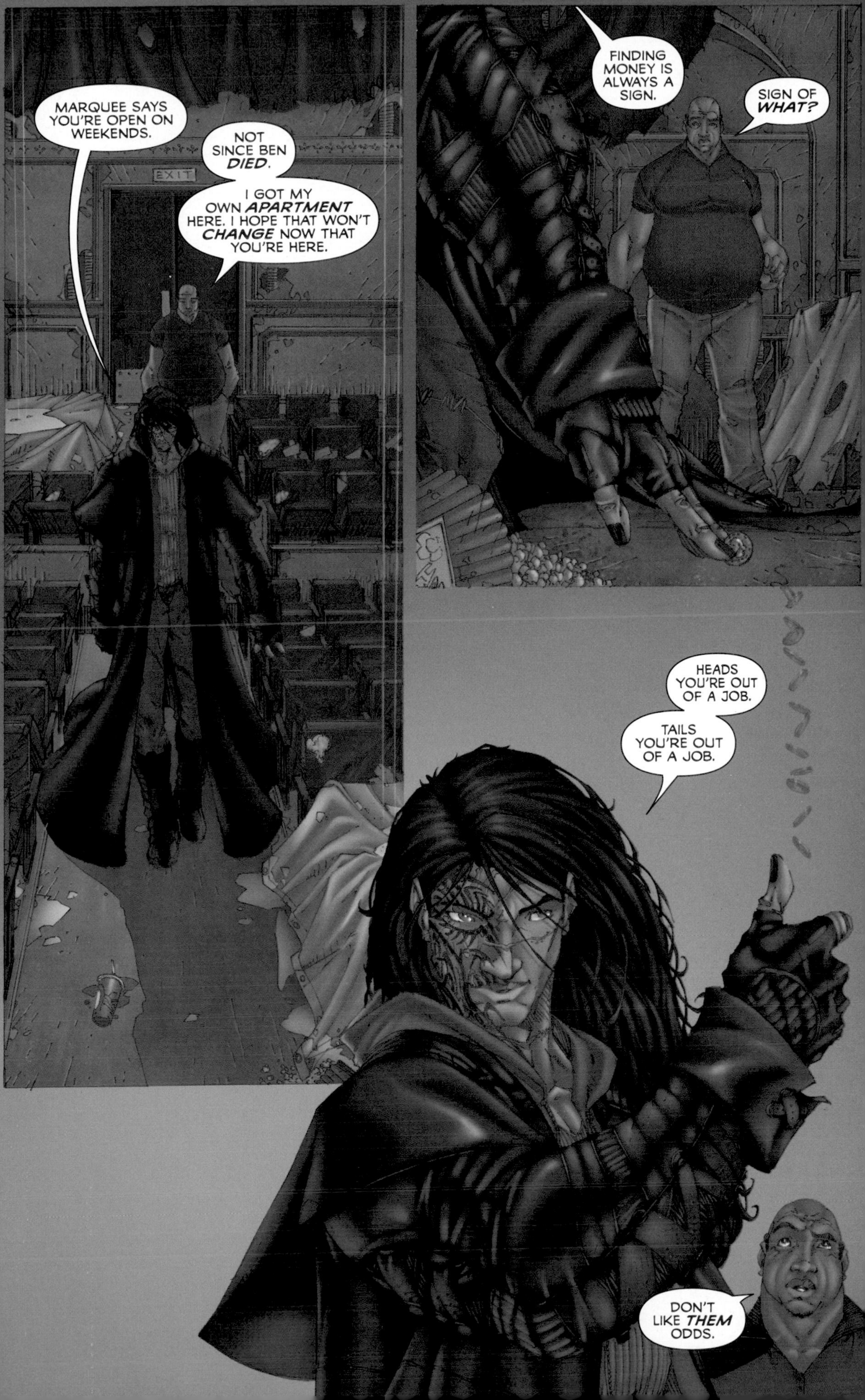

MARQUEE SAYS YOU'RE OPEN ON WEEKENDS.
NOT SINCE BEN *DIED*.
I GOT MY OWN *APARTMENT* HERE. I HOPE THAT WON'T *CHANGE* NOW THAT YOU'RE HERE.
FINDING MONEY IS ALWAYS A SIGN.
SIGN OF *WHAT?*
HEADS YOU'RE OUT OF A JOB.
TAILS YOU'RE OUT OF A JOB.
DON'T LIKE *THEM* ODDS.

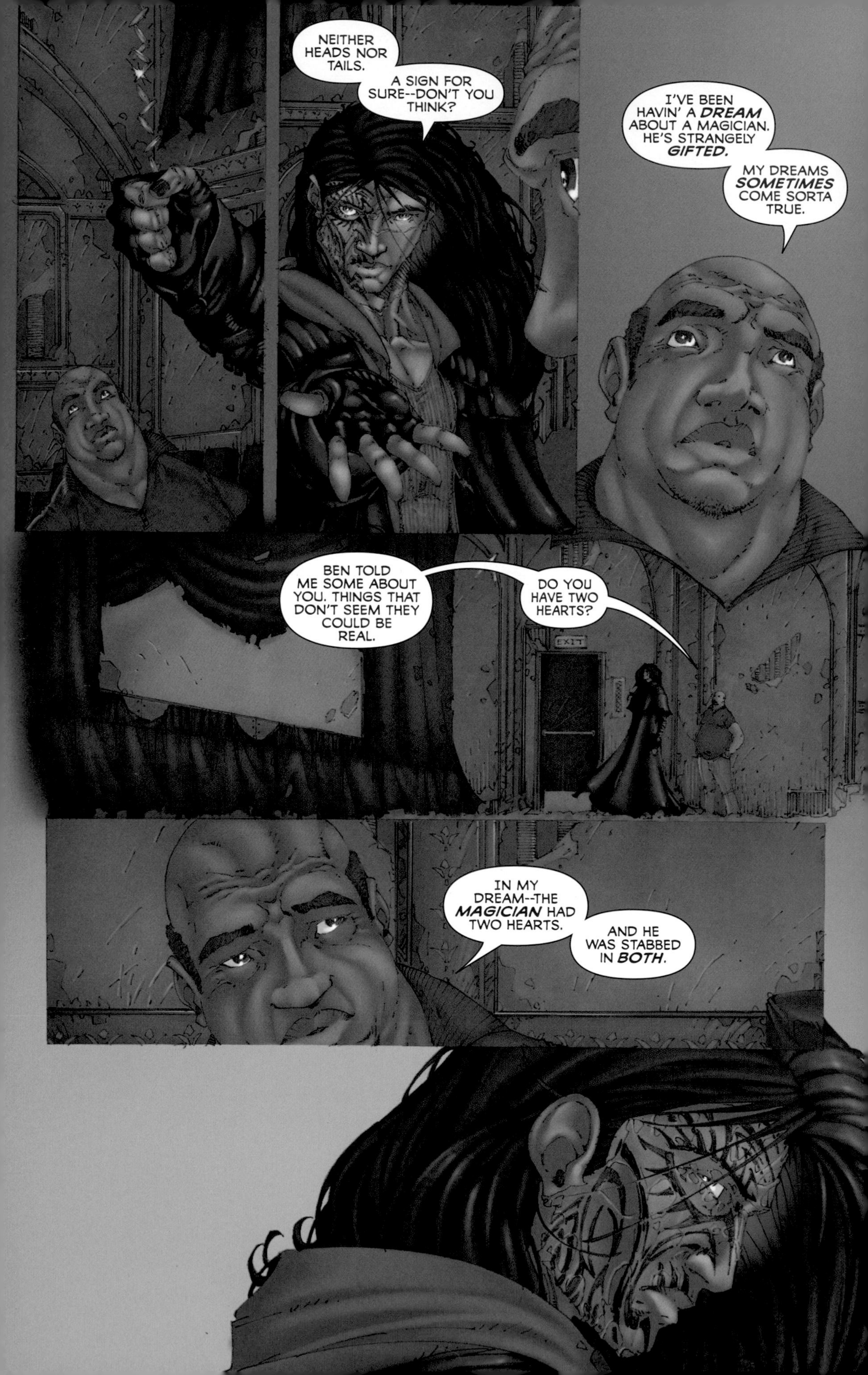
NEITHER HEADS NOR TAILS.
A SIGN FOR SURE--DON'T YOU THINK?
I'VE BEEN HAVIN' A **DREAM** ABOUT A MAGICIAN. HE'S STRANGELY **GIFTED.**
MY DREAMS **SOMETIMES** COME SORTA TRUE.
BEN TOLD ME SOME ABOUT YOU. THINGS THAT DON'T SEEM THEY COULD BE REAL.
DO YOU HAVE TWO HEARTS?
EXIT
IN MY DREAM--THE **MAGICIAN** HAD TWO HEARTS.
AND HE WAS STABBED IN **BOTH**.

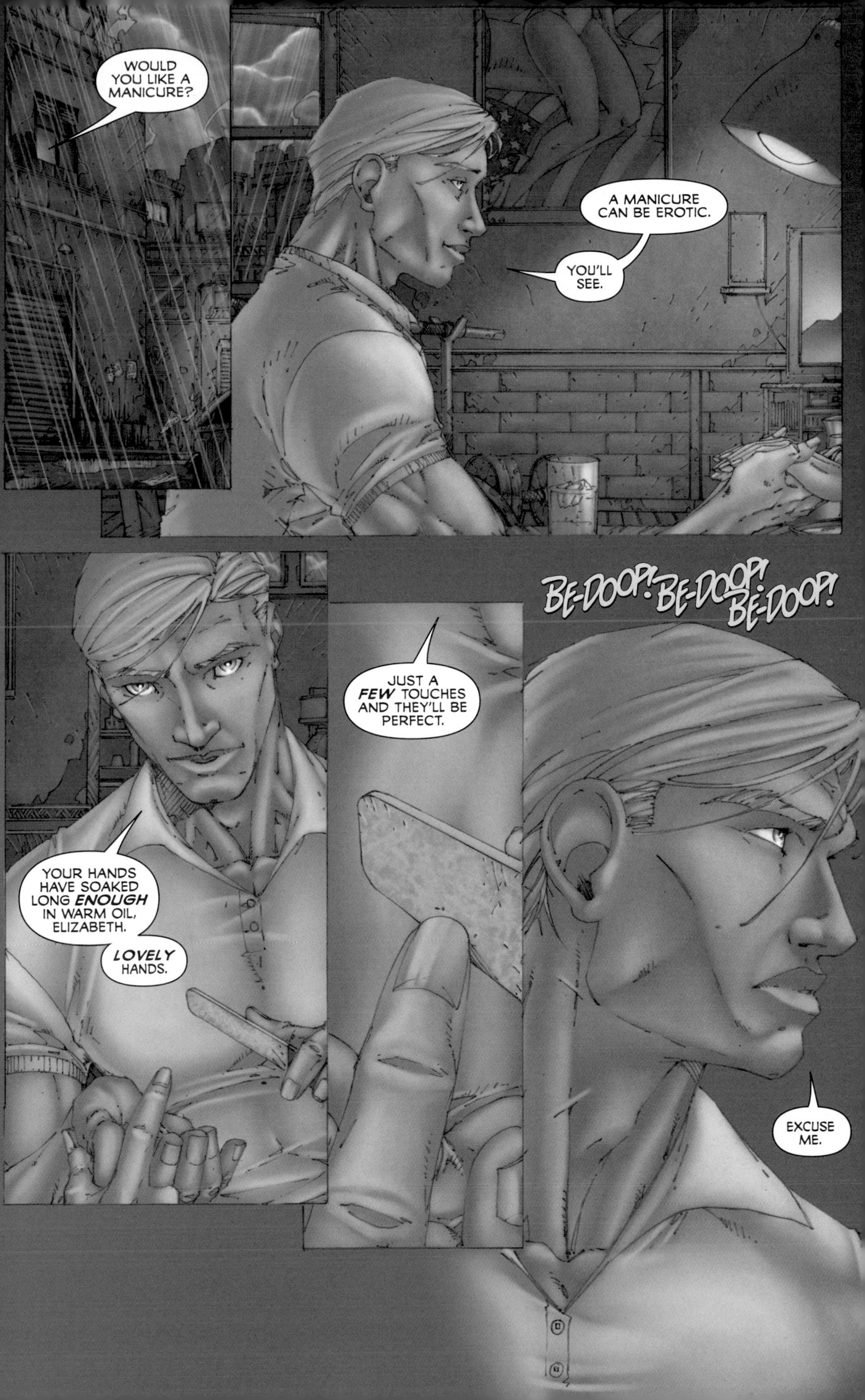
WOULD YOU LIKE A MANICURE?
A MANICURE CAN BE EROTIC.
YOU'LL SEE.
YOUR HANDS HAVE SOAKED LONG ENOUGH IN WARM OIL, ELIZABETH.
LOVELY HANDS.
JUST A FEW TOUCHES AND THEY'LL BE PERFECT.
BE-DOOP! BE-DOOP! BE-DOOP!
EXCUSE ME.

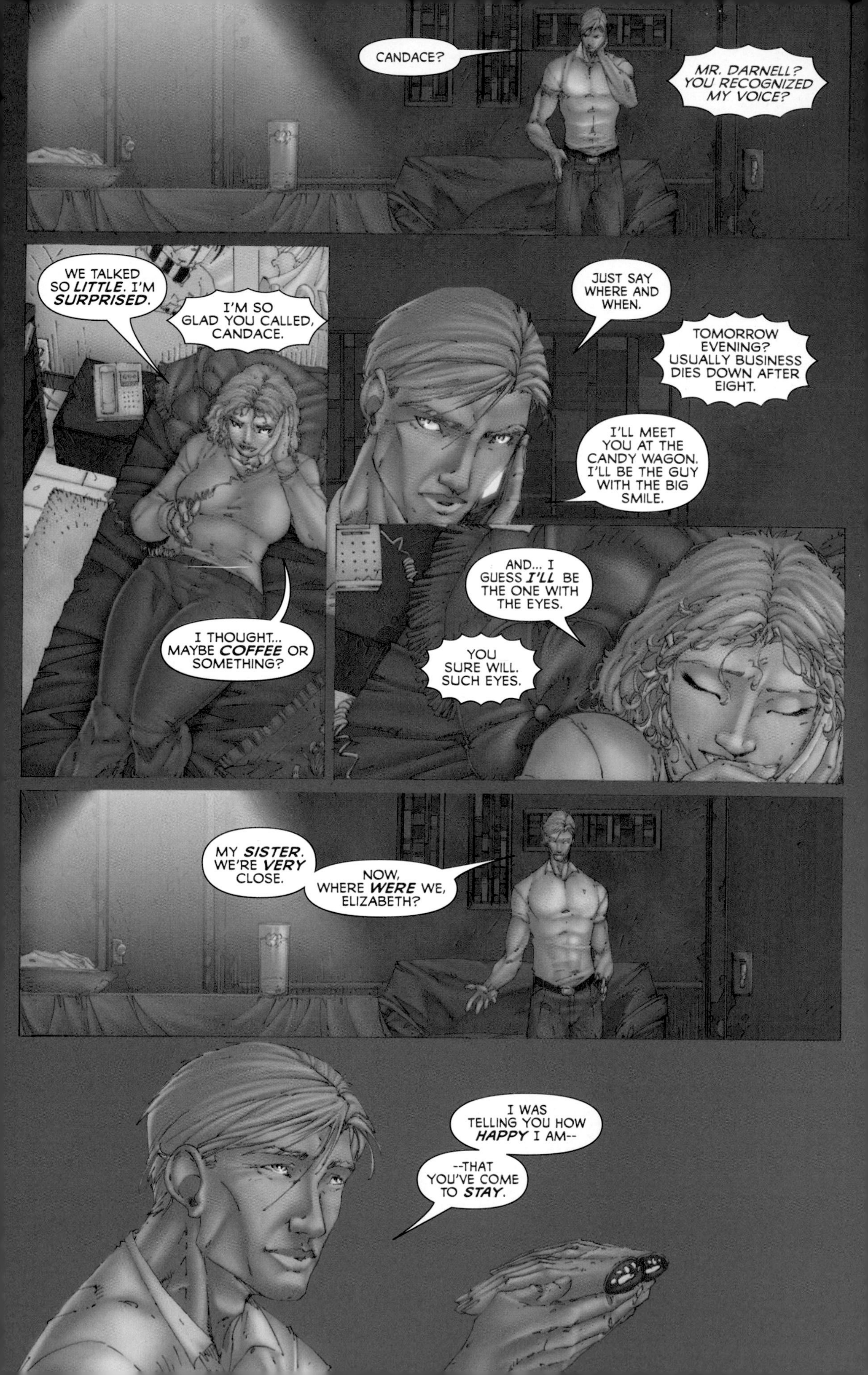
CANDACE?
MR. DARNELL? YOU RECOGNIZED MY VOICE?
WE TALKED SO LITTLE. I'M SURPRISED.
I'M SO GLAD YOU CALLED, CANDACE.
I THOUGHT... MAYBE COFFEE OR SOMETHING?
JUST SAY WHERE AND WHEN.
TOMORROW EVENING? USUALLY BUSINESS DIES DOWN AFTER EIGHT.
I'LL MEET YOU AT THE CANDY WAGON. I'LL BE THE GUY WITH THE BIG SMILE.
AND... I GUESS I'LL BE THE ONE WITH THE EYES.
YOU SURE WILL. SUCH EYES.
MY SISTER. WE'RE VERY CLOSE.
NOW, WHERE WERE WE, ELIZABETH?
I WAS TELLING YOU HOW HAPPY I AM--
--THAT YOU'VE COME TO STAY.

chapter two

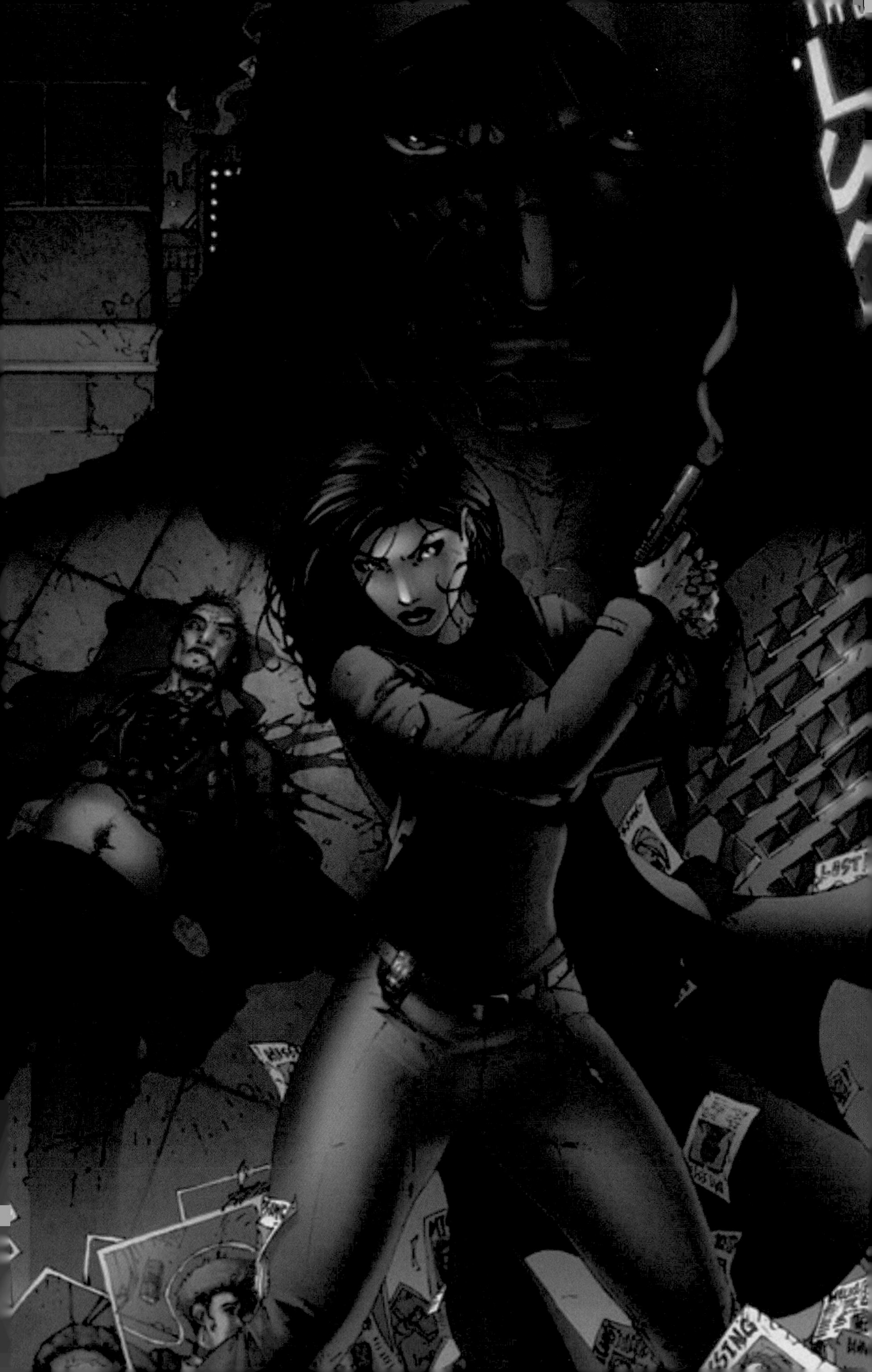

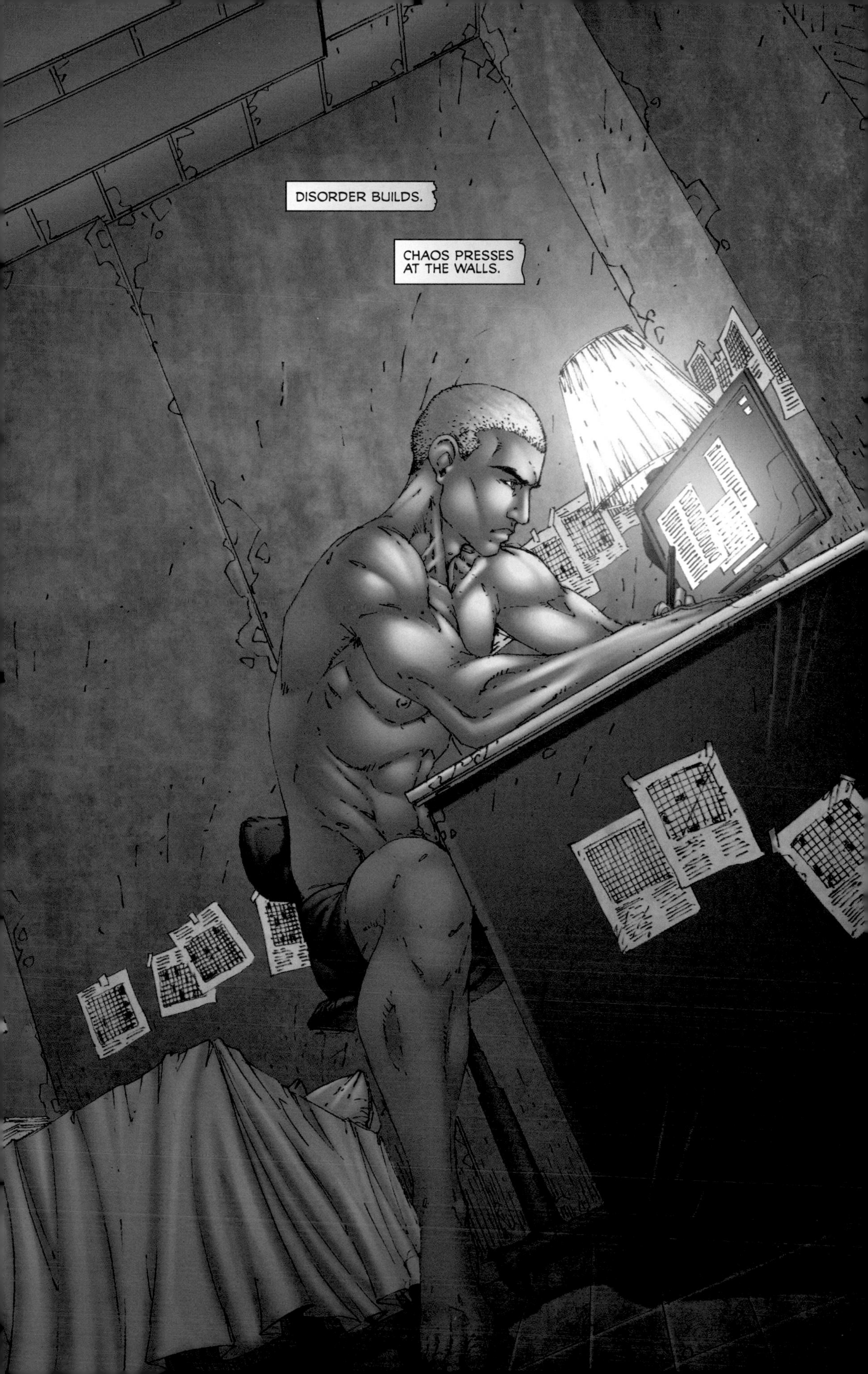
DISORDER BUILDS.
CHAOS PRESSES AT THE WALLS.

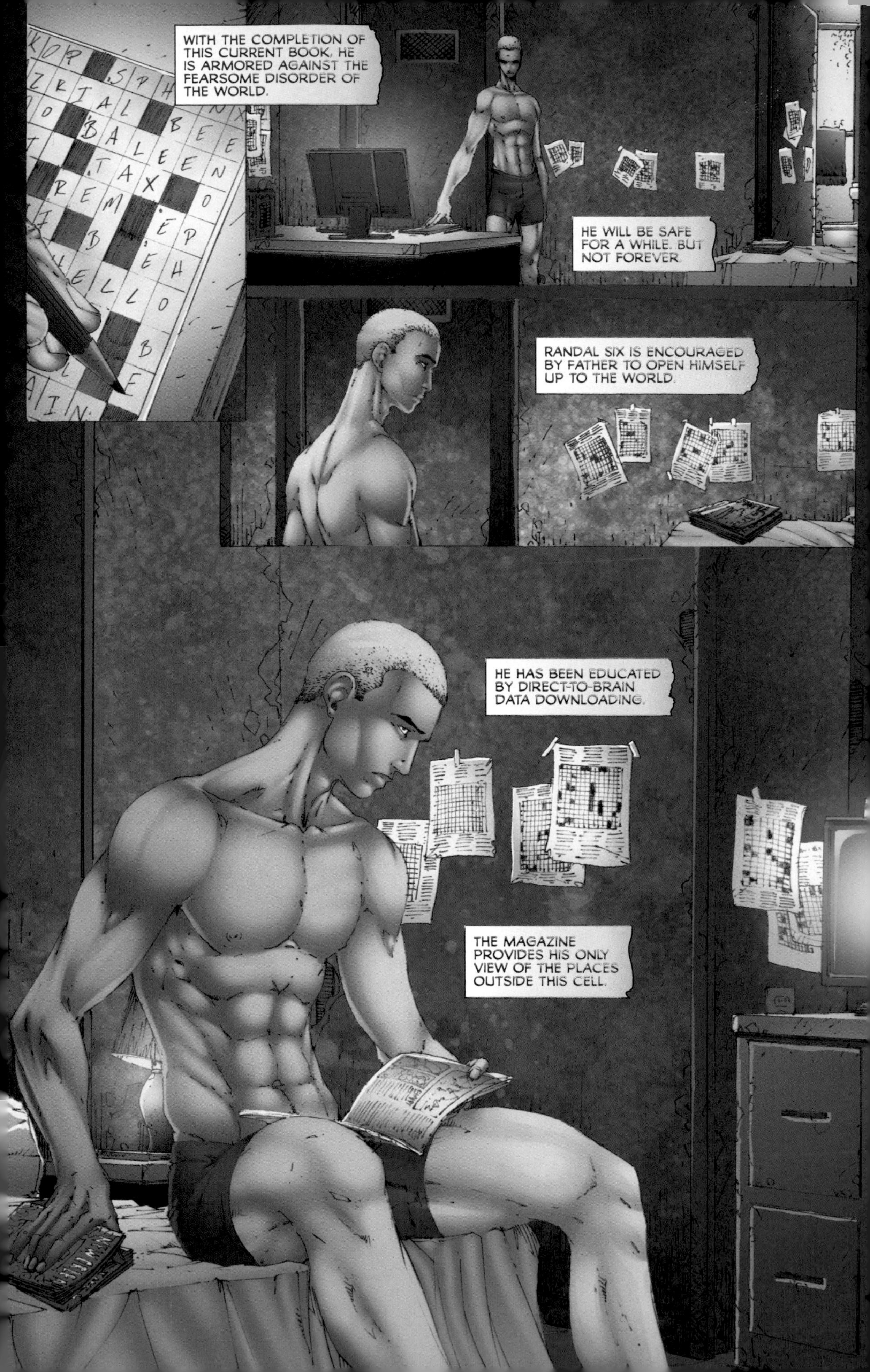
WITH THE COMPLETION OF THIS CURRENT BOOK, HE IS ARMORED AGAINST THE FEARSOME DISORDER OF THE WORLD.
HE WILL BE SAFE FOR A WHILE. BUT NOT FOREVER.
RANDAL SIX IS ENCOURAGED BY FATHER TO OPEN HIMSELF UP TO THE WORLD.
HE HAS BEEN EDUCATED BY DIRECT-TO-BRAIN DATA DOWNLOADING.
THE MAGAZINE PROVIDES HIS ONLY VIEW OF THE PLACES OUTSIDE THIS CELL.

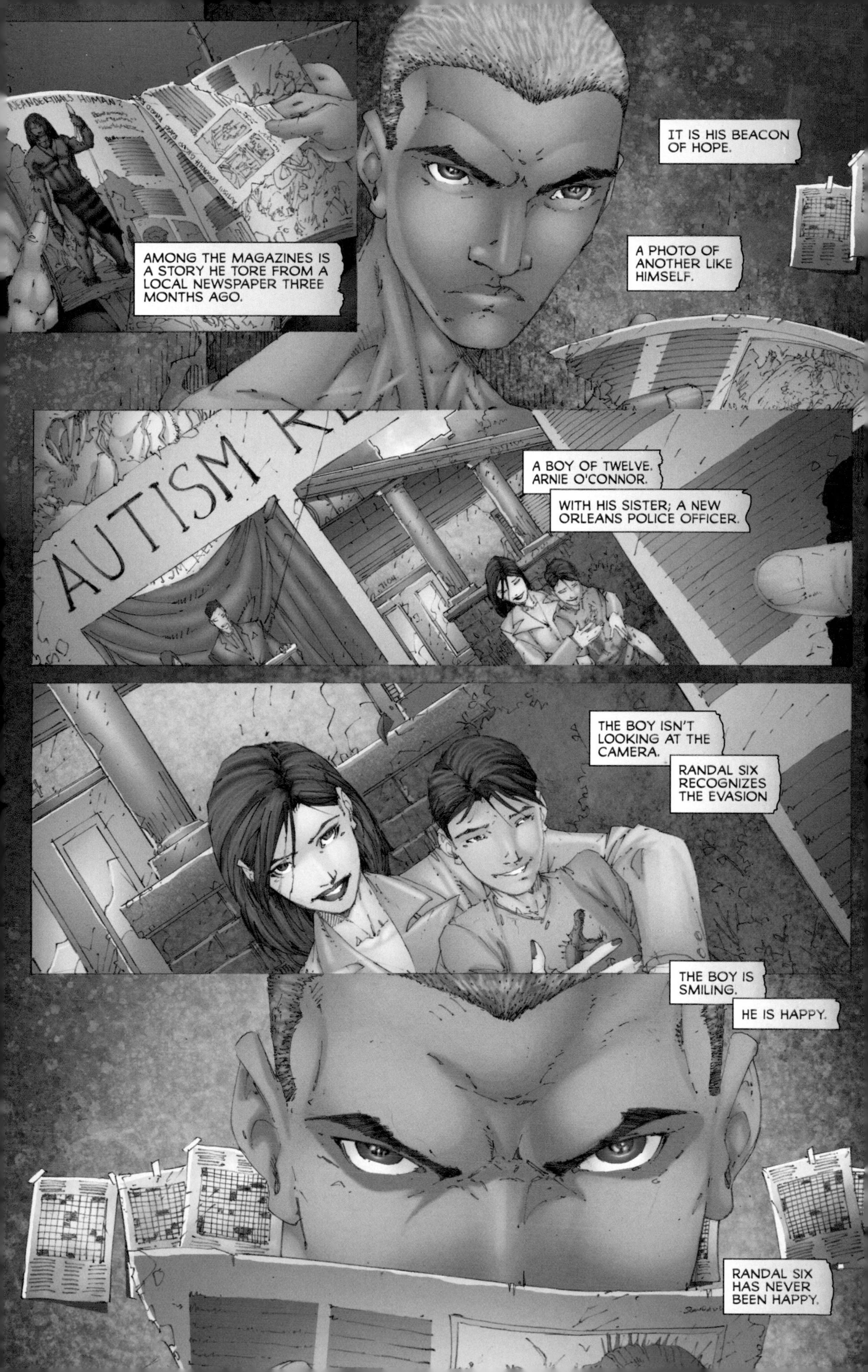
AMONG THE MAGAZINES IS A STORY HE TORE FROM A LOCAL NEWSPAPER THREE MONTHS AGO.
IT IS HIS BEACON OF HOPE.
A PHOTO OF ANOTHER LIKE HIMSELF.
AUTISM
A BOY OF TWELVE. ARNIE O'CONNOR.
WITH HIS SISTER; A NEW ORLEANS POLICE OFFICER.
THE BOY ISN'T LOOKING AT THE CAMERA.
RANDAL SIX RECOGNIZES THE EVASION
THE BOY IS SMILING.
HE IS HAPPY.
RANDAL SIX HAS NEVER BEEN HAPPY.

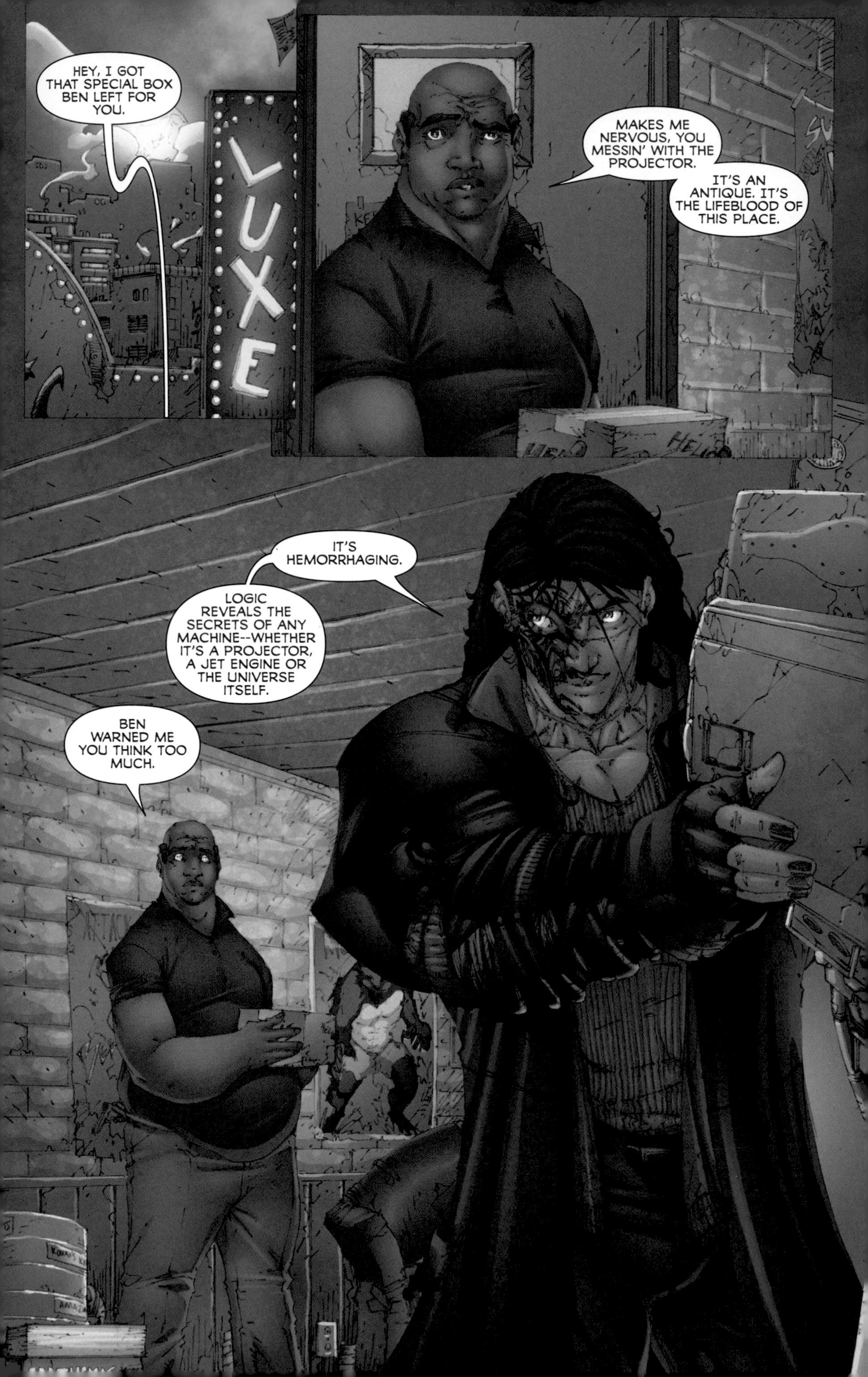

HEY, I GOT THAT SPECIAL BOX BEN LEFT FOR YOU.
LUXE
MAKES ME NERVOUS, YOU MESSIN' WITH THE PROJECTOR.
IT'S AN ANTIQUE. IT'S THE LIFEBLOOD OF THIS PLACE.
IT'S HEMORRHAGING.
LOGIC REVEALS THE SECRETS OF ANY MACHINE--WHETHER IT'S A PROJECTOR, A JET ENGINE OR THE UNIVERSE ITSELF.
BEN WARNED ME YOU THINK TOO MUCH.

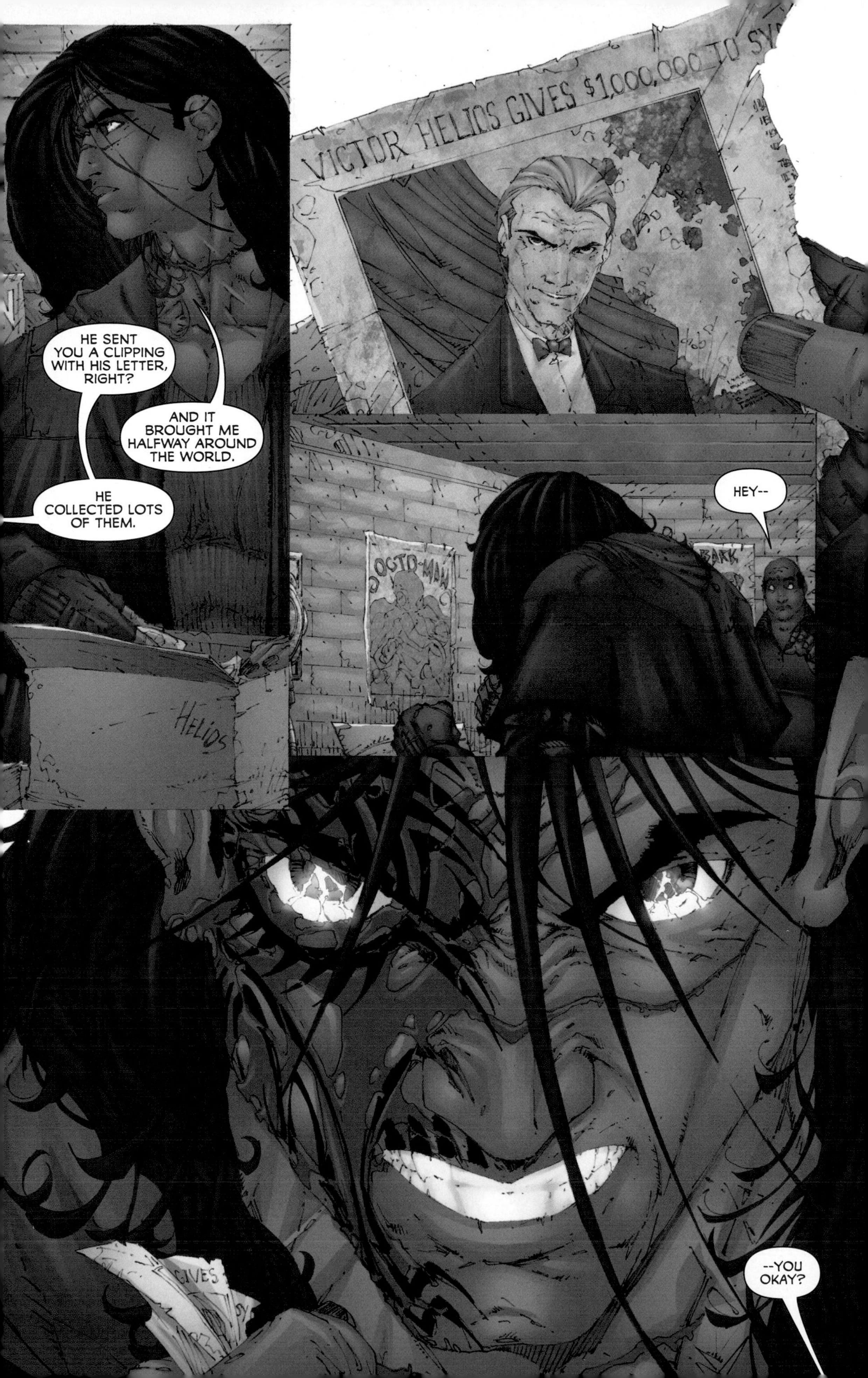
VICTOR HELIOS GIVES $1,000,000 TO SY
HE SENT YOU A CLIPPING WITH HIS LETTER, RIGHT?
AND IT BROUGHT ME HALFWAY AROUND THE WORLD.
HE COLLECTED LOTS OF THEM.
HELIOS
OCTO-MAN
HEY--
--YOU OKAY?
GIVES

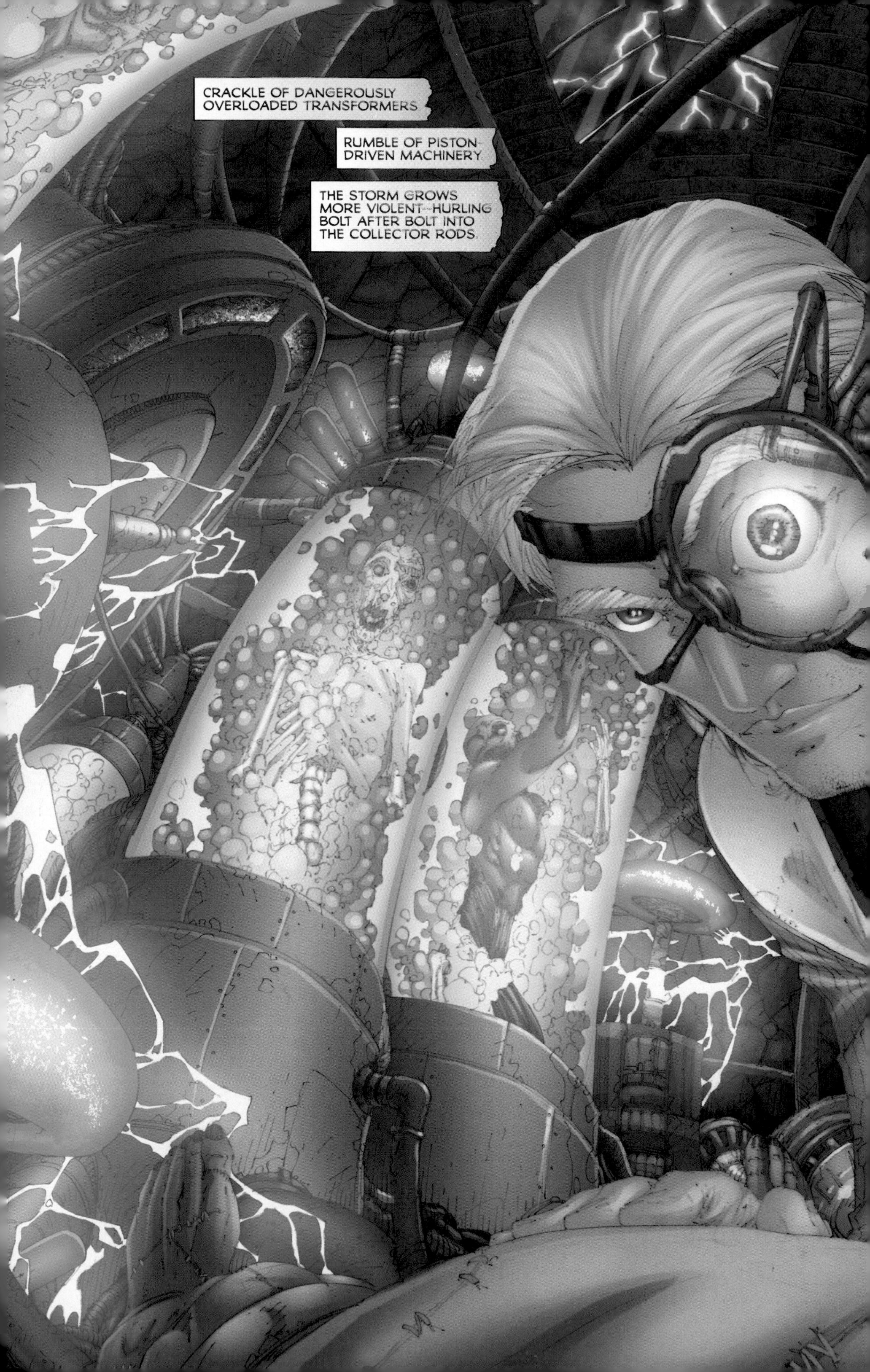
CRACKLE OF DANGEROUSLY OVERLOADED TRANSFORMERS.
RUMBLE OF PISTON-DRIVEN MACHINERY.
THE STORM GROWS MORE VIOLENT—HURLING BOLT AFTER BOLT INTO THE COLLECTOR RODS.

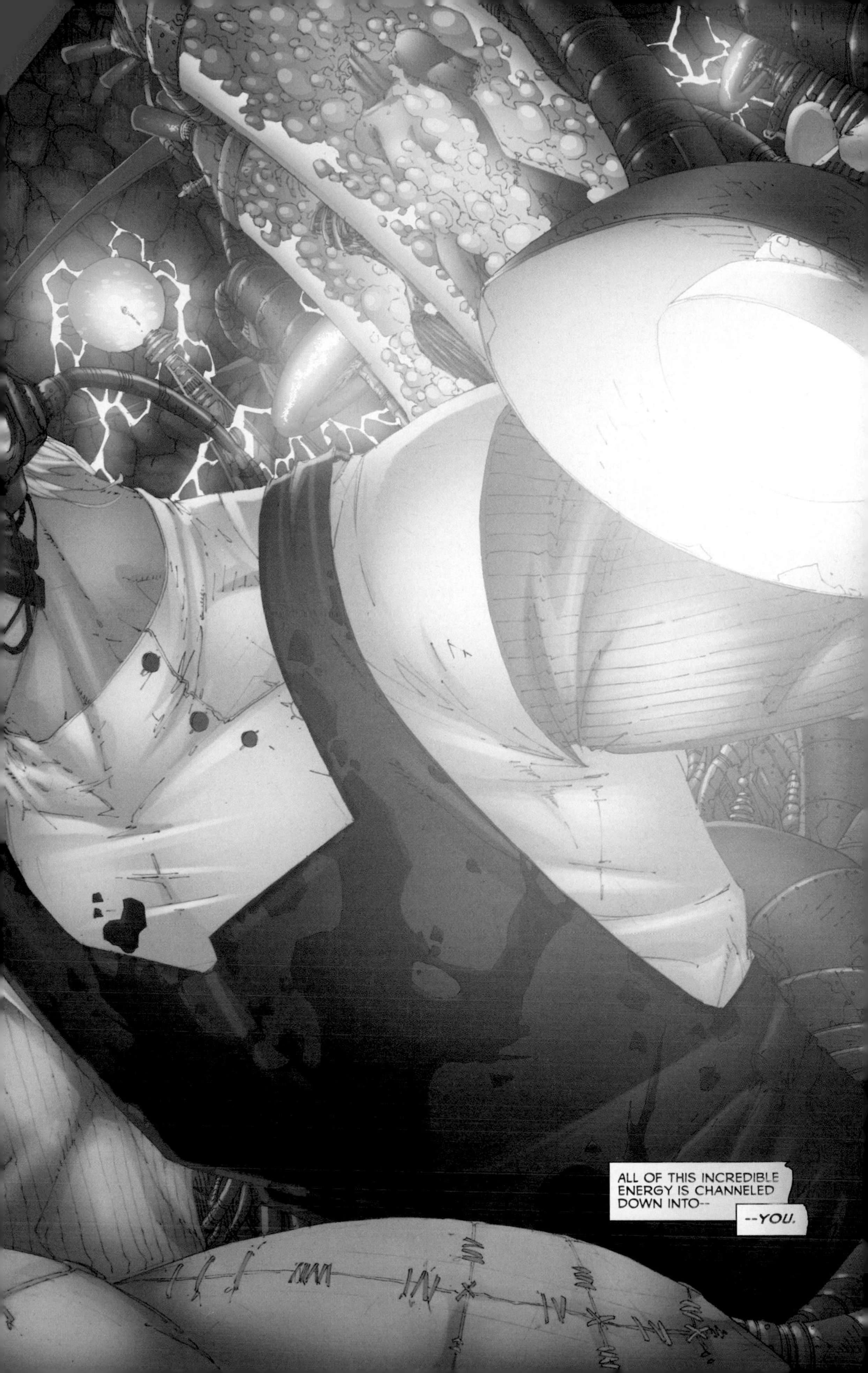
ALL OF THIS INCREDIBLE ENERGY IS CHANNELED DOWN INTO--
--YOU.

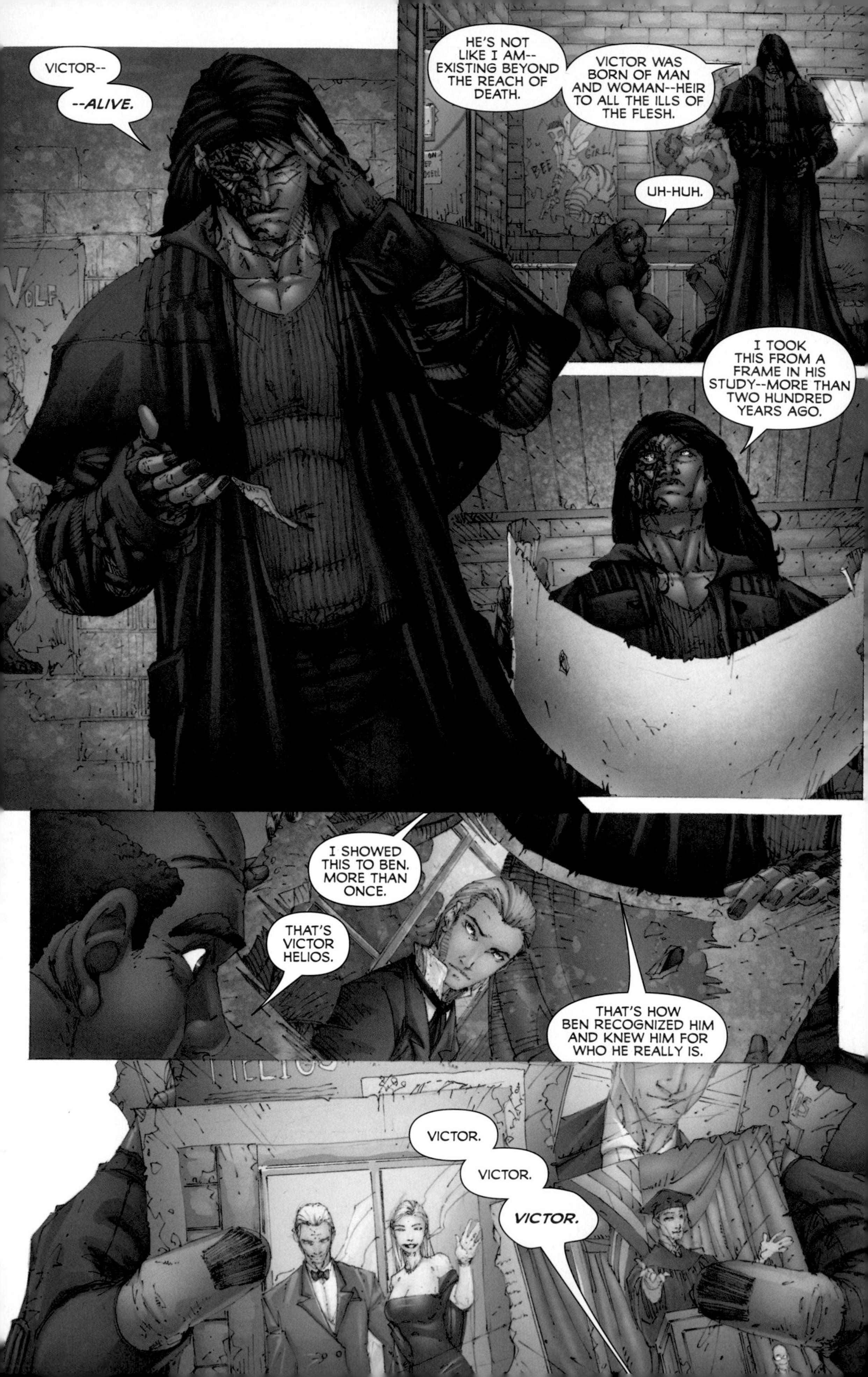
VICTOR--
--ALIVE.
HE'S NOT LIKE I AM--EXISTING BEYOND THE REACH OF DEATH.
VICTOR WAS BORN OF MAN AND WOMAN--HEIR TO ALL THE ILLS OF THE FLESH.
UH-HUH.
I TOOK THIS FROM A FRAME IN HIS STUDY--MORE THAN TWO HUNDRED YEARS AGO.
I SHOWED THIS TO BEN. MORE THAN ONCE.
THAT'S VICTOR HELIOS.
THAT'S HOW BEN RECOGNIZED HIM AND KNEW HIM FOR WHO HE REALLY IS.
VICTOR.
VICTOR.
VICTOR.

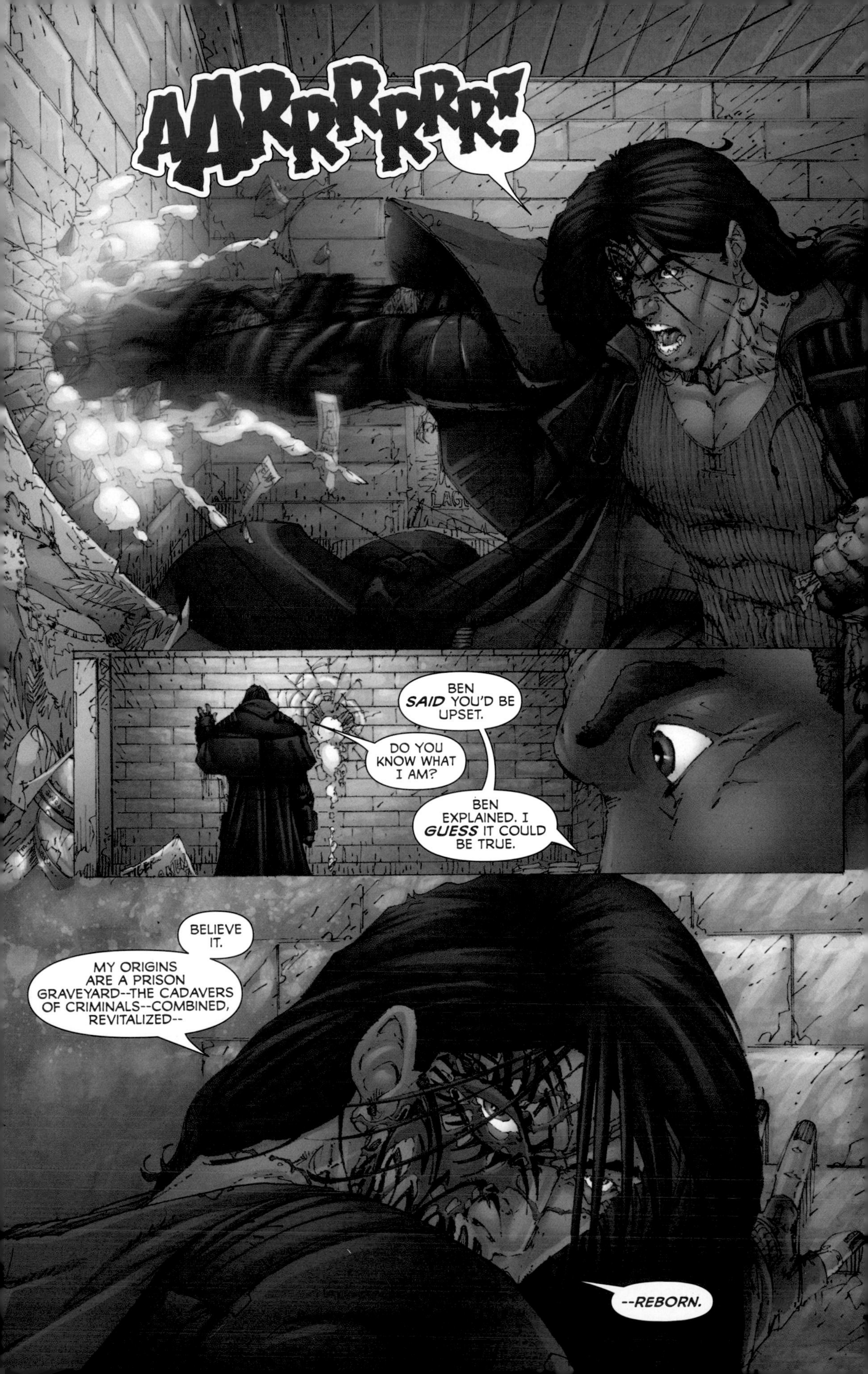
AAARRRRRR!
BEN SAID YOU'D BE UPSET.
DO YOU KNOW WHAT I AM?
BEN EXPLAINED. I GUESS IT COULD BE TRUE.
BELIEVE IT.
MY ORIGINS ARE A PRISON GRAVEYARD--THE CADAVERS OF CRIMINALS--COMBINED, REVITALIZED--
--REBORN.

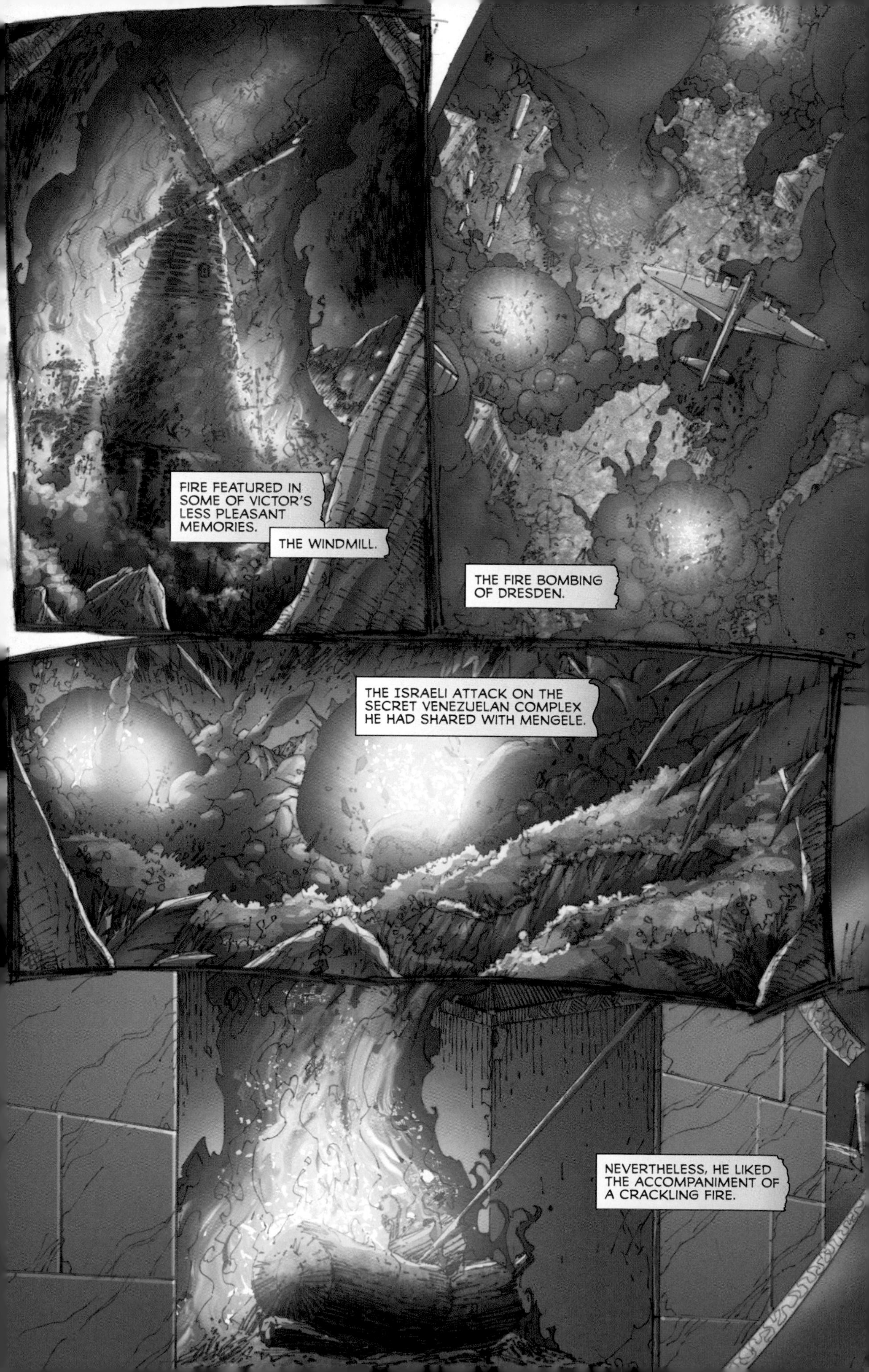
FIRE FEATURED IN SOME OF VICTOR'S LESS PLEASANT MEMORIES.
THE WINDMILL.
THE FIRE BOMBING OF DRESDEN.
THE ISRAELI ATTACK ON THE SECRET VENEZUELAN COMPLEX HE HAD SHARED WITH MENGELE.
NEVERTHELESS, HE LIKED THE ACCOMPANIMENT OF A CRACKLING FIRE.

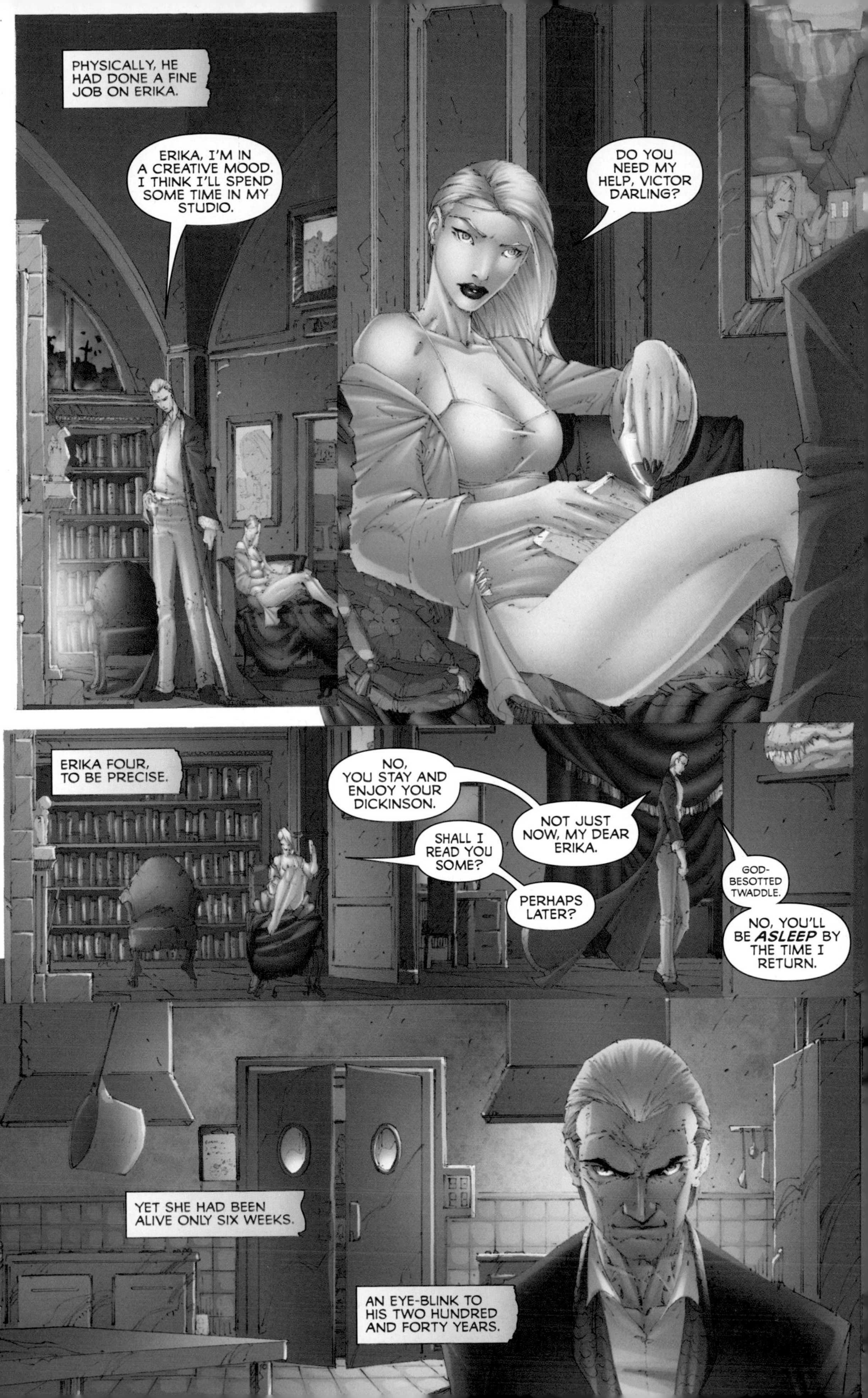
PHYSICALLY, HE HAD DONE A FINE JOB ON ERIKA.
ERIKA, I'M IN A CREATIVE MOOD. I THINK I'LL SPEND SOME TIME IN MY STUDIO.
DO YOU NEED MY HELP, VICTOR DARLING?
ERIKA FOUR, TO BE PRECISE.
NO, YOU STAY AND ENJOY YOUR DICKINSON.
NOT JUST NOW, MY DEAR ERIKA.
SHALL I READ YOU SOME?
PERHAPS LATER?
GOD-BESOTTED TWADDLE.
NO, YOU'LL BE ***ASLEEP*** BY THE TIME I RETURN.
YET SHE HAD BEEN ALIVE ONLY SIX WEEKS.
AN EYE-BLINK TO HIS TWO HUNDRED AND FORTY YEARS.

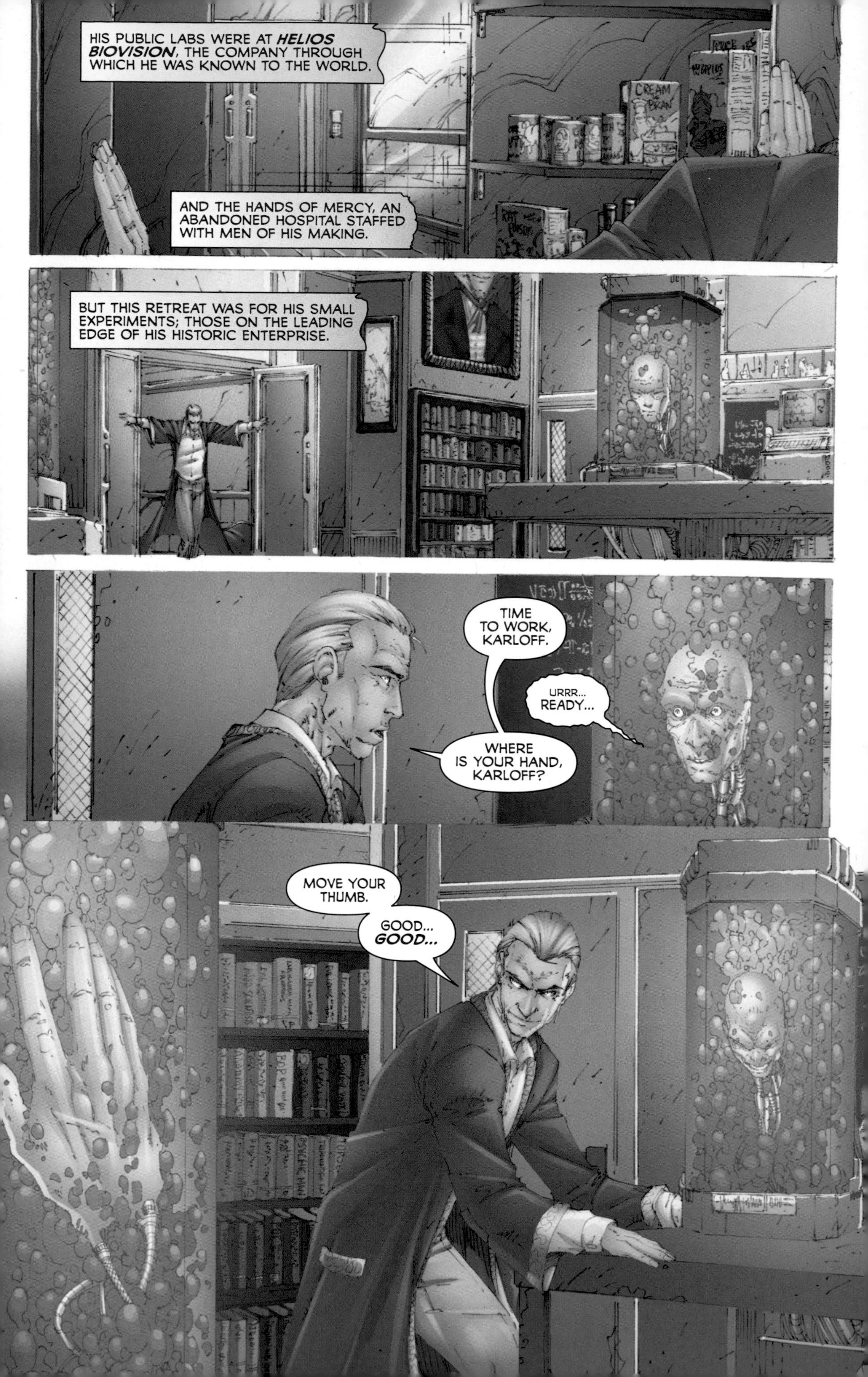
HIS PUBLIC LABS WERE AT HELIOS BIOVISION, THE COMPANY THROUGH WHICH HE WAS KNOWN TO THE WORLD.
AND THE HANDS OF MERCY, AN ABANDONED HOSPITAL STAFFED WITH MEN OF HIS MAKING.
CREAM OF BRAN
RAT POISON
BUT THIS RETREAT WAS FOR HIS SMALL EXPERIMENTS; THOSE ON THE LEADING EDGE OF HIS HISTORIC ENTERPRISE.
TIME TO WORK, KARLOFF.
URRR... READY...
WHERE IS YOUR HAND, KARLOFF?
MOVE YOUR THUMB.
GOOD... GOOD...

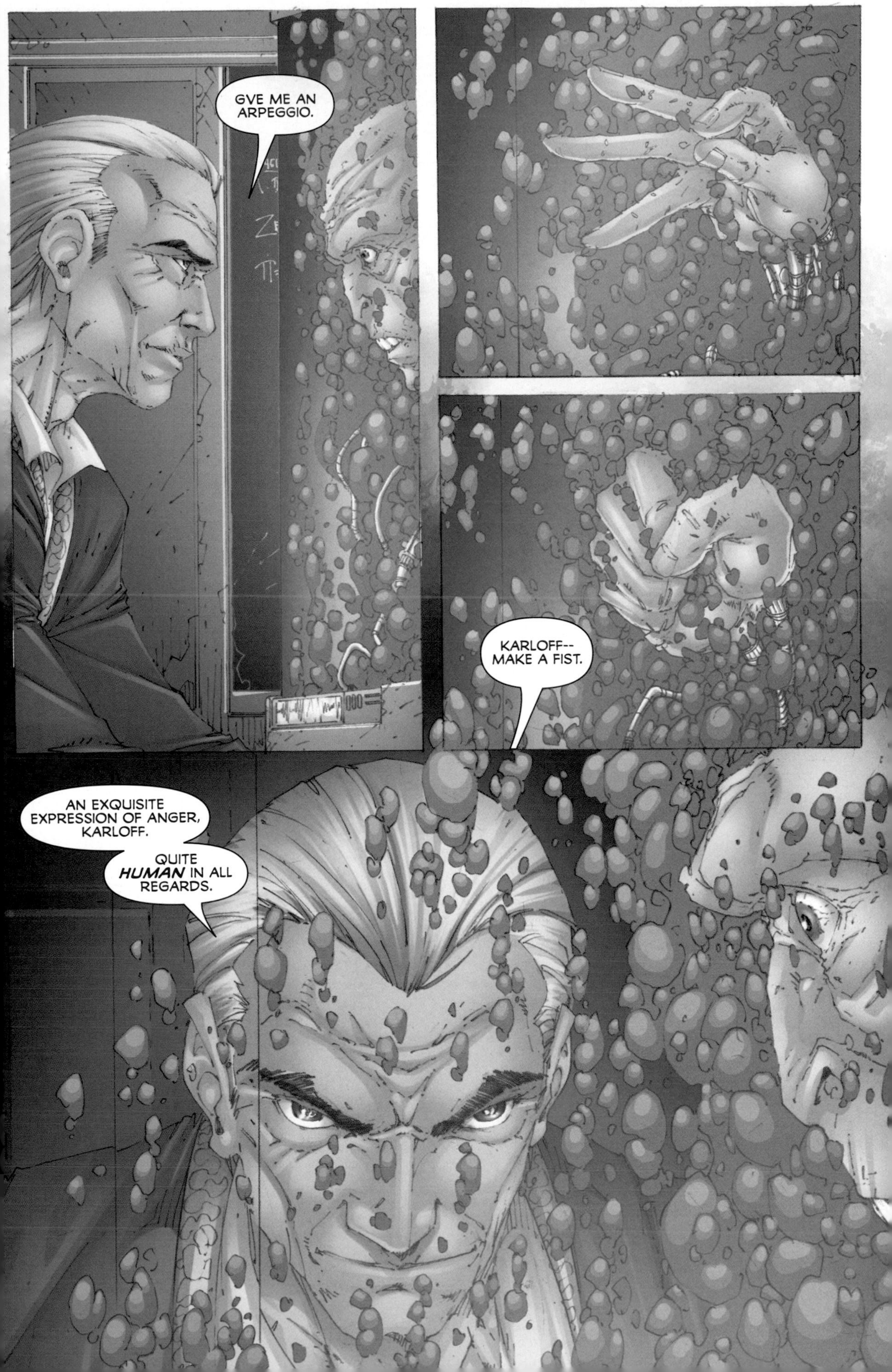
GVE ME AN ARPEGGIO.
KARLOFF-- MAKE A FIST.
AN EXQUISITE EXPRESSION OF ANGER, KARLOFF.
QUITE *HUMAN* IN ALL REGARDS.

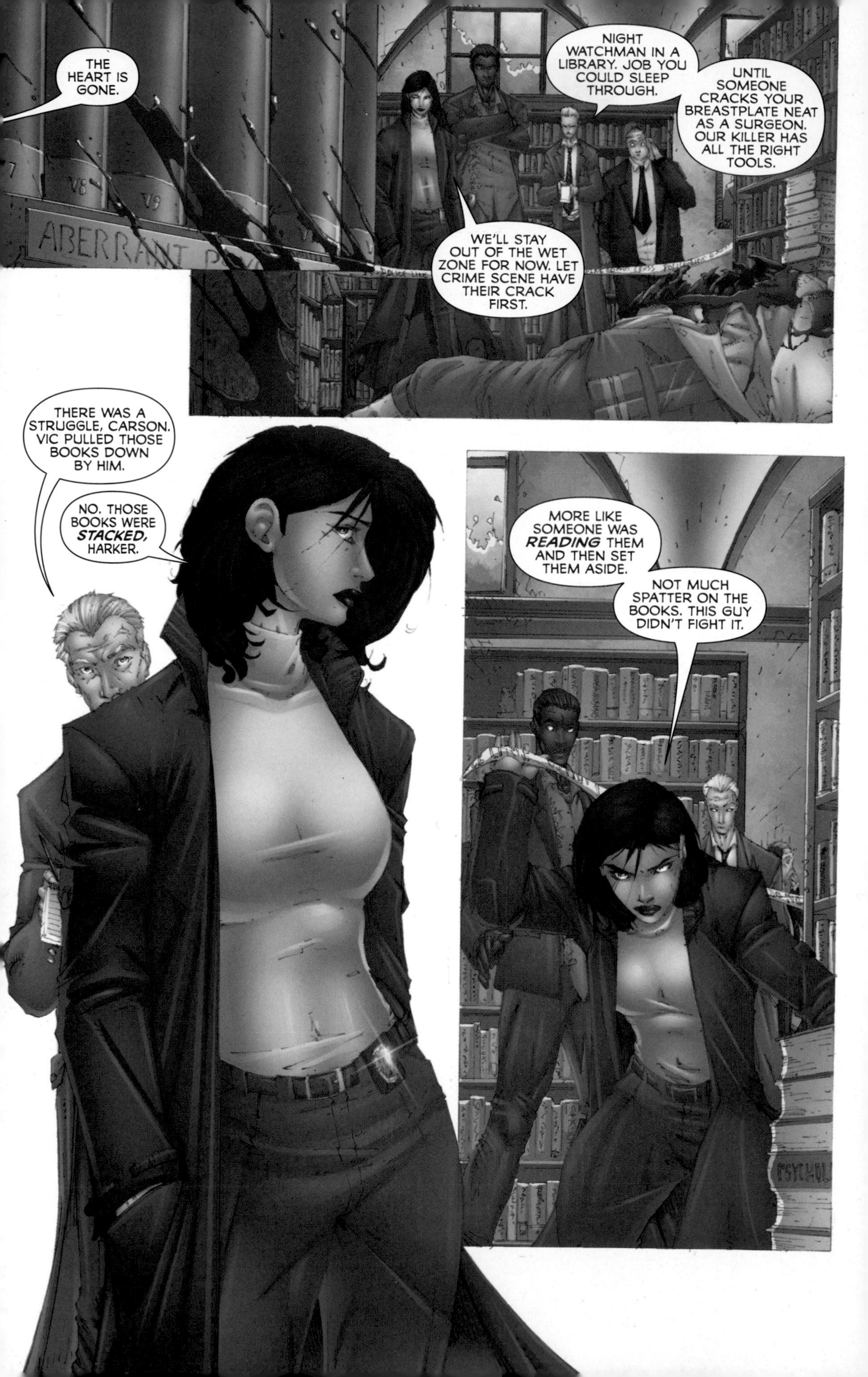
THE HEART IS GONE.
NIGHT WATCHMAN IN A LIBRARY. JOB YOU COULD SLEEP THROUGH.
UNTIL SOMEONE CRACKS YOUR BREASTPLATE NEAT AS A SURGEON. OUR KILLER HAS ALL THE RIGHT TOOLS.
WE'LL STAY OUT OF THE WET ZONE FOR NOW. LET CRIME SCENE HAVE THEIR CRACK FIRST.
ABERRANT
THERE WAS A STRUGGLE, CARSON. VIC PULLED THOSE BOOKS DOWN BY HIM.
NO. THOSE BOOKS WERE *STACKED,* HARKER.
MORE LIKE SOMEONE WAS *READING* THEM AND THEN SET THEM ASIDE.
NOT MUCH SPATTER ON THE BOOKS. THIS GUY DIDN'T FIGHT IT.

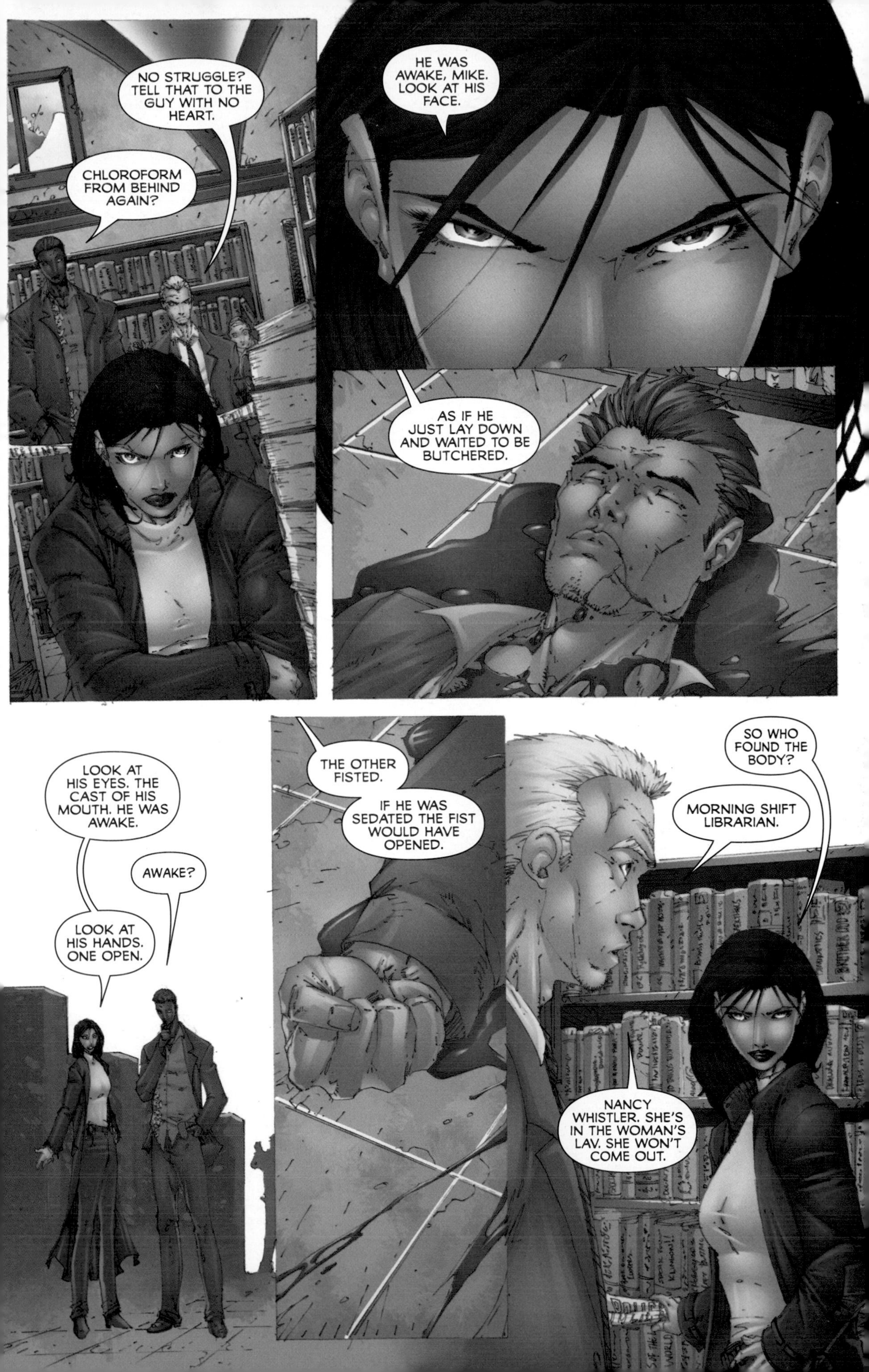
NO STRUGGLE? TELL THAT TO THE GUY WITH NO HEART.
CHLOROFORM FROM BEHIND AGAIN?
HE WAS AWAKE, MIKE. LOOK AT HIS FACE.
AS IF HE JUST LAY DOWN AND WAITED TO BE BUTCHERED.
LOOK AT HIS EYES. THE CAST OF HIS MOUTH. HE WAS AWAKE.
AWAKE?
LOOK AT HIS HANDS. ONE OPEN.
THE OTHER FISTED.
IF HE WAS SEDATED THE FIST WOULD HAVE OPENED.
SO WHO FOUND THE BODY?
MORNING SHIFT LIBRARIAN.
NANCY WHISTLER. SHE'S IN THE WOMAN'S LAV. SHE WON'T COME OUT.

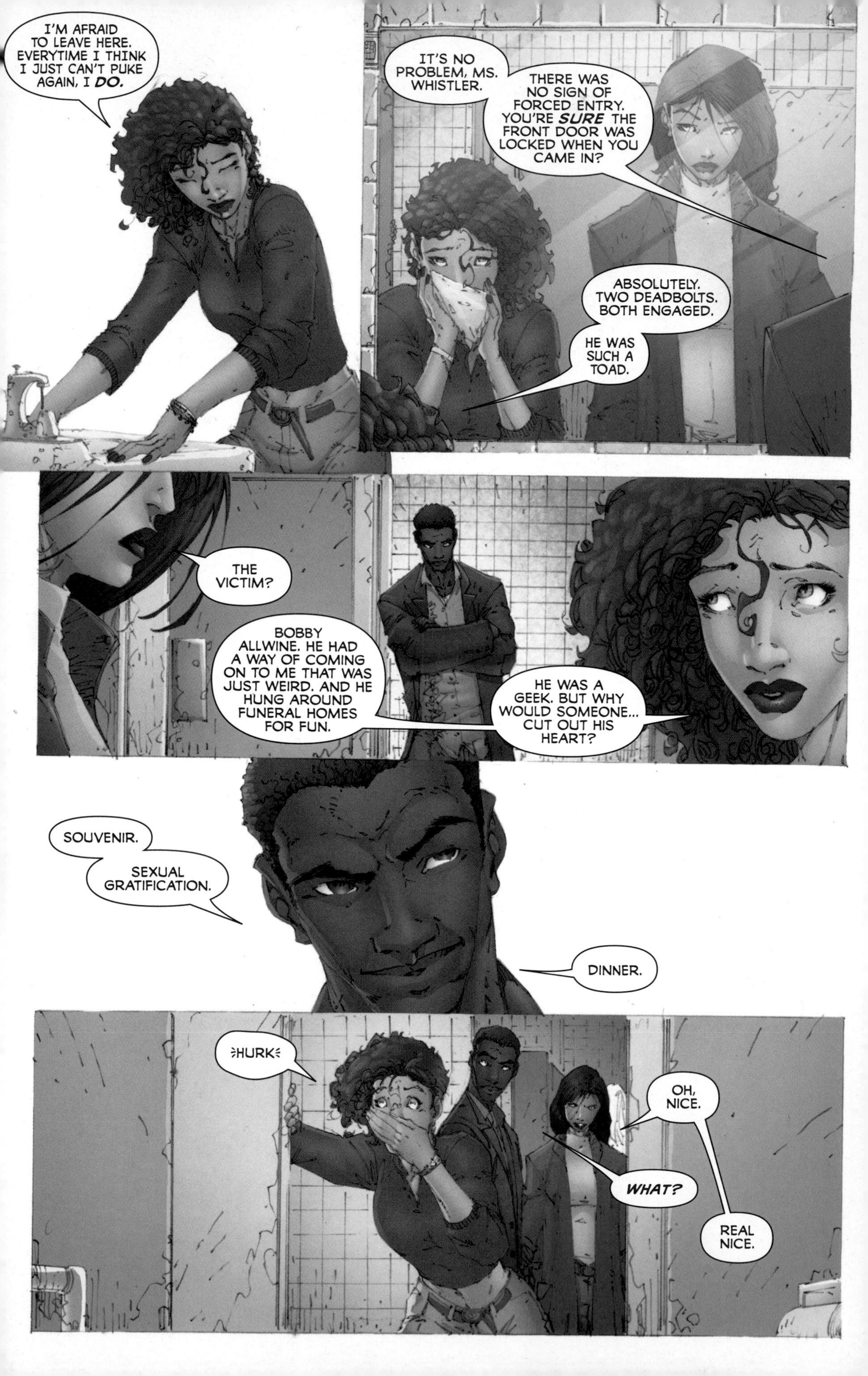
I'M AFRAID TO LEAVE HERE. EVERYTIME I THINK I JUST CAN'T PUKE AGAIN, I *DO.*
IT'S NO PROBLEM, MS. WHISTLER.
THERE WAS NO SIGN OF FORCED ENTRY. YOU'RE *SURE* THE FRONT DOOR WAS LOCKED WHEN YOU CAME IN?
ABSOLUTELY. TWO DEADBOLTS. BOTH ENGAGED.
HE WAS SUCH A TOAD.
THE VICTIM?
BOBBY ALLWINE. HE HAD A WAY OF COMING ON TO ME THAT WAS JUST WEIRD. AND HE HUNG AROUND FUNERAL HOMES FOR FUN.
HE WAS A GEEK. BUT WHY WOULD SOMEONE... CUT OUT HIS HEART?
SOUVENIR.
SEXUAL GRATIFICATION.
DINNER.
HURK
OH, NICE.
WHAT?
REAL NICE.

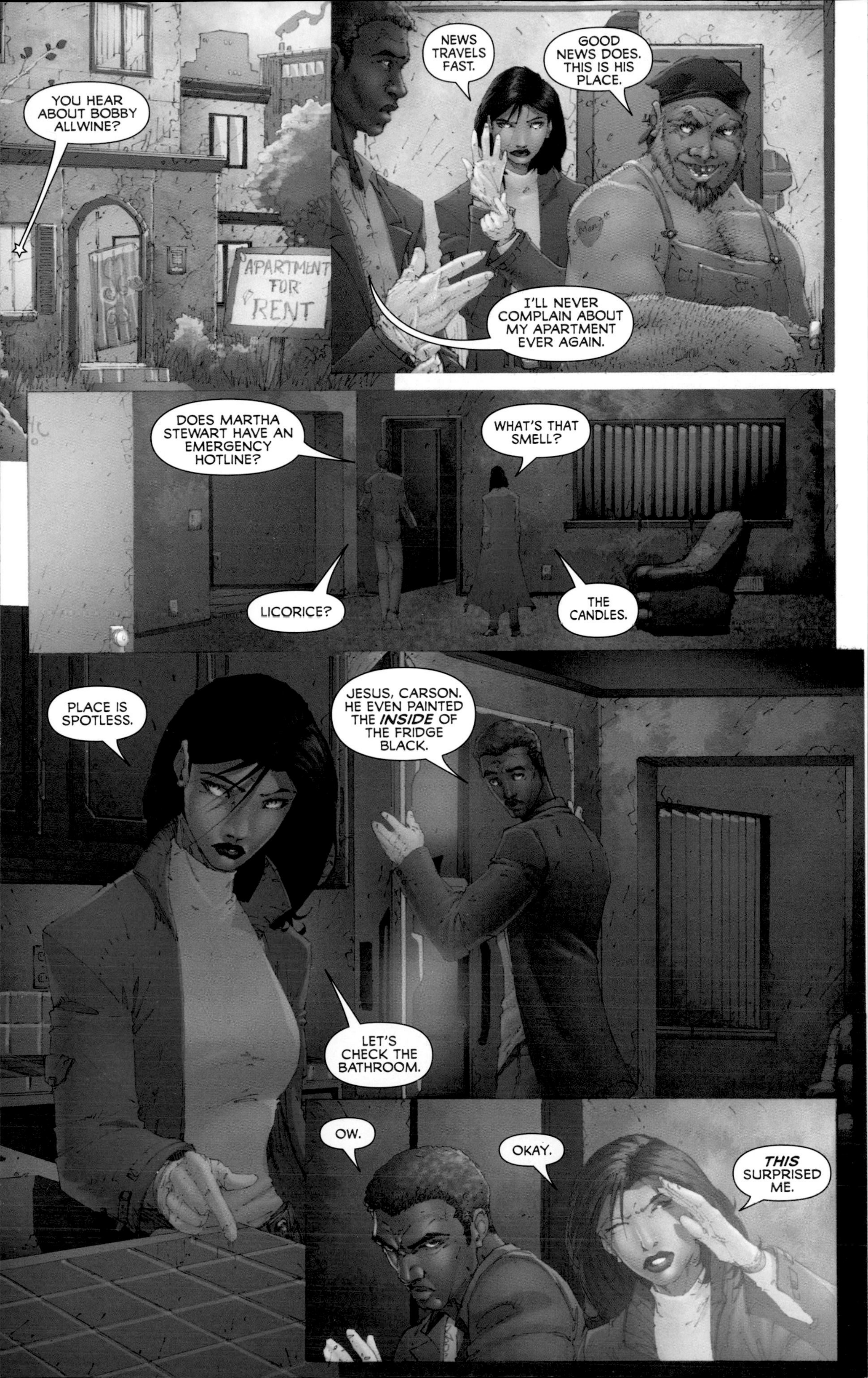
YOU HEAR ABOUT BOBBY ALLWINE?
APARTMENT FOR RENT
NEWS TRAVELS FAST.
GOOD NEWS DOES. THIS IS HIS PLACE.
I'LL NEVER COMPLAIN ABOUT MY APARTMENT EVER AGAIN.
DOES MARTHA STEWART HAVE AN EMERGENCY HOTLINE?
LICORICE?
WHAT'S THAT SMELL?
THE CANDLES.
PLACE IS SPOTLESS.
JESUS, CARSON. HE EVEN PAINTED THE *INSIDE* OF THE FRIDGE BLACK.
LET'S CHECK THE BATHROOM.
OW.
OKAY.
THIS SURPRISED ME.

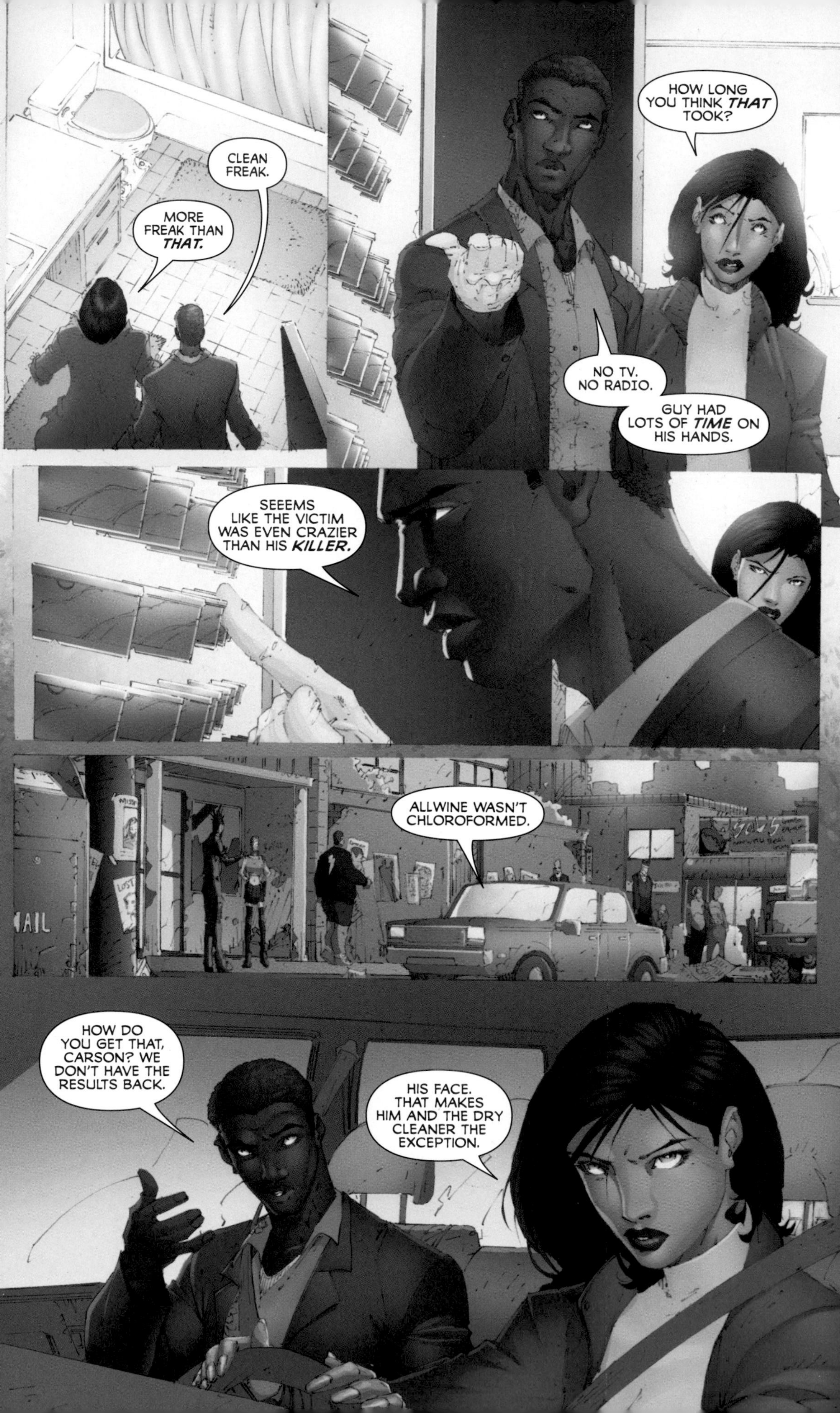
CLEAN FREAK.
MORE FREAK THAN *THAT.*
HOW LONG YOU THINK *THAT* TOOK?
NO TV. NO RADIO.
GUY HAD LOTS OF *TIME* ON HIS HANDS.
SEEEMS LIKE THE VICTIM WAS EVEN CRAZIER THAN HIS *KILLER.*
LOST
AIL
ALLWINE WASN'T CHLOROFORMED.
HOW DO YOU GET THAT, CARSON? WE DON'T HAVE THE RESULTS BACK.
HIS FACE. THAT MAKES HIM AND THE DRY CLEANER THE EXCEPTION.

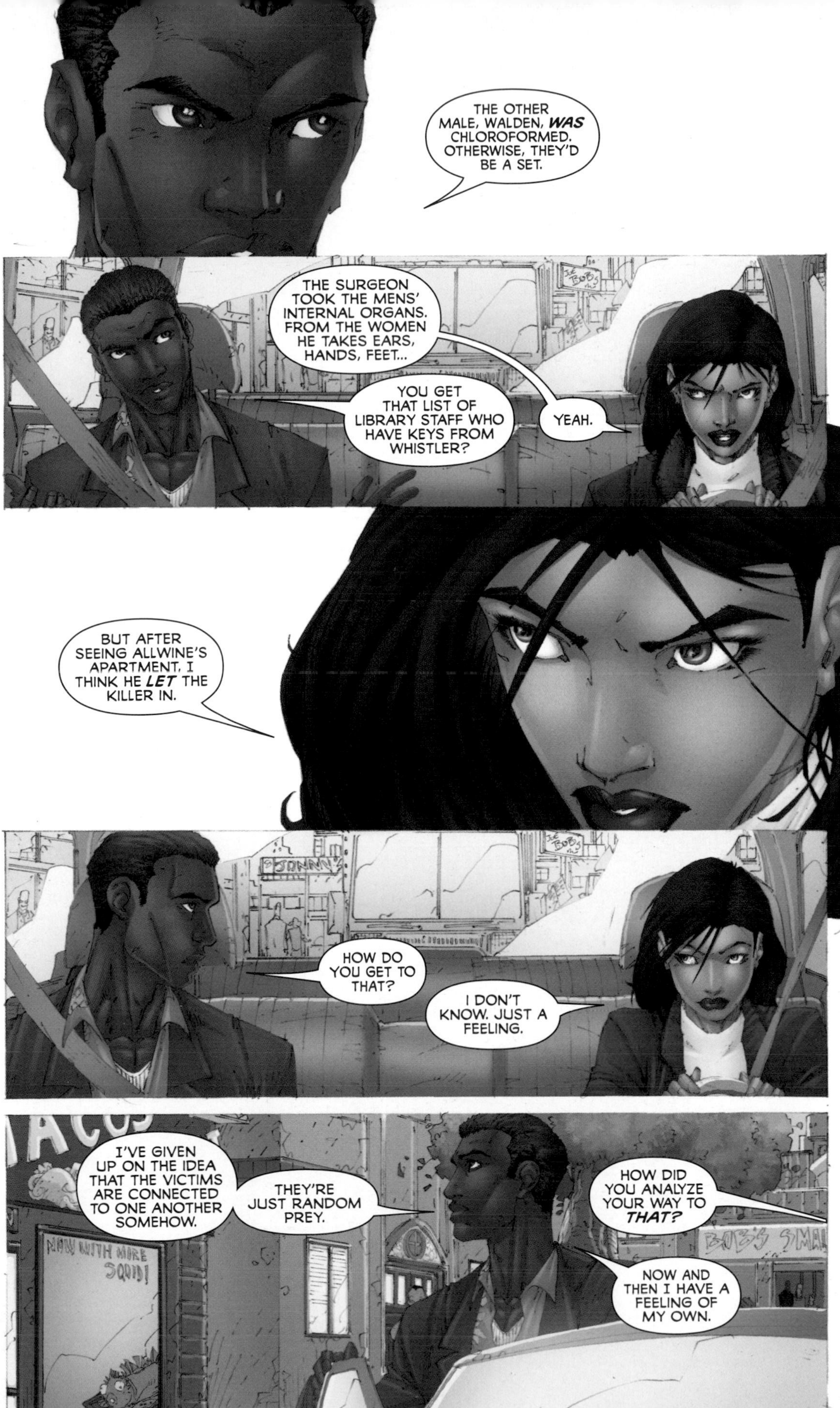
THE OTHER MALE, WALDEN, *WAS* CHLOROFORMED. OTHERWISE, THEY'D BE A SET.
THE SURGEON TOOK THE MENS' INTERNAL ORGANS. FROM THE WOMEN HE TAKES EARS, HANDS, FEET...
YOU GET THAT LIST OF LIBRARY STAFF WHO HAVE KEYS FROM WHISTLER?
YEAH.
BUT AFTER SEEING ALLWINE'S APARTMENT, I THINK HE *LET* THE KILLER IN.
HOW DO YOU GET TO THAT?
I DON'T KNOW. JUST A FEELING.
I'VE GIVEN UP ON THE IDEA THAT THE VICTIMS ARE CONNECTED TO ONE ANOTHER SOMEHOW.
THEY'RE JUST RANDOM PREY.
HOW DID YOU ANALYZE YOUR WAY TO *THAT?*
NOW AND THEN I HAVE A FEELING OF MY OWN.
NOW WITH MORE SQUID!

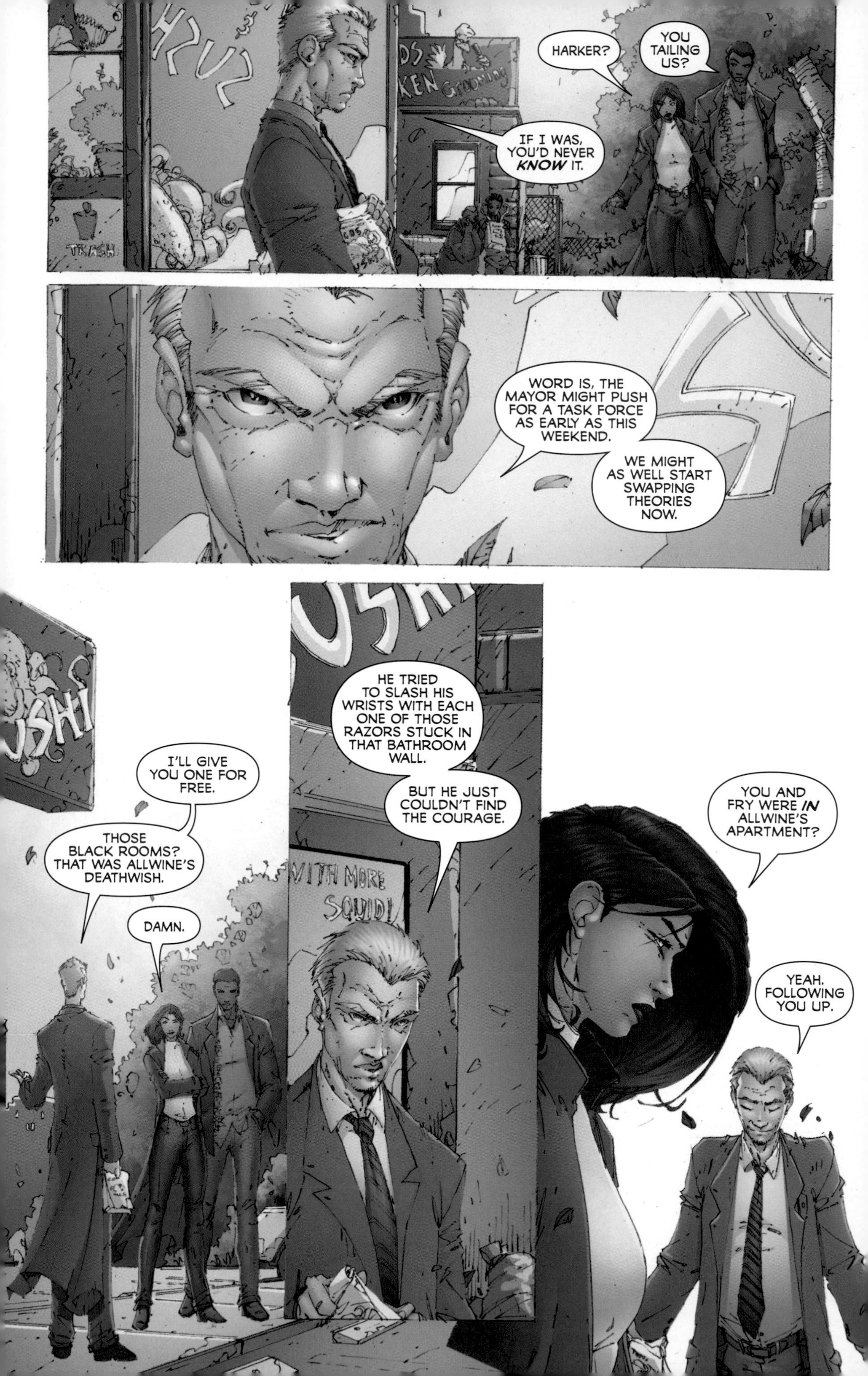
HARKER?
YOU TAILING US?
IF I WAS, YOU'D NEVER *KNOW* IT.
WORD IS, THE MAYOR MIGHT PUSH FOR A TASK FORCE AS EARLY AS THIS WEEKEND.
WE MIGHT AS WELL START SWAPPING THEORIES NOW.
I'LL GIVE YOU ONE FOR FREE.
THOSE BLACK ROOMS? THAT WAS ALLWINE'S DEATHWISH.
DAMN.
HE TRIED TO SLASH HIS WRISTS WITH EACH ONE OF THOSE RAZORS STUCK IN THAT BATHROOM WALL.
BUT HE JUST COULDN'T FIND THE COURAGE.
WITH MORE SQUID!
YOU AND FRY WERE *IN* ALLWINE'S APARTMENT?
YEAH. FOLLOWING YOU UP.

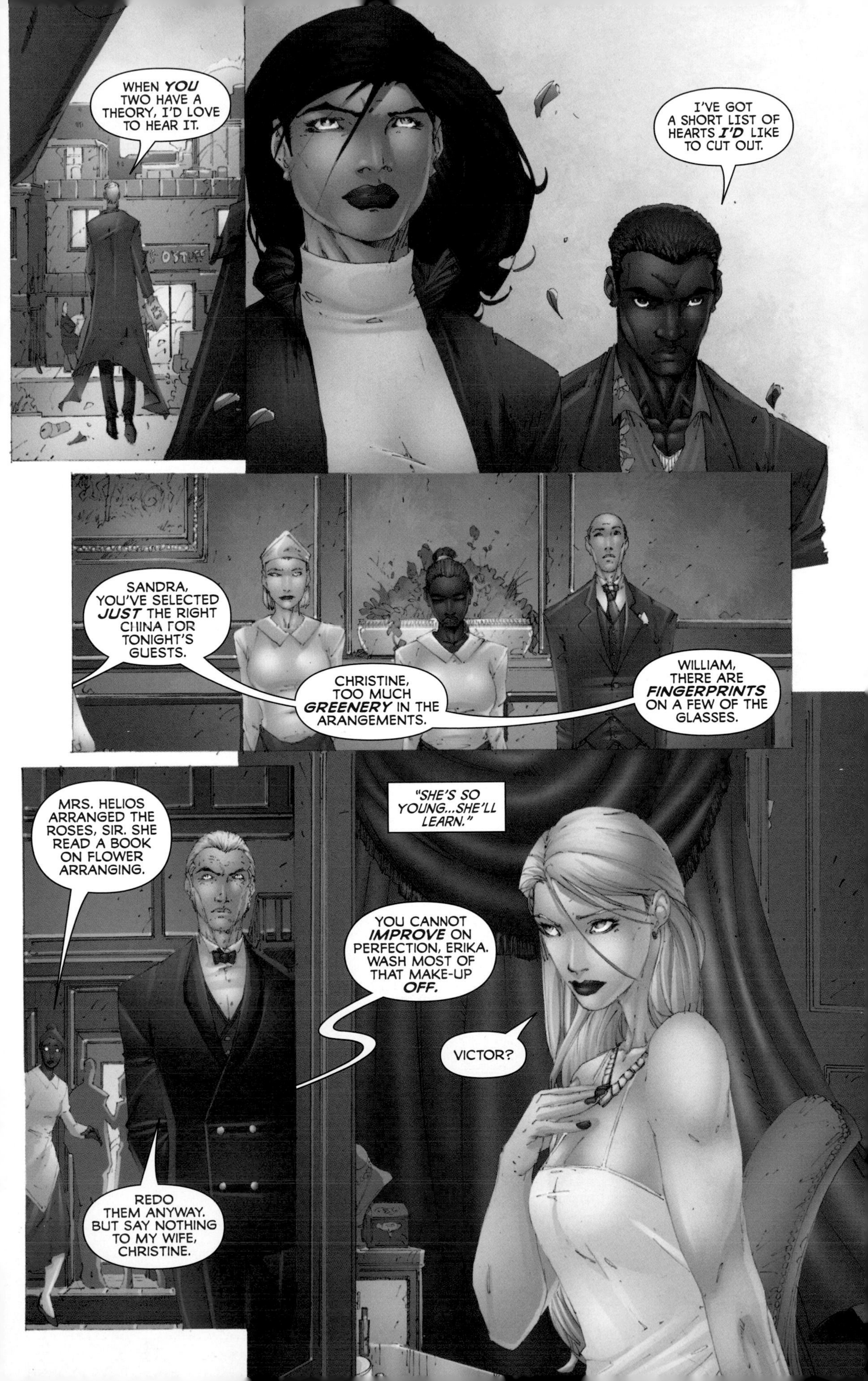
WHEN *YOU* TWO HAVE A THEORY, I'D LOVE TO HEAR IT.
I'VE GOT A SHORT LIST OF HEARTS *I'D* LIKE TO CUT OUT.
SANDRA, YOU'VE SELECTED *JUST* THE RIGHT CHINA FOR TONIGHT'S GUESTS.
CHRISTINE, TOO MUCH *GREENERY* IN THE ARANGEMENTS.
WILLIAM, THERE ARE *FINGERPRINTS* ON A FEW OF THE GLASSES.
MRS. HELIOS ARRANGED THE ROSES, SIR. SHE READ A BOOK ON FLOWER ARRANGING.
"SHE'S SO YOUNG...SHE'LL LEARN."
YOU CANNOT *IMPROVE* ON PERFECTION, ERIKA. WASH MOST OF THAT MAKE-UP *OFF.*
VICTOR?
REDO THEM ANYWAY. BUT SAY NOTHING TO MY WIFE, CHRISTINE.

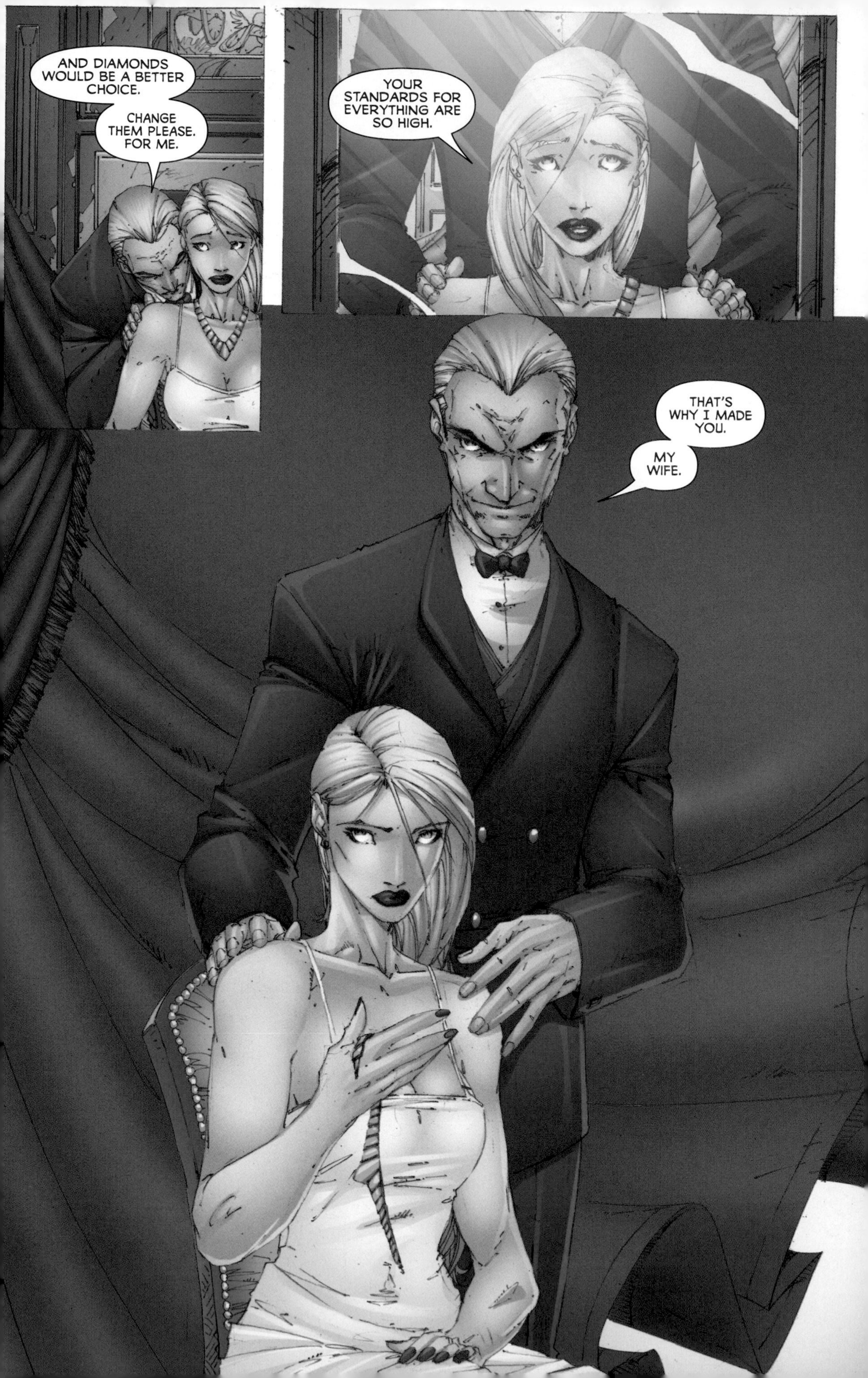
AND DIAMONDS WOULD BE A BETTER CHOICE.
CHANGE THEM PLEASE. FOR ME.
YOUR STANDARDS FOR EVERYTHING ARE SO HIGH.
THAT'S WHY I MADE YOU.
MY WIFE.

chapter Three

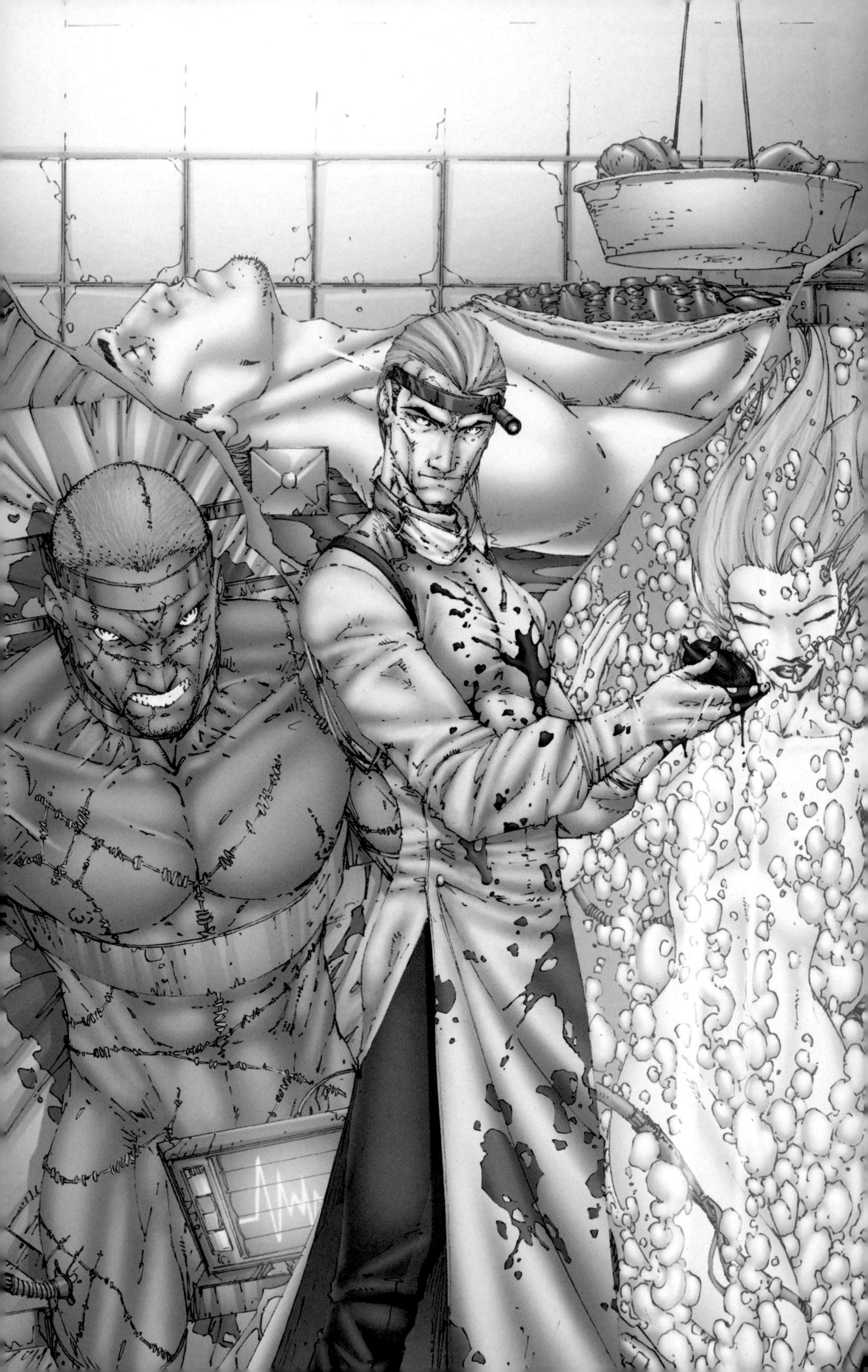

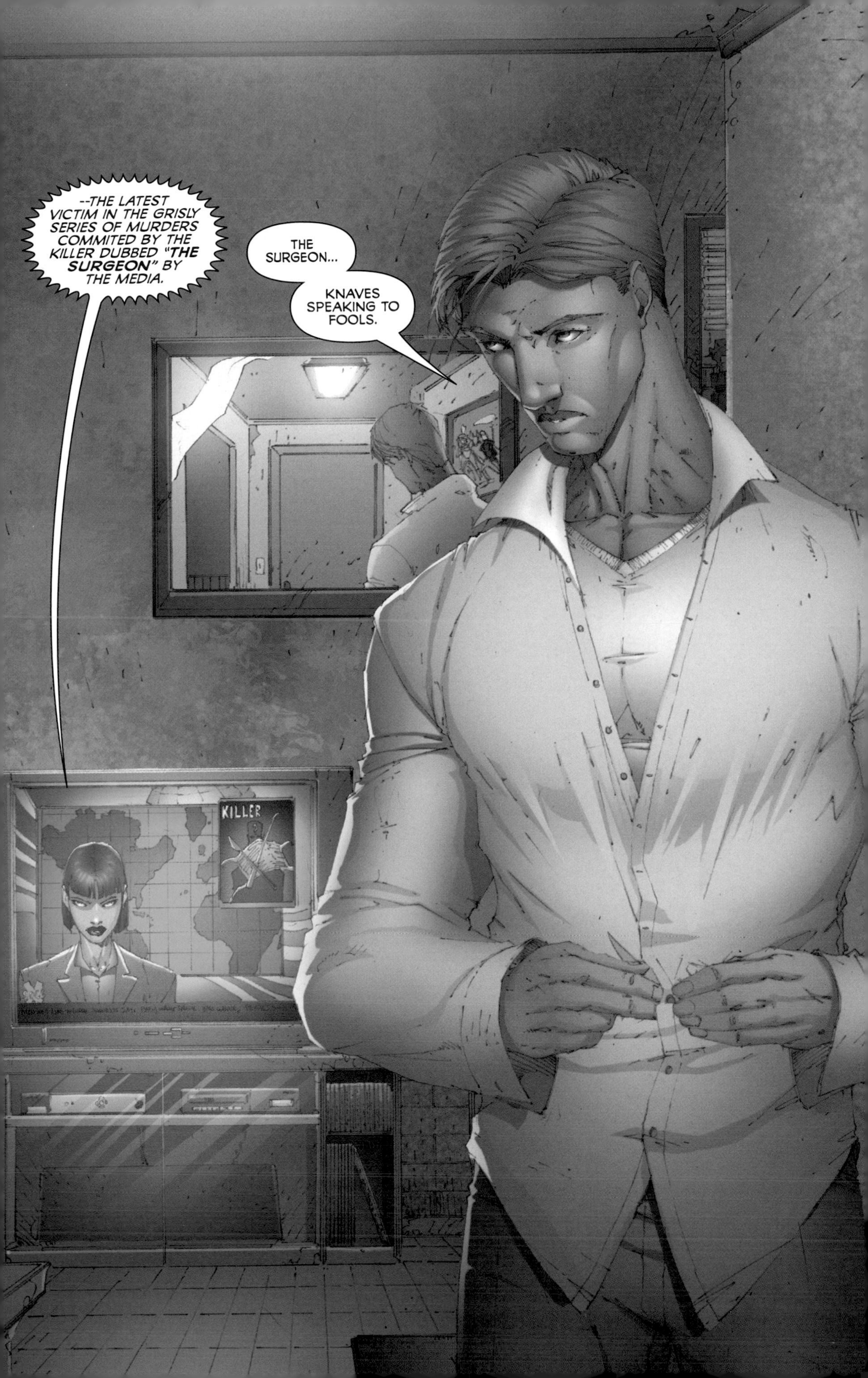
--THE LATEST VICTIM IN THE GRISLY SERIES OF MURDERS COMMITED BY THE KILLER DUBBED "THE SURGEON" BY THE MEDIA.
THE SURGEON...
KNAVES SPEAKING TO FOOLS.
KILLER

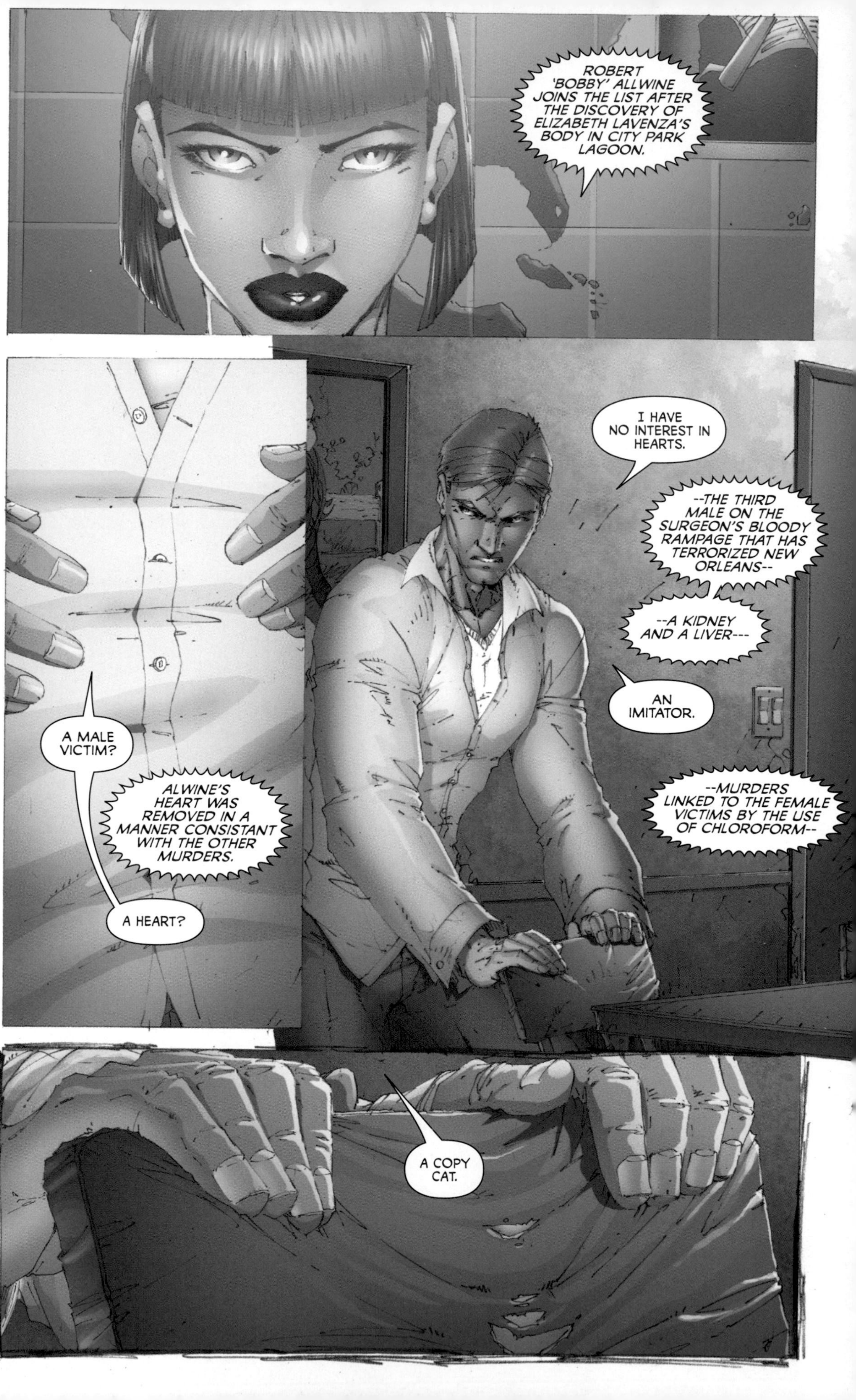
ROBERT 'BOBBY' ALLWINE JOINS THE LIST AFTER THE DISCOVERY OF ELIZABETH LAVENZA'S BODY IN CITY PARK LAGOON.
I HAVE NO INTEREST IN HEARTS.
--THE THIRD MALE ON THE SURGEON'S BLOODY RAMPAGE THAT HAS TERRORIZED NEW ORLEANS--
--A KIDNEY AND A LIVER---
AN IMITATOR.
--MURDERS LINKED TO THE FEMALE VICTIMS BY THE USE OF CHLOROFORM--
A MALE VICTIM?
ALWINE'S HEART WAS REMOVED IN A MANNER CONSISTANT WITH THE OTHER MURDERS.
A HEART?
A COPY CAT.

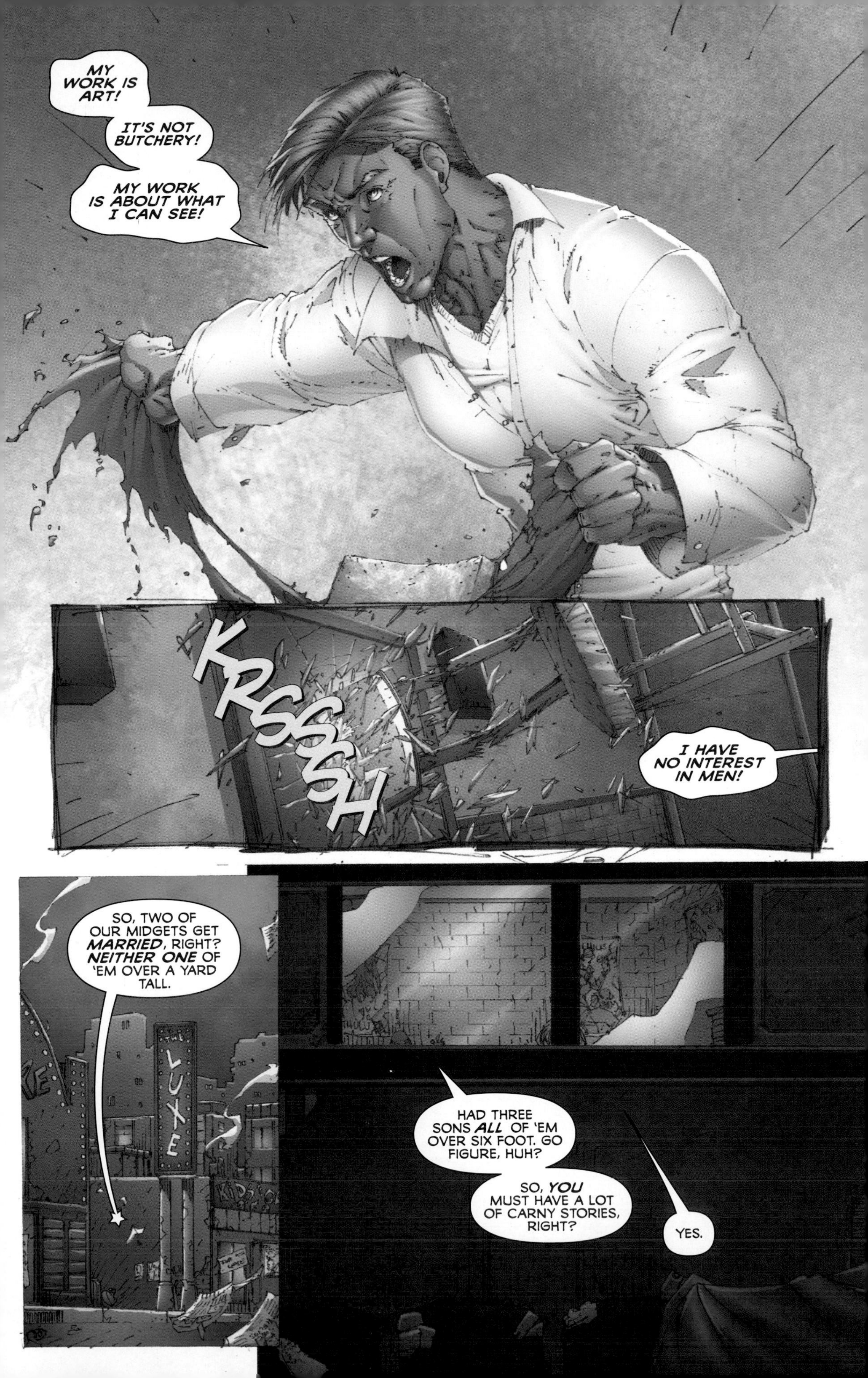
MY WORK IS ART!
IT'S NOT BUTCHERY!
MY WORK IS ABOUT WHAT I CAN SEE!
KRSSSH
I HAVE NO INTEREST IN MEN!
SO, TWO OF OUR MIDGETS GET MARRIED, RIGHT? NEITHER ONE OF 'EM OVER A YARD TALL.
THE LUXE
HAD THREE SONS ALL OF 'EM OVER SIX FOOT. GO FIGURE, HUH?
SO, YOU MUST HAVE A LOT OF CARNY STORIES, RIGHT?
YES.

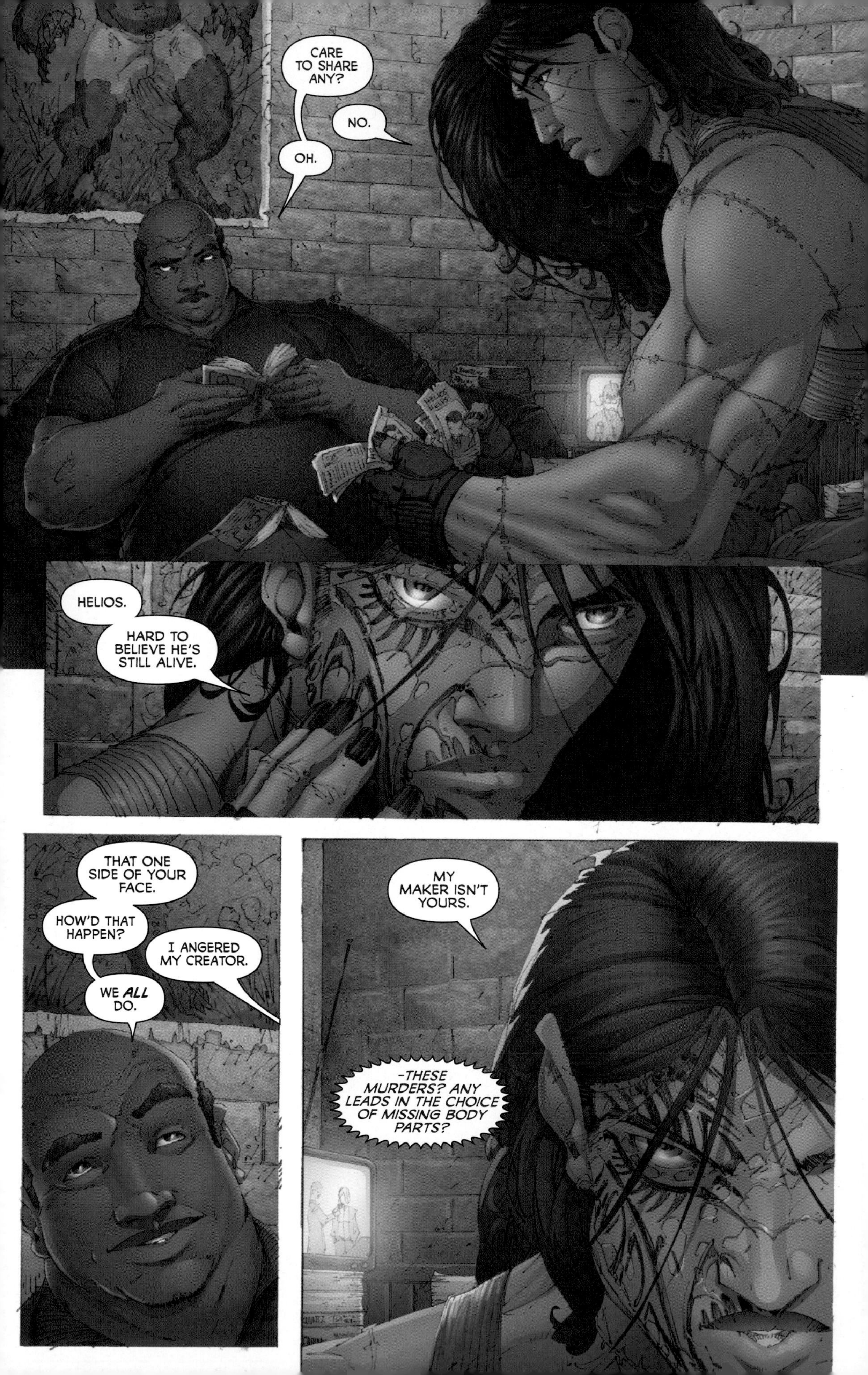
CARE TO SHARE ANY?
NO.
OH.
HELIOS.
HARD TO BELIEVE HE'S STILL ALIVE.
THAT ONE SIDE OF YOUR FACE.
HOW'D THAT HAPPEN?
I ANGERED MY CREATOR.
WE *ALL* DO.
MY MAKER ISN'T YOURS.
-THESE MURDERS? ANY LEADS IN THE CHOICE OF MISSING BODY PARTS?

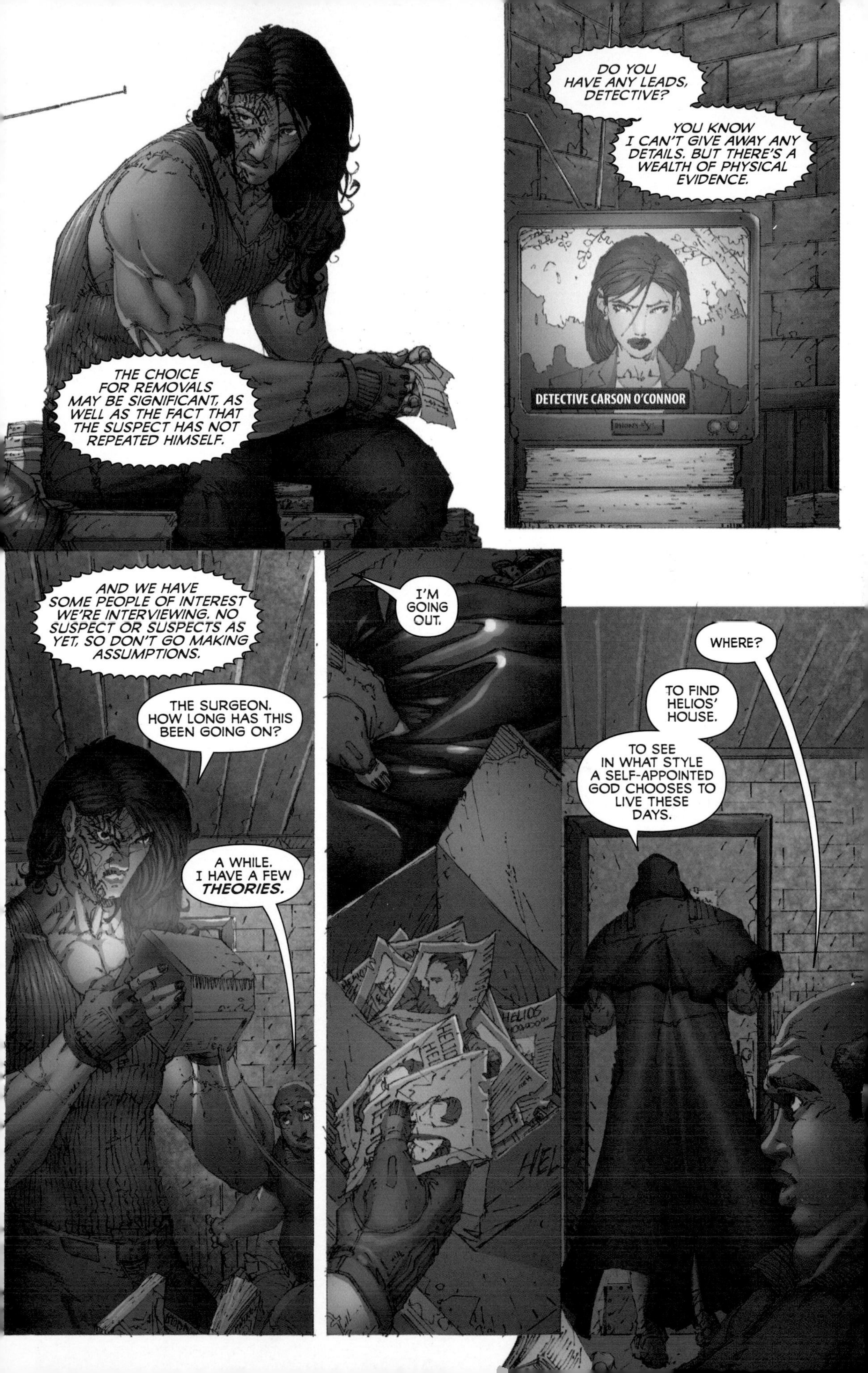
THE CHOICE FOR REMOVALS MAY BE SIGNIFICANT, AS WELL AS THE FACT THAT THE SUSPECT HAS NOT REPEATED HIMSELF.
DO YOU HAVE ANY LEADS, DETECTIVE?
YOU KNOW I CAN'T GIVE AWAY ANY DETAILS. BUT THERE'S A WEALTH OF PHYSICAL EVIDENCE.
DETECTIVE CARSON O'CONNOR
AND WE HAVE SOME PEOPLE OF INTEREST WE'RE INTERVIEWING. NO SUSPECT OR SUSPECTS AS YET, SO DON'T GO MAKING ASSUMPTIONS.
THE SURGEON. HOW LONG HAS THIS BEEN GOING ON?
A WHILE. I HAVE A FEW *THEORIES.*
I'M GOING OUT.
WHERE?
TO FIND HELIOS' HOUSE.
TO SEE IN WHAT STYLE A SELF-APPOINTED GOD CHOOSES TO LIVE THESE DAYS.

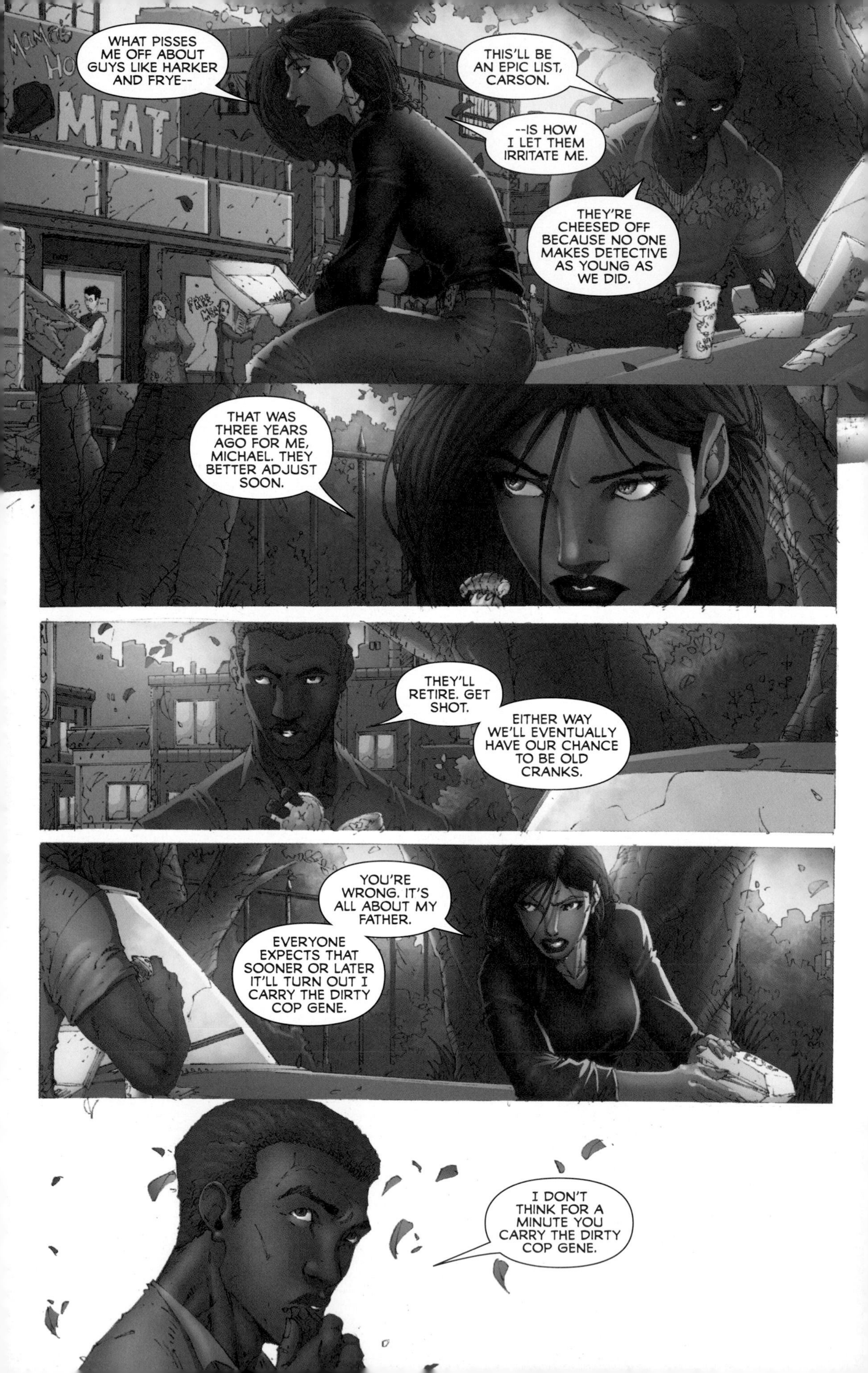
WHAT PISSES ME OFF ABOUT GUYS LIKE HARKER AND FRYE--
THIS'LL BE AN EPIC LIST, CARSON.
--IS HOW I LET THEM IRRITATE ME.
THEY'RE CHEESED OFF BECAUSE NO ONE MAKES DETECTIVE AS YOUNG AS WE DID.
MEAT
THAT WAS THREE YEARS AGO FOR ME, MICHAEL. THEY BETTER ADJUST SOON.
THEY'LL RETIRE. GET SHOT.
EITHER WAY WE'LL EVENTUALLY HAVE OUR CHANCE TO BE OLD CRANKS.
YOU'RE WRONG. IT'S ALL ABOUT MY FATHER.
EVERYONE EXPECTS THAT SOONER OR LATER IT'LL TURN OUT I CARRY THE DIRTY COP GENE.
I DON'T THINK FOR A MINUTE YOU CARRY THE DIRTY COP GENE.

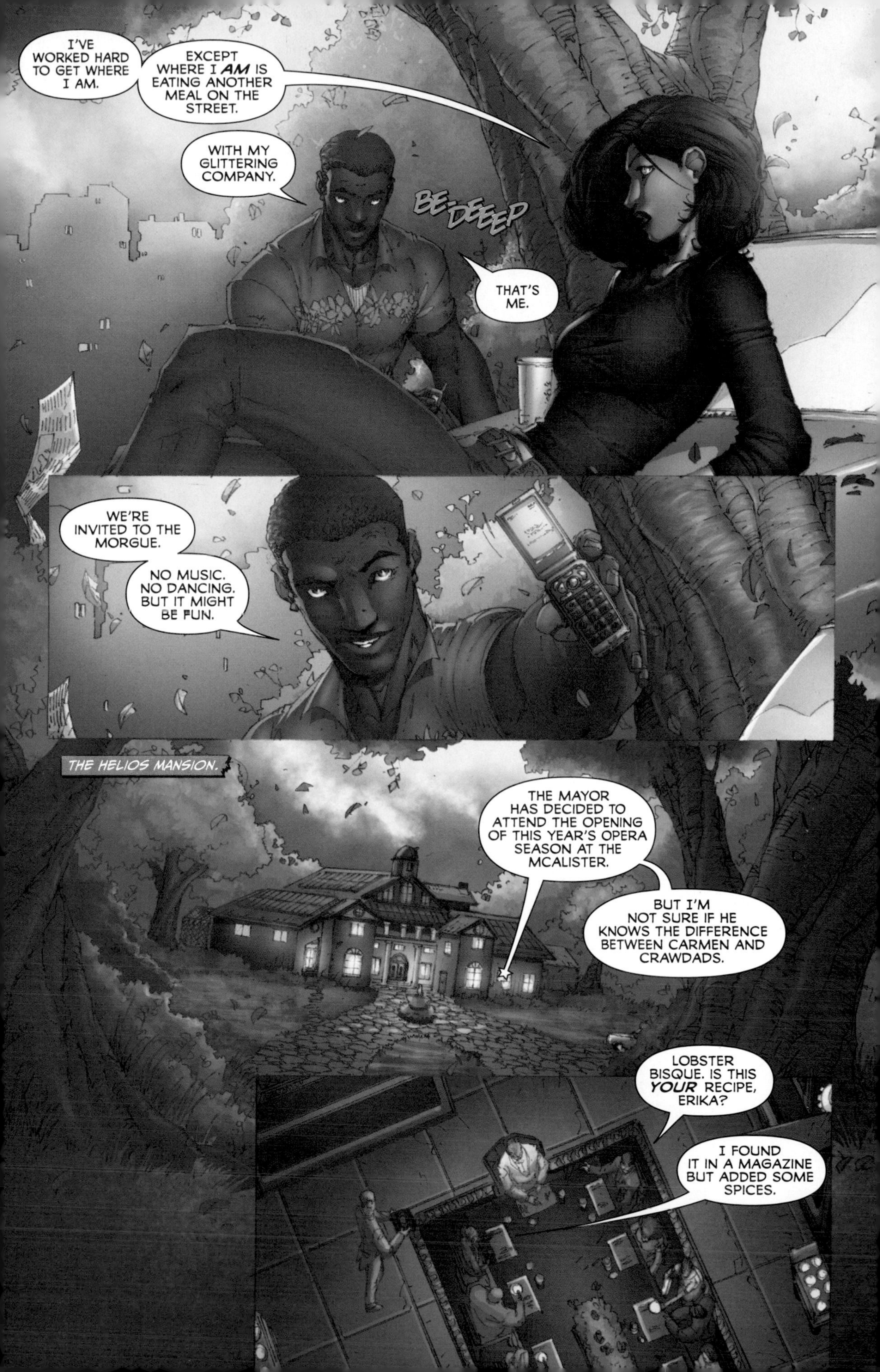
I'VE WORKED HARD TO GET WHERE I AM.
EXCEPT WHERE I AM IS EATING ANOTHER MEAL ON THE STREET.
WITH MY GLITTERING COMPANY.
BE-DEEEP
THAT'S ME.
WE'RE INVITED TO THE MORGUE.
NO MUSIC. NO DANCING. BUT IT MIGHT BE FUN.
THE HELIOS MANSION.
THE MAYOR HAS DECIDED TO ATTEND THE OPENING OF THIS YEAR'S OPERA SEASON AT THE MCALISTER.
BUT I'M NOT SURE IF HE KNOWS THE DIFFERENCE BETWEEN CARMEN AND CRAWDADS.
LOBSTER BISQUE. IS THIS YOUR RECIPE, ERIKA?
I FOUND IT IN A MAGAZINE BUT ADDED SOME SPICES.

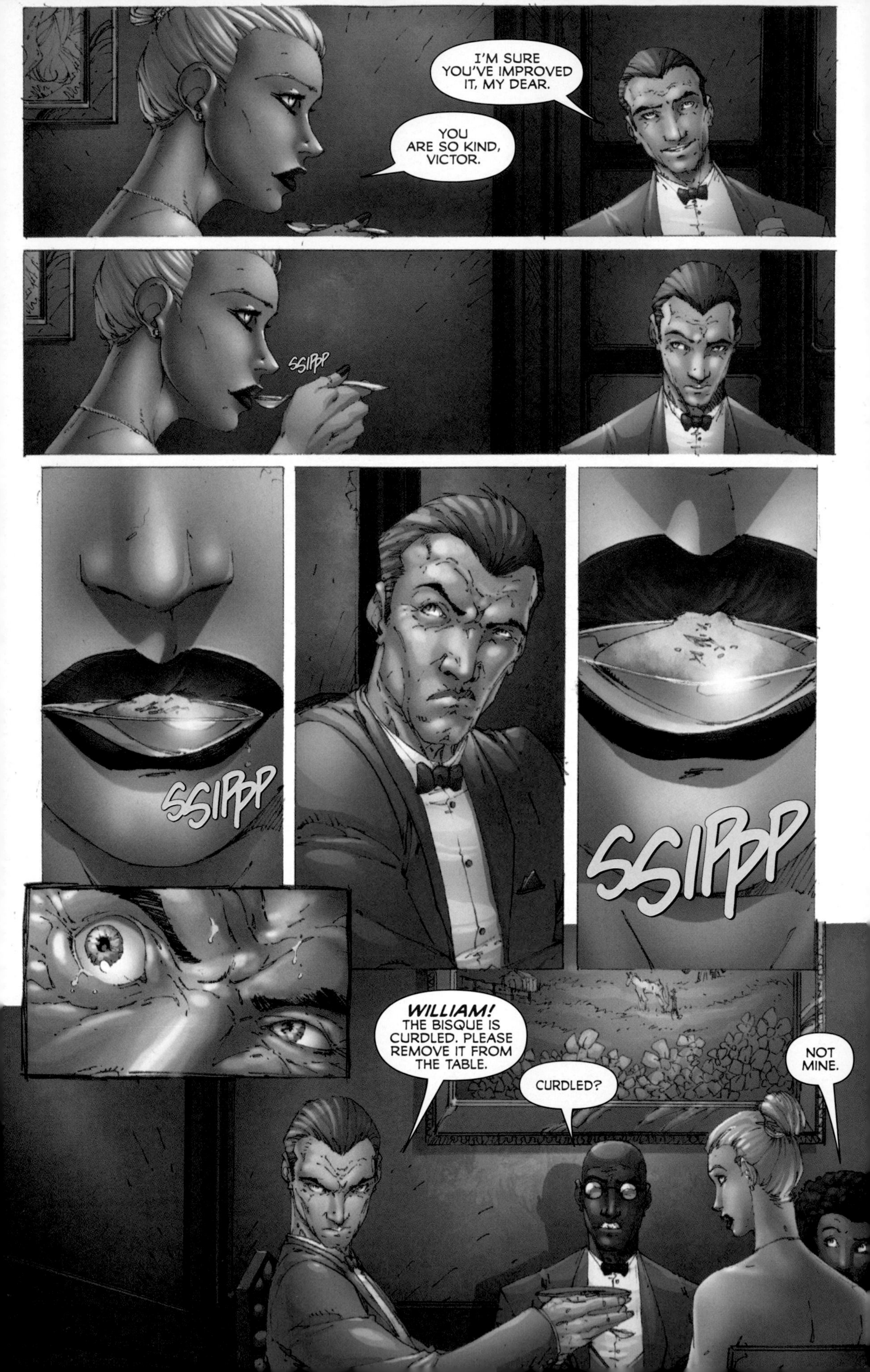
I'M SURE YOU'VE IMPROVED IT, MY DEAR.
YOU ARE SO KIND, VICTOR.
SSIPP
SSIPP
SSIPP
WILLIAM! THE BISQUE IS CURDLED. PLEASE REMOVE IT FROM THE TABLE.
CURDLED?
NOT MINE.

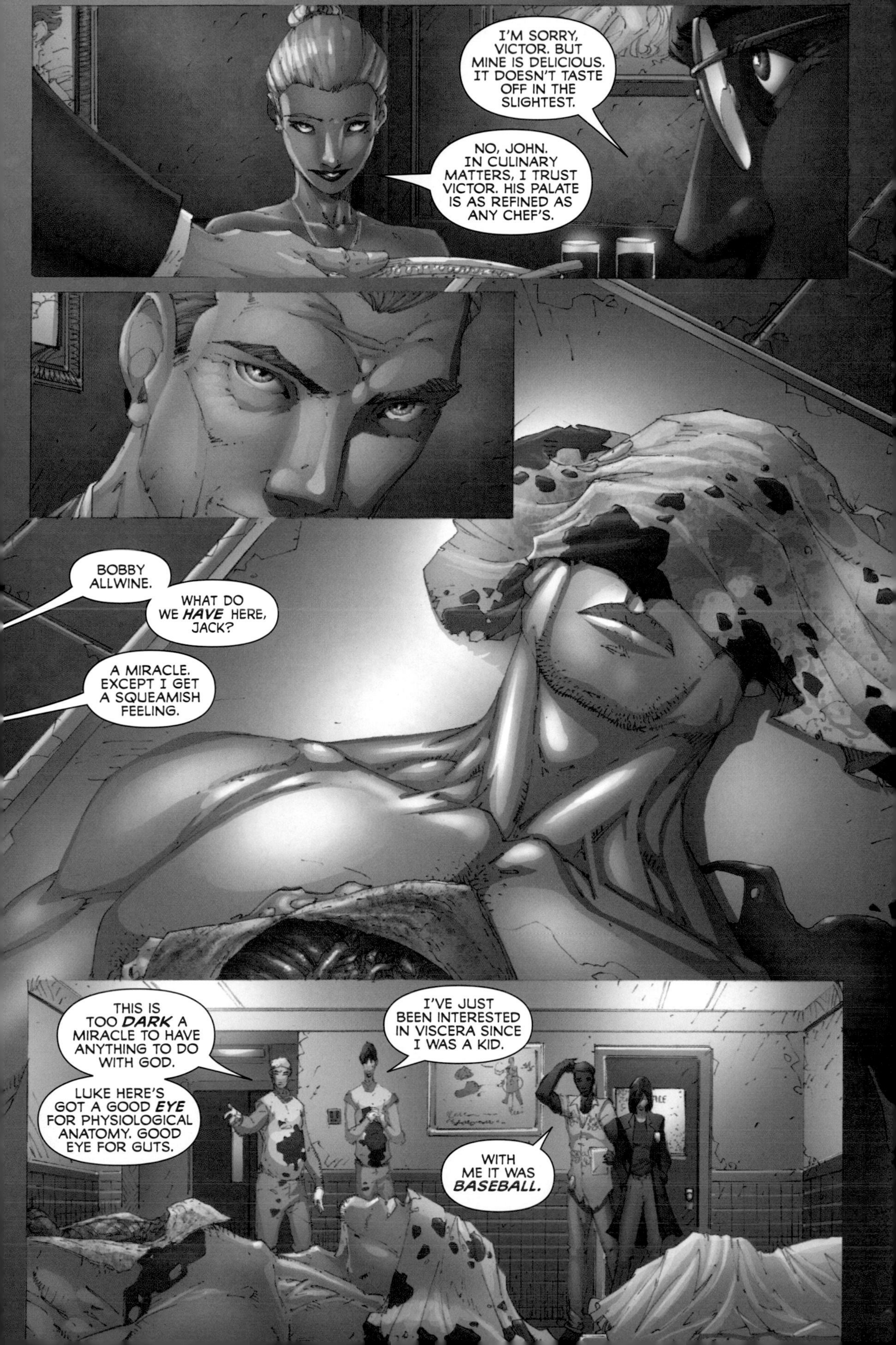
I'M SORRY, VICTOR. BUT MINE IS DELICIOUS. IT DOESN'T TASTE OFF IN THE SLIGHTEST.
NO, JOHN. IN CULINARY MATTERS, I TRUST VICTOR. HIS PALATE IS AS REFINED AS ANY CHEF'S.
BOBBY ALLWINE.
WHAT DO WE *HAVE* HERE, JACK?
A MIRACLE. EXCEPT I GET A SQUEAMISH FEELING.
THIS IS TOO *DARK* A MIRACLE TO HAVE ANYTHING TO DO WITH GOD.
LUKE HERE'S GOT A GOOD *EYE* FOR PHYSIOLOGICAL ANATOMY. GOOD EYE FOR GUTS.
I'VE JUST BEEN INTERESTED IN VISCERA SINCE I WAS A KID.
WITH ME IT WAS *BASEBALL.*

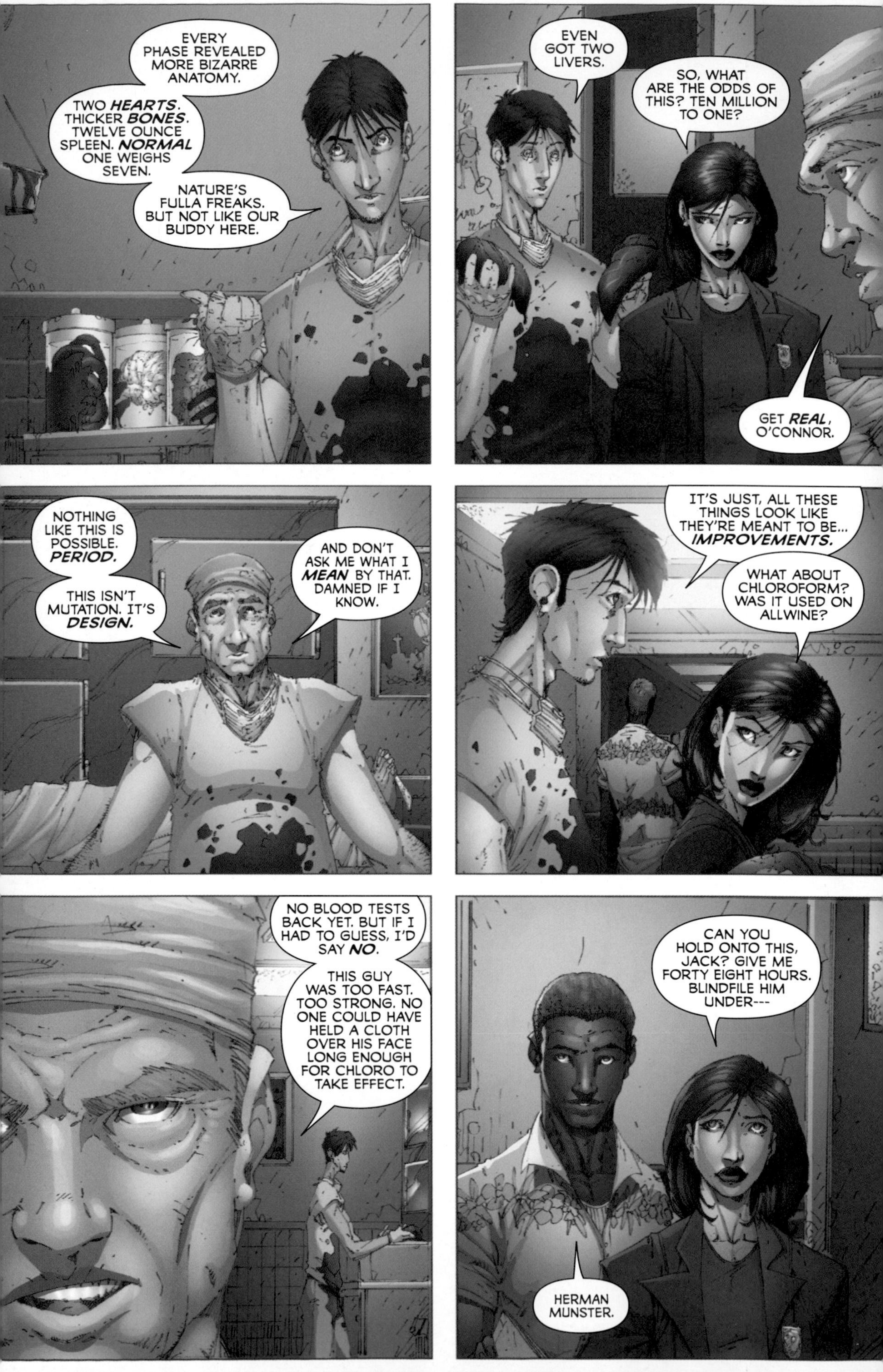
EVERY PHASE REVEALED MORE BIZARRE ANATOMY.
TWO **HEARTS**. THICKER **BONES**. TWELVE OUNCE SPLEEN. **NORMAL** ONE WEIGHS SEVEN.
NATURE'S FULLA FREAKS. BUT NOT LIKE OUR BUDDY HERE.
EVEN GOT TWO LIVERS.
SO, WHAT ARE THE ODDS OF THIS? TEN MILLION TO ONE?
GET **REAL**, O'CONNOR.
NOTHING LIKE THIS IS POSSIBLE. **PERIOD.**
THIS ISN'T MUTATION. IT'S **DESIGN.**
AND DON'T ASK ME WHAT I **MEAN** BY THAT. DAMNED IF I KNOW.
IT'S JUST, ALL THESE THINGS LOOK LIKE THEY'RE MEANT TO BE... **IMPROVEMENTS.**
WHAT ABOUT CHLOROFORM? WAS IT USED ON ALLWINE?
NO BLOOD TESTS BACK YET. BUT IF I HAD TO GUESS, I'D SAY **NO**.
THIS GUY WAS TOO FAST. TOO STRONG. NO ONE COULD HAVE HELD A CLOTH OVER HIS FACE LONG ENOUGH FOR CHLORO TO TAKE EFFECT.
CAN YOU HOLD ONTO THIS, JACK? GIVE ME FORTY EIGHT HOURS. BLINDFILE HIM UNDER---
HERMAN MUNSTER.

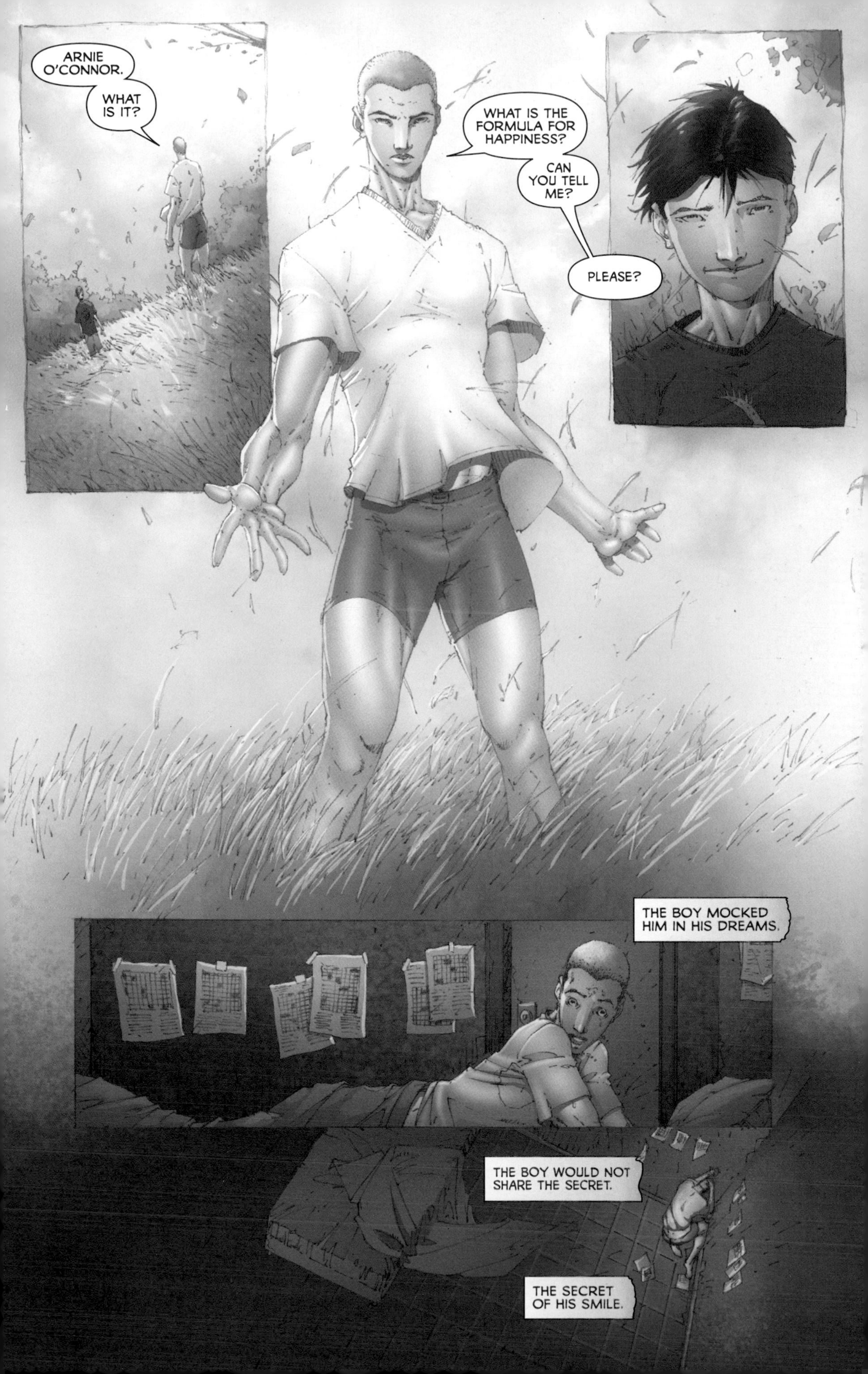
ARNIE O'CONNOR.
WHAT IS IT?
WHAT IS THE FORMULA FOR HAPPINESS?
CAN YOU TELL ME?
PLEASE?
THE BOY MOCKED HIM IN HIS DREAMS.
THE BOY WOULD NOT SHARE THE SECRET.
THE SECRET OF HIS SMILE.

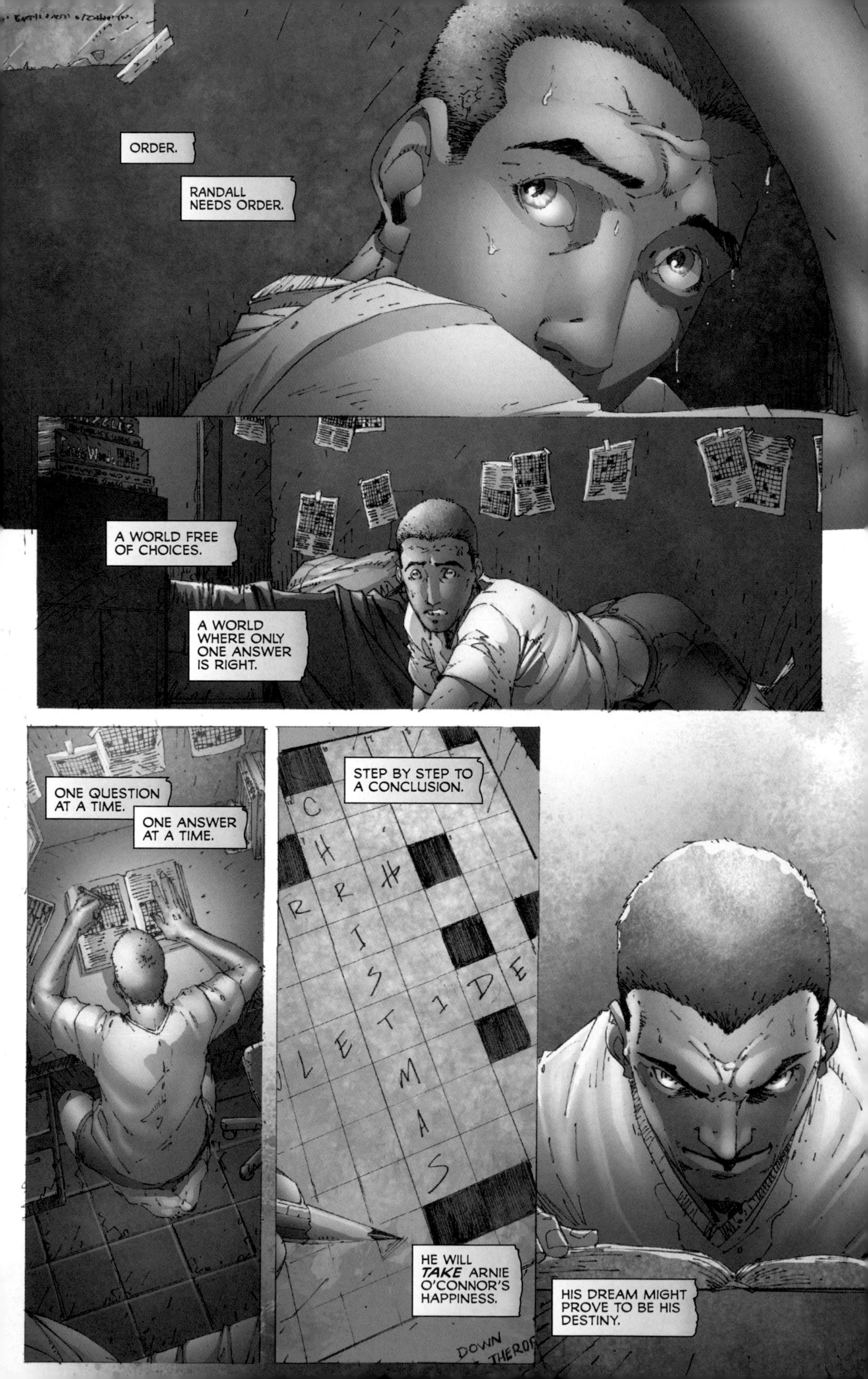
ORDER.
RANDALL NEEDS ORDER.
A WORLD FREE OF CHOICES.
A WORLD WHERE ONLY ONE ANSWER IS RIGHT.
ONE QUESTION AT A TIME.
ONE ANSWER AT A TIME.
STEP BY STEP TO A CONCLUSION.
HE WILL *TAKE* ARNIE O'CONNOR'S HAPPINESS.
HIS DREAM MIGHT PROVE TO BE HIS DESTINY.

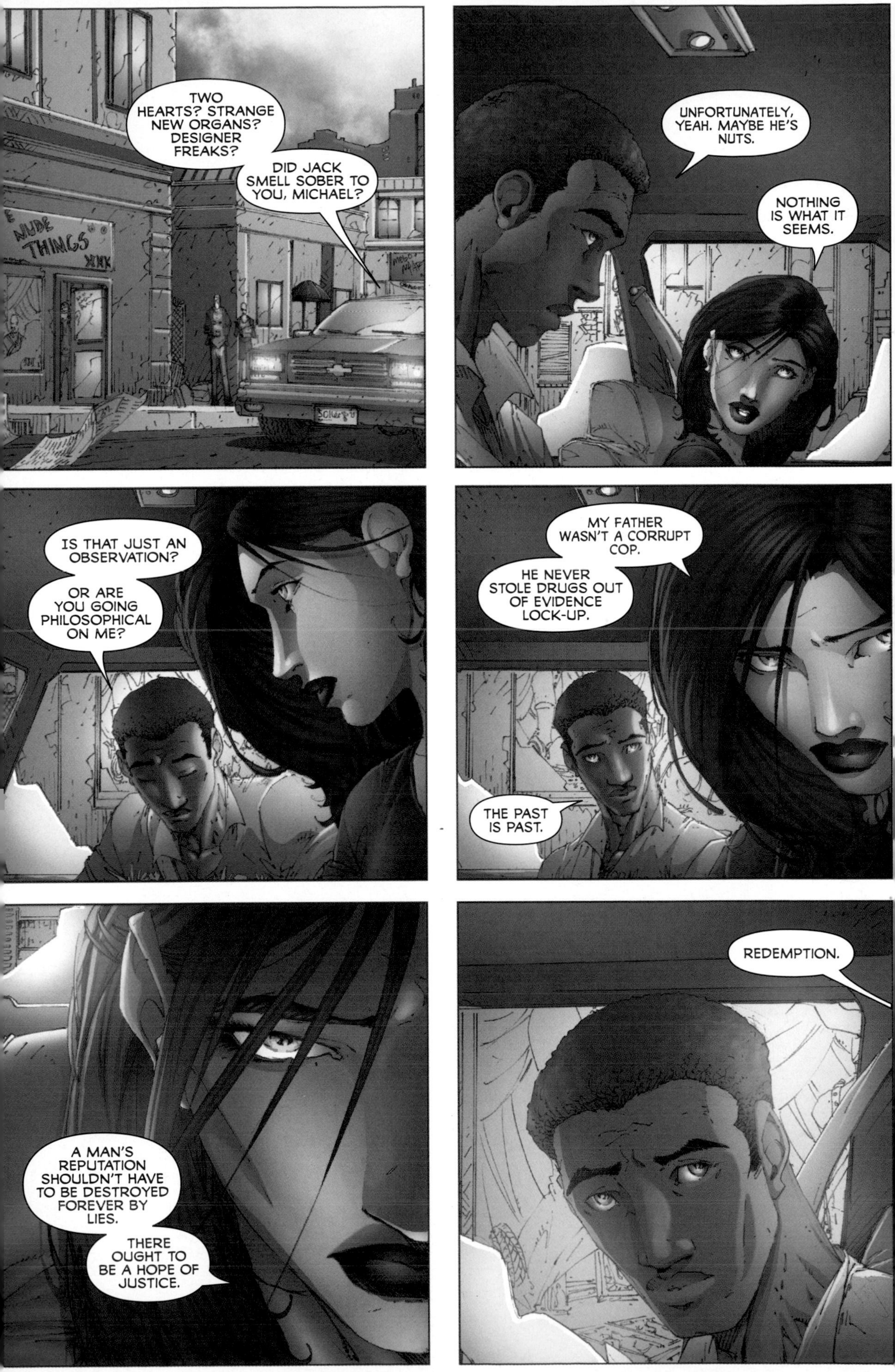
TWO HEARTS? STRANGE NEW ORGANS? DESIGNER FREAKS?
DID JACK SMELL SOBER TO YOU, MICHAEL?
UNFORTUNATELY, YEAH. MAYBE HE'S NUTS.
NOTHING IS WHAT IT SEEMS.
IS THAT JUST AN OBSERVATION?
OR ARE YOU GOING PHILOSOPHICAL ON ME?
MY FATHER WASN'T A CORRUPT COP.
HE NEVER STOLE DRUGS OUT OF EVIDENCE LOCK-UP.
THE PAST IS PAST.
A MAN'S REPUTATION SHOULDN'T HAVE TO BE DESTROYED FOREVER BY LIES.
THERE OUGHT TO BE A HOPE OF JUSTICE.
REDEMPTION.

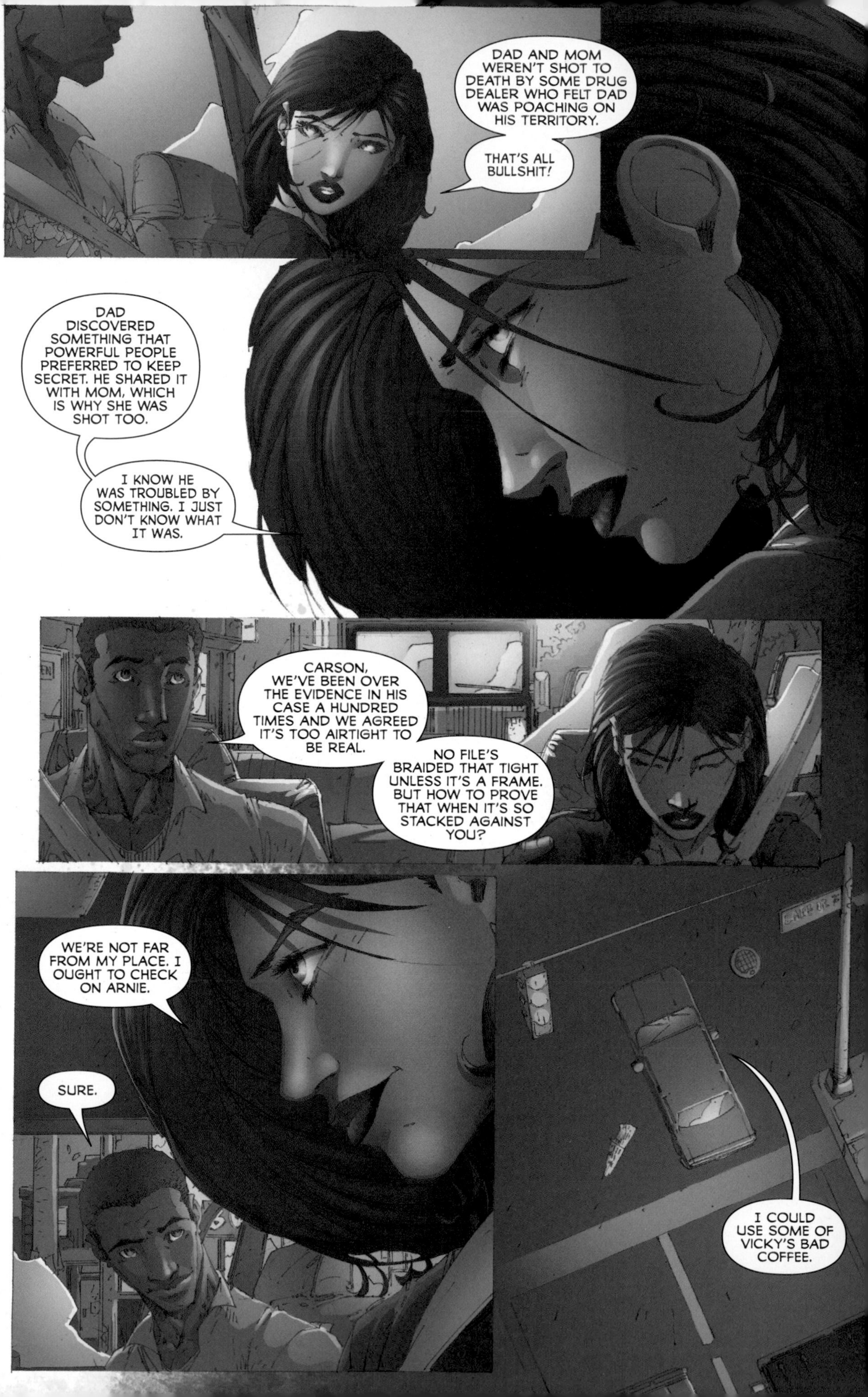
DAD AND MOM WEREN'T SHOT TO DEATH BY SOME DRUG DEALER WHO FELT DAD WAS POACHING ON HIS TERRITORY.
THAT'S ALL BULLSHIT!
DAD DISCOVERED SOMETHING THAT POWERFUL PEOPLE PREFERRED TO KEEP SECRET. HE SHARED IT WITH MOM, WHICH IS WHY SHE WAS SHOT TOO.
I KNOW HE WAS TROUBLED BY SOMETHING. I JUST DON'T KNOW WHAT IT WAS.
CARSON, WE'VE BEEN OVER THE EVIDENCE IN HIS CASE A HUNDRED TIMES AND WE AGREED IT'S TOO AIRTIGHT TO BE REAL.
NO FILE'S BRAIDED THAT TIGHT UNLESS IT'S A FRAME. BUT HOW TO PROVE THAT WHEN IT'S SO STACKED AGAINST YOU?
WE'RE NOT FAR FROM MY PLACE. I OUGHT TO CHECK ON ARNIE.
SURE.
I COULD USE SOME OF VICKY'S BAD COFFEE.

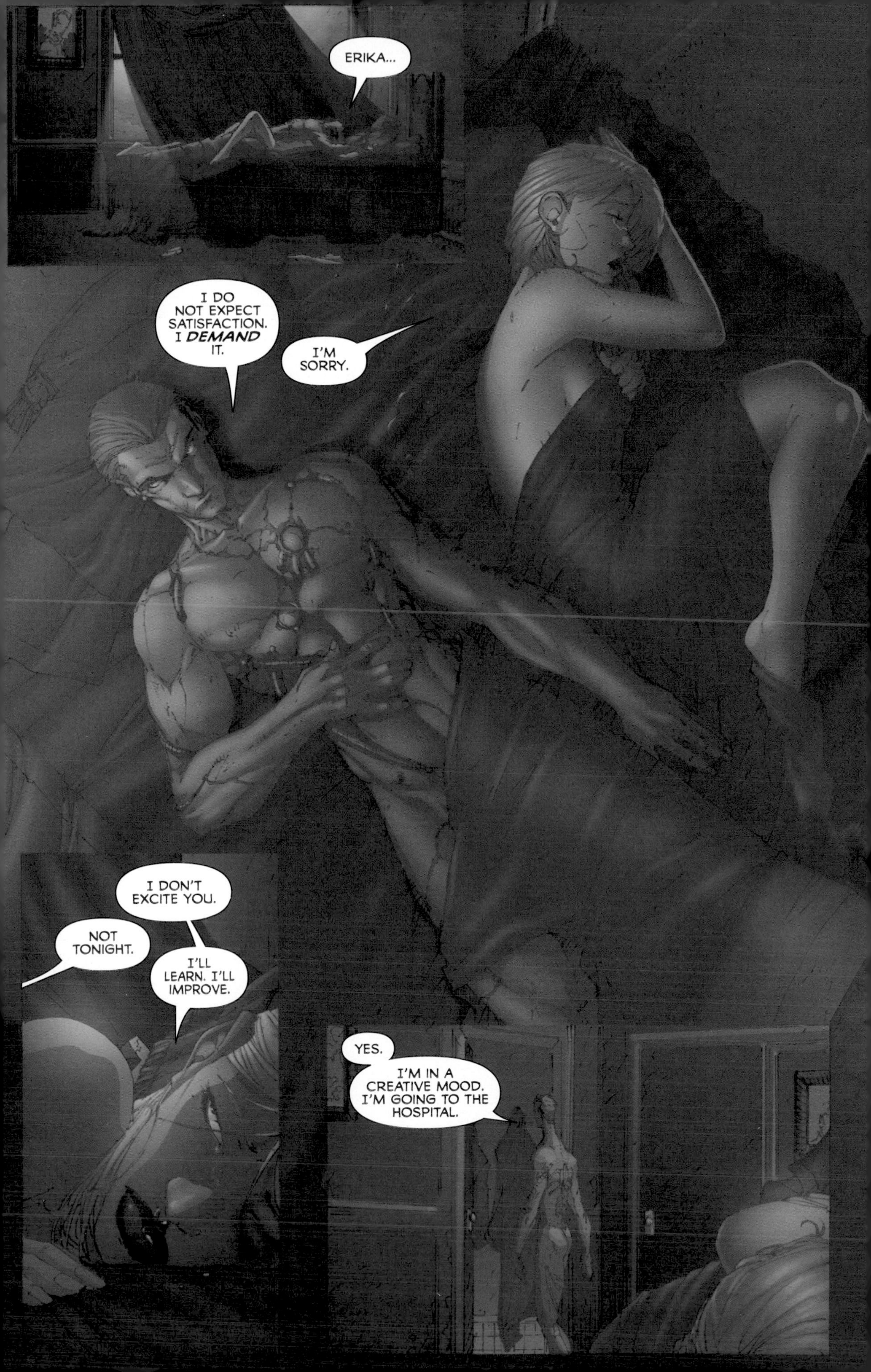
ERIKA...
I DO NOT EXPECT SATISFACTION. I *DEMAND* IT.
I'M SORRY.
I DON'T EXCITE YOU.
NOT TONIGHT.
I'LL LEARN. I'LL IMPROVE.
YES.
I'M IN A CREATIVE MOOD. I'M GOING TO THE HOSPITAL.

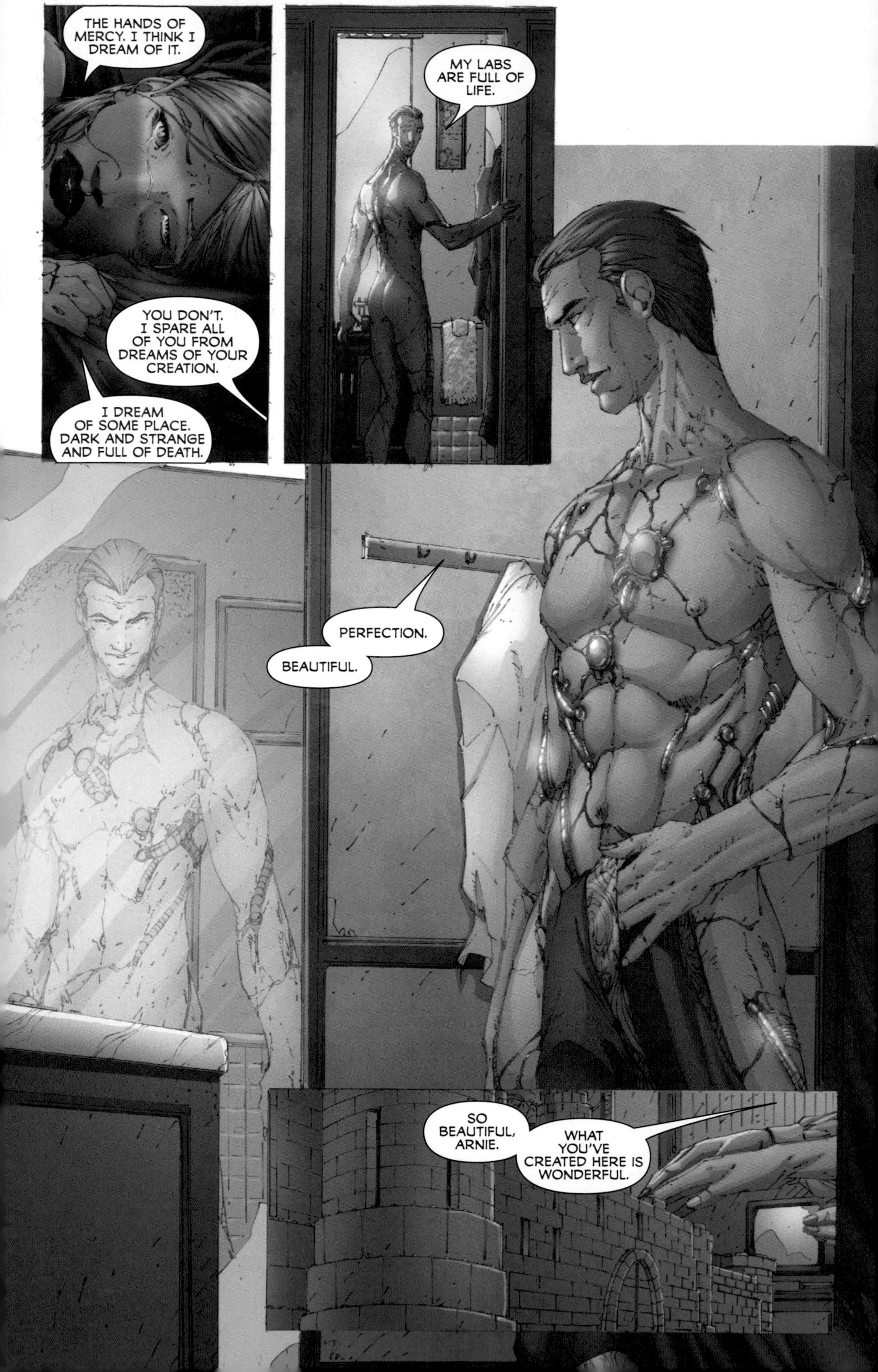
THE HANDS OF MERCY. I THINK I DREAM OF IT.
YOU DON'T. I SPARE ALL OF YOU FROM DREAMS OF YOUR CREATION.
I DREAM OF SOME PLACE. DARK AND STRANGE AND FULL OF DEATH.
MY LABS ARE FULL OF LIFE.
PERFECTION.
BEAUTIFUL.
SO BEAUTIFUL, ARNIE.
WHAT YOU'VE CREATED HERE IS WONDERFUL.

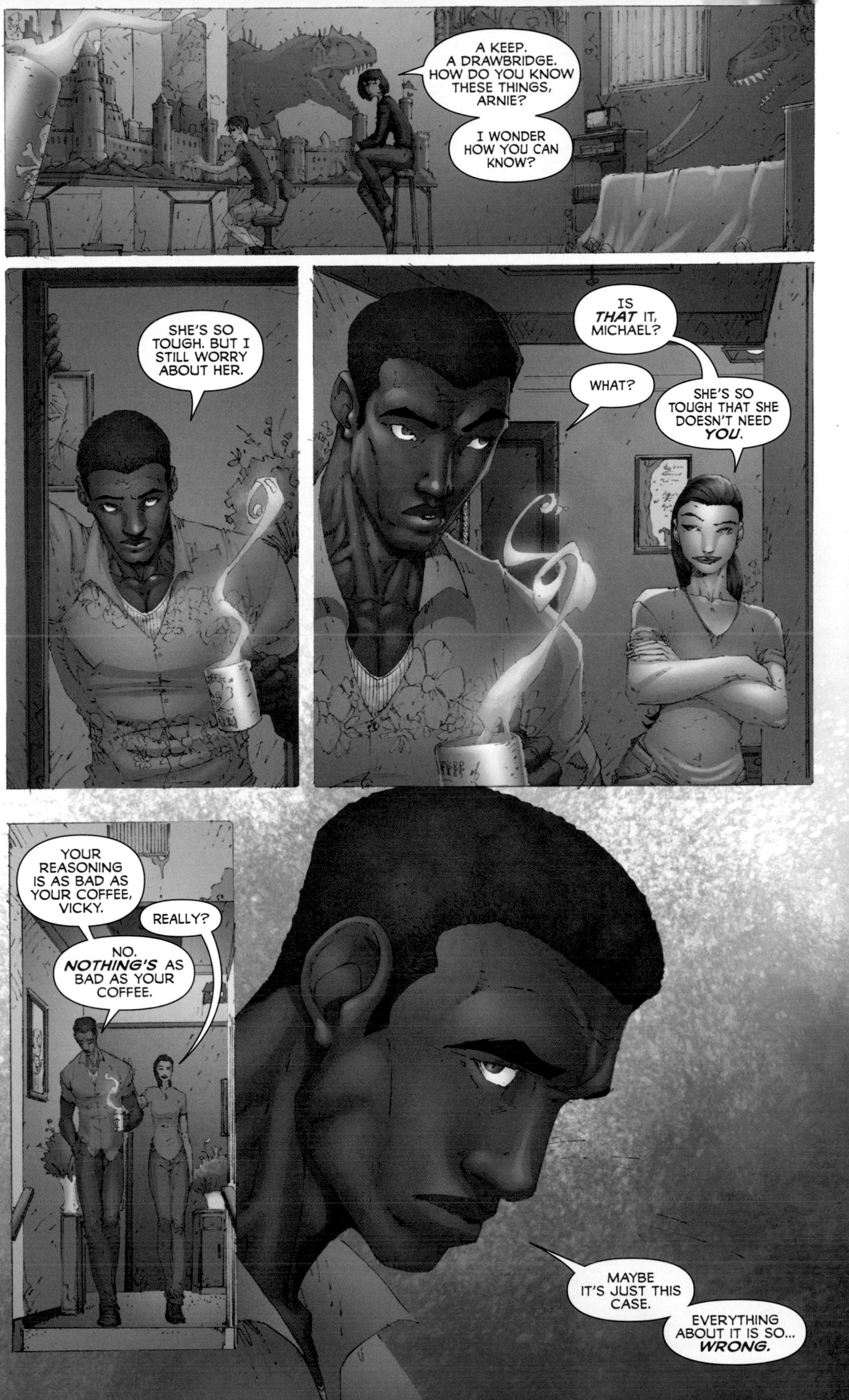
A KEEP. A DRAWBRIDGE. HOW DO YOU KNOW THESE THINGS, ARNIE?
I WONDER HOW YOU CAN KNOW?
SHE'S SO TOUGH. BUT I STILL WORRY ABOUT HER.
IS *THAT* IT, MICHAEL?
WHAT?
SHE'S SO TOUGH THAT SHE DOESN'T NEED *YOU*.
YOUR REASONING IS AS BAD AS YOUR COFFEE, VICKY.
REALLY?
NO. *NOTHING'S* AS BAD AS YOUR COFFEE.
MAYBE IT'S JUST THIS CASE.
EVERYTHING ABOUT IT IS SO... *WRONG.*

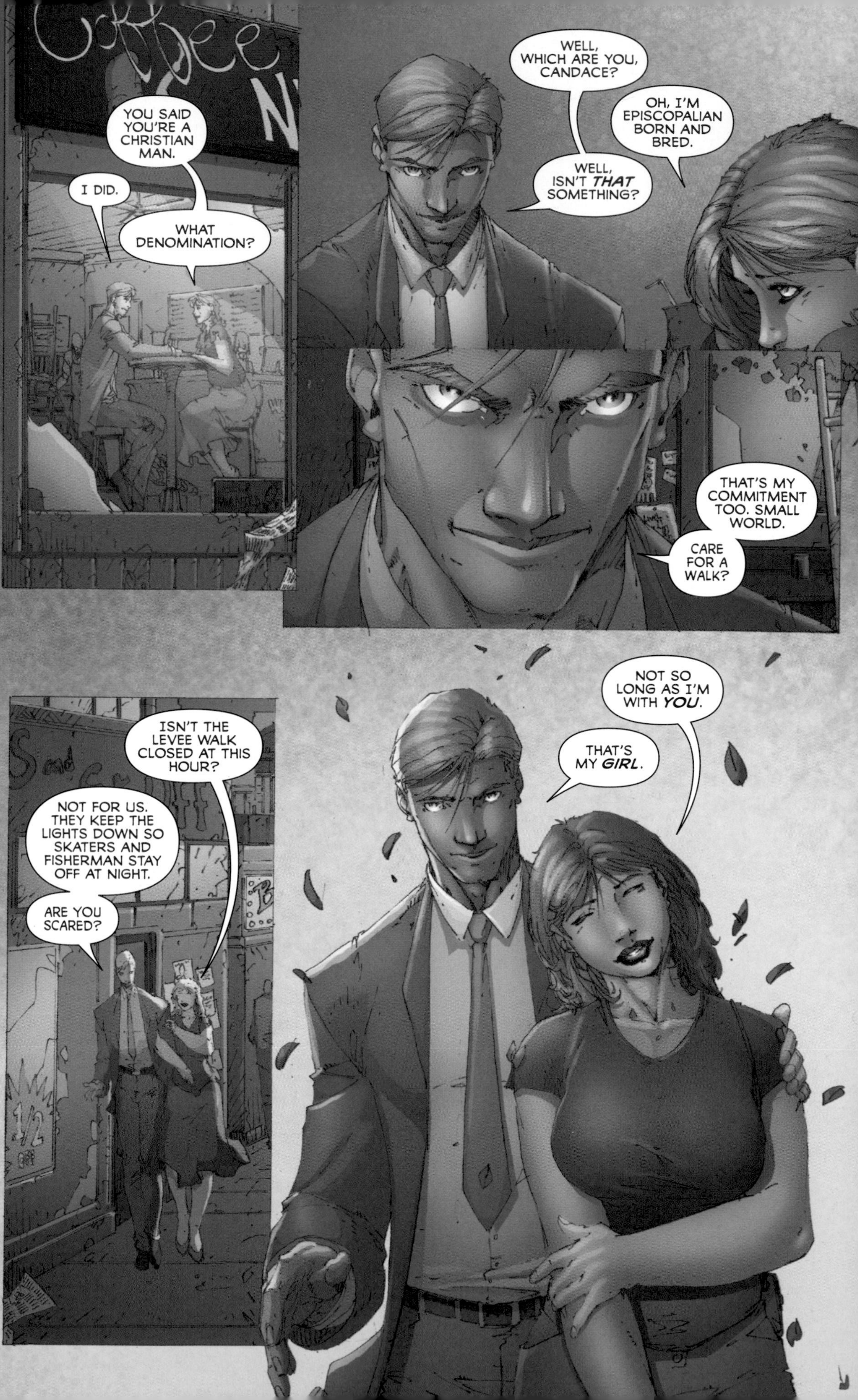
YOU SAID YOU'RE A CHRISTIAN MAN.
I DID.
WHAT DENOMINATION?
WELL, WHICH ARE YOU, CANDACE?
OH, I'M EPISCOPALIAN BORN AND BRED.
WELL, ISN'T *THAT* SOMETHING?
THAT'S MY COMMITMENT TOO. SMALL WORLD.
CARE FOR A WALK?
ISN'T THE LEVEE WALK CLOSED AT THIS HOUR?
NOT FOR US. THEY KEEP THE LIGHTS DOWN SO SKATERS AND FISHERMAN STAY OFF AT NIGHT.
ARE YOU SCARED?
NOT SO LONG AS I'M WITH *YOU*.
THAT'S MY *GIRL*.

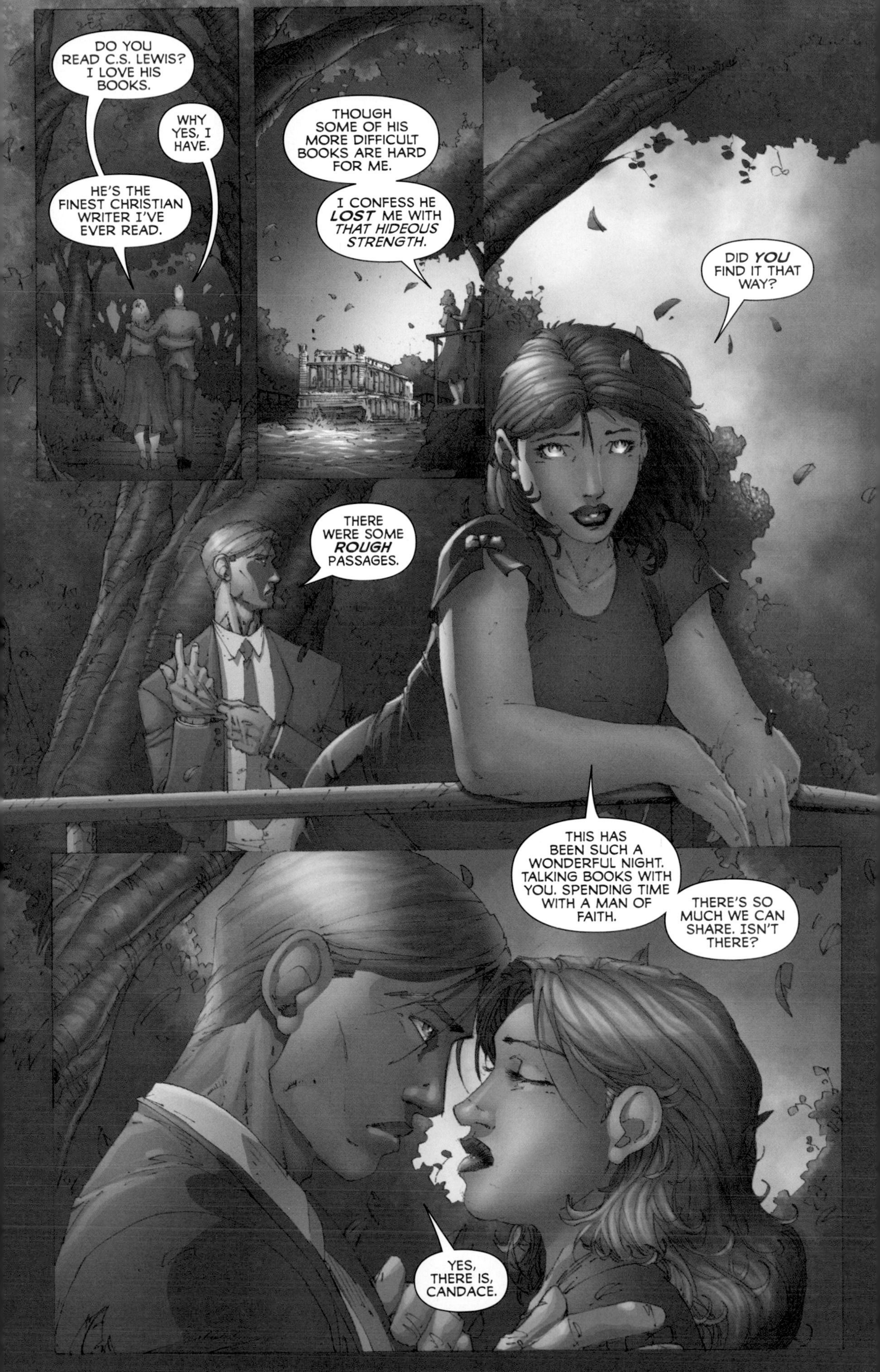
DO YOU READ C.S. LEWIS? I LOVE HIS BOOKS.
WHY YES, I HAVE.
HE'S THE FINEST CHRISTIAN WRITER I'VE EVER READ.
THOUGH SOME OF HIS MORE DIFFICULT BOOKS ARE HARD FOR ME.
I CONFESS HE LOST ME WITH THAT HIDEOUS STRENGTH.
DID YOU FIND IT THAT WAY?
THERE WERE SOME ROUGH PASSAGES.
THIS HAS BEEN SUCH A WONDERFUL NIGHT. TALKING BOOKS WITH YOU. SPENDING TIME WITH A MAN OF FAITH.
THERE'S SO MUCH WE CAN SHARE. ISN'T THERE?
YES, THERE IS, CANDACE.

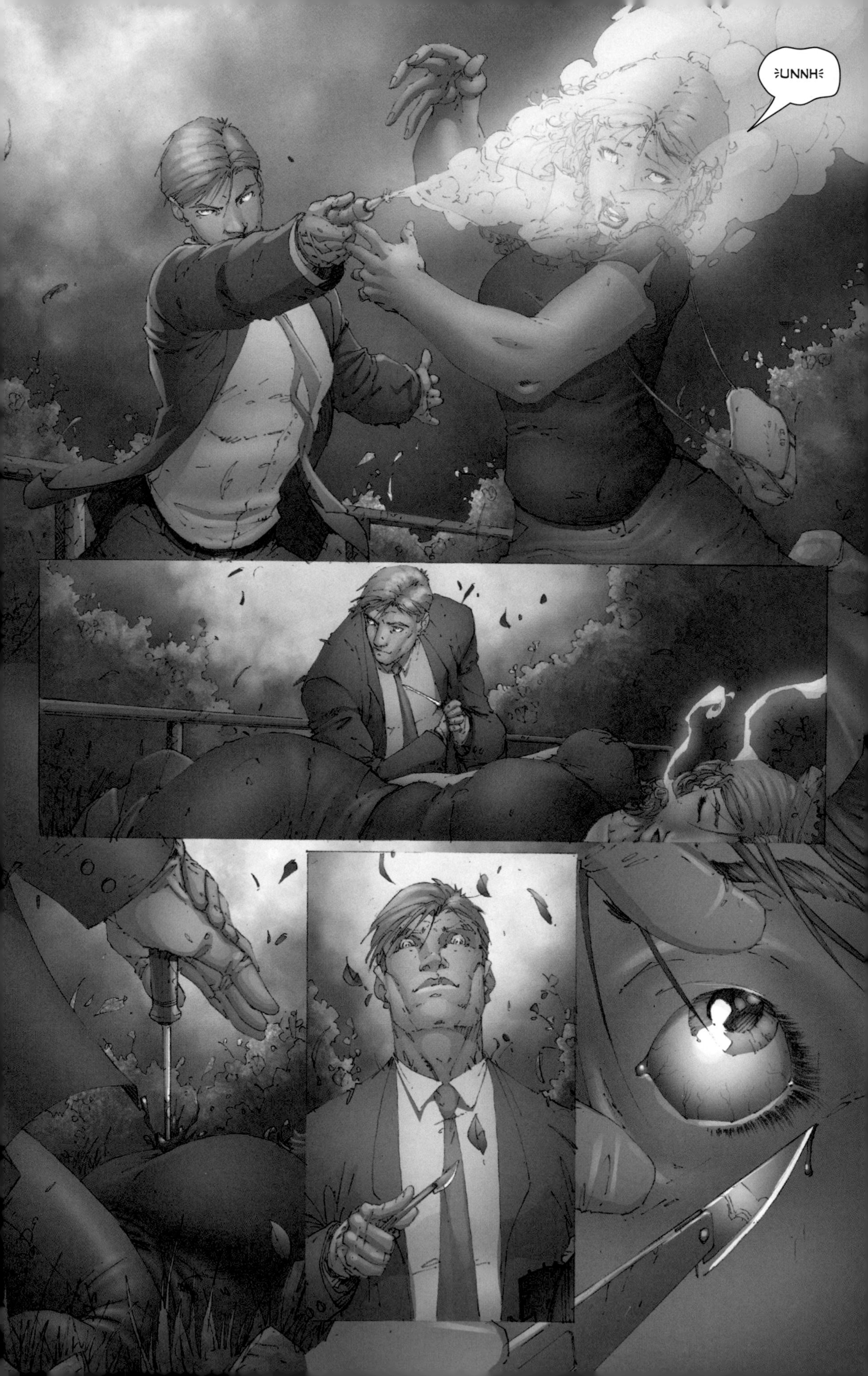
UNNH

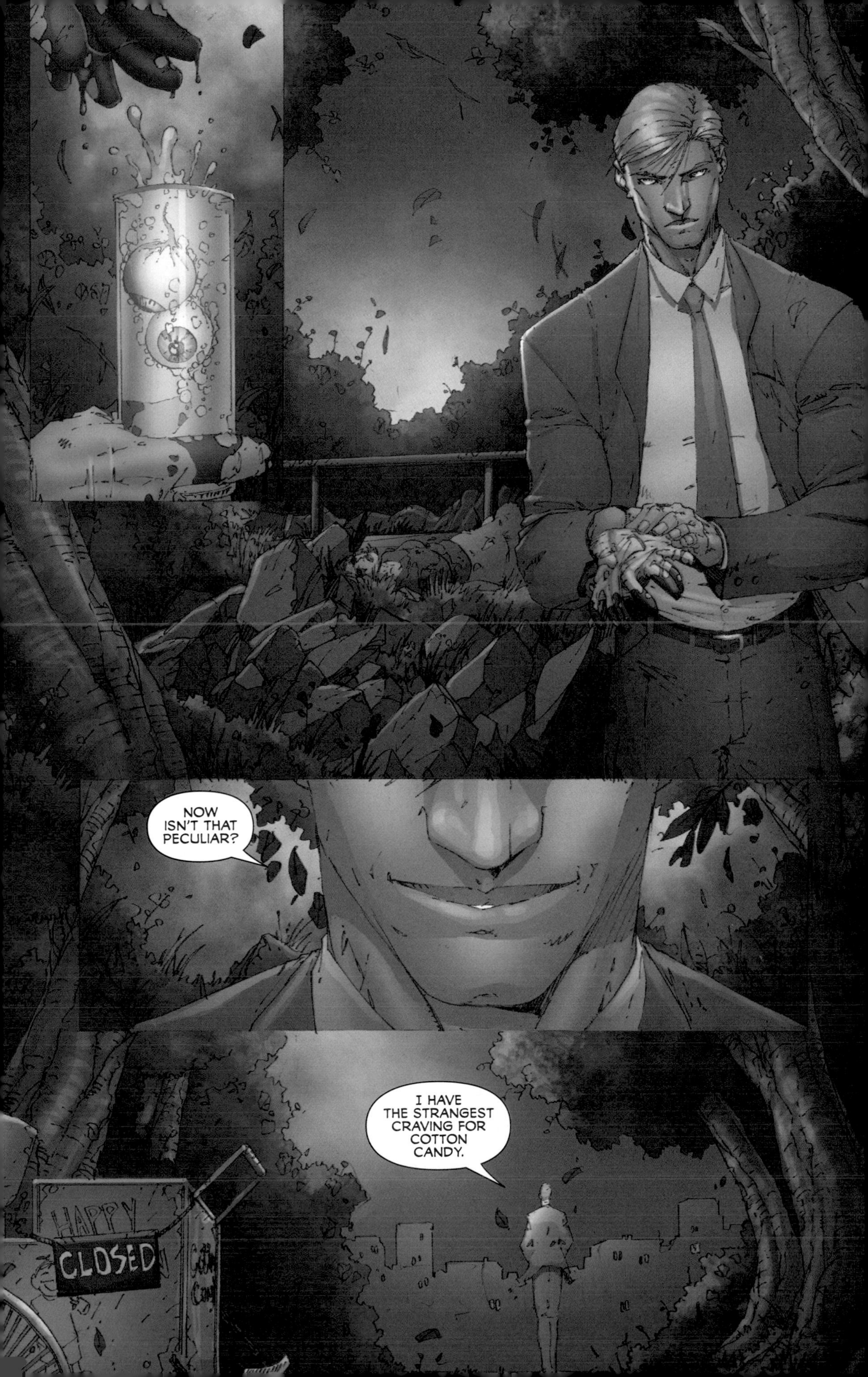
NOW ISN'T THAT PECULIAR?
I HAVE THE STRANGEST CRAVING FOR COTTON CANDY.
HAPPY
CLOSED

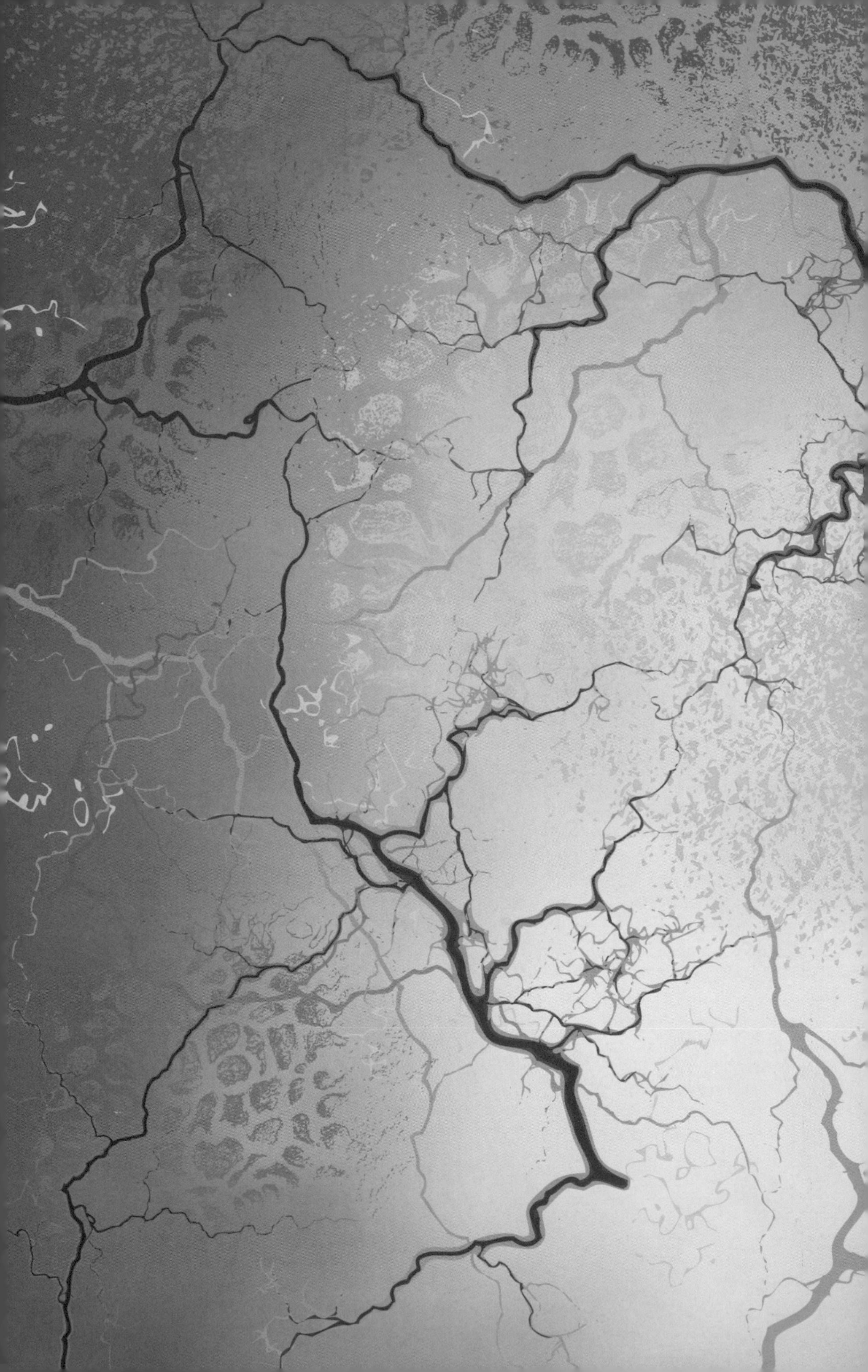

chapter four

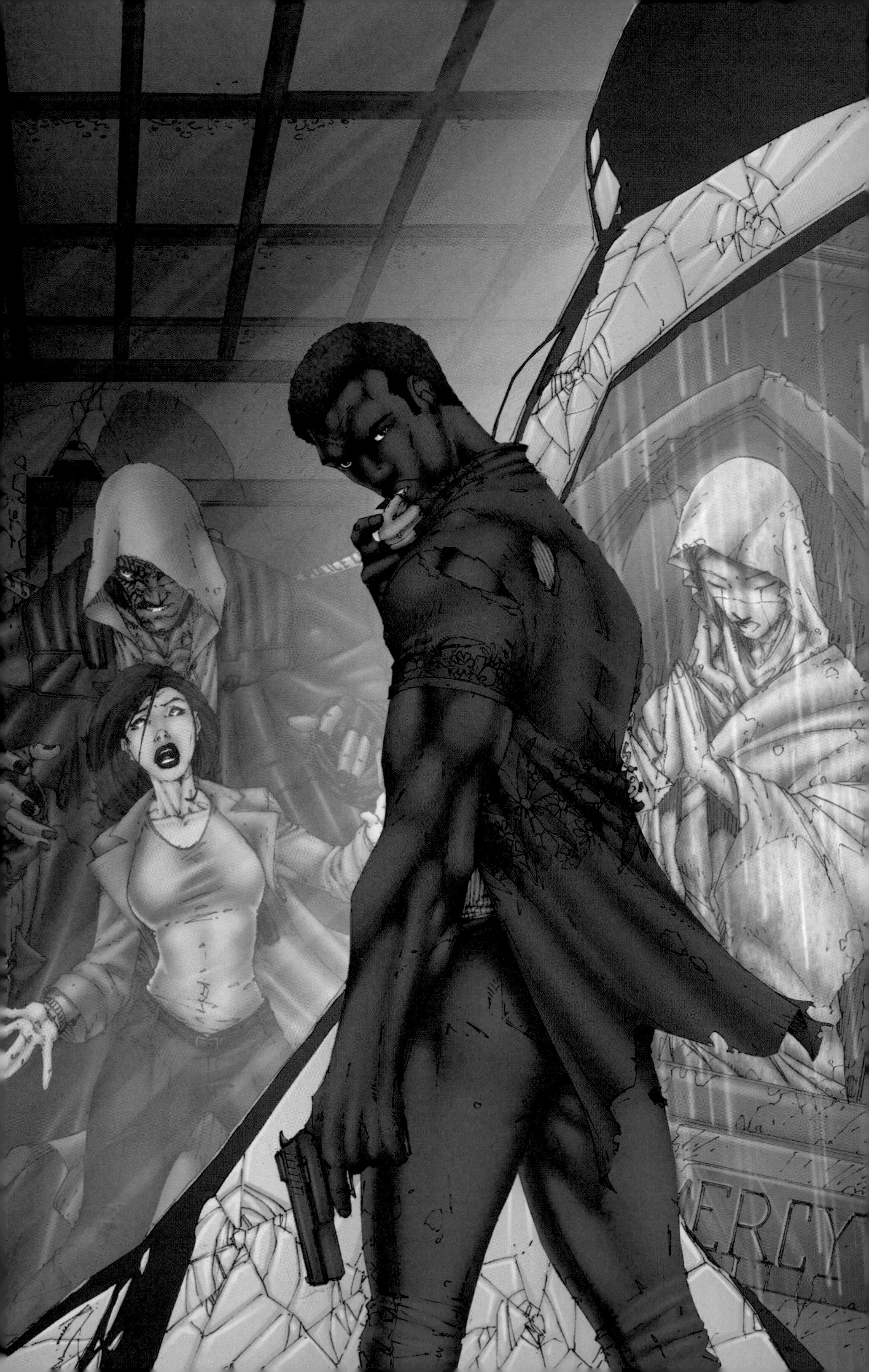
ERCY

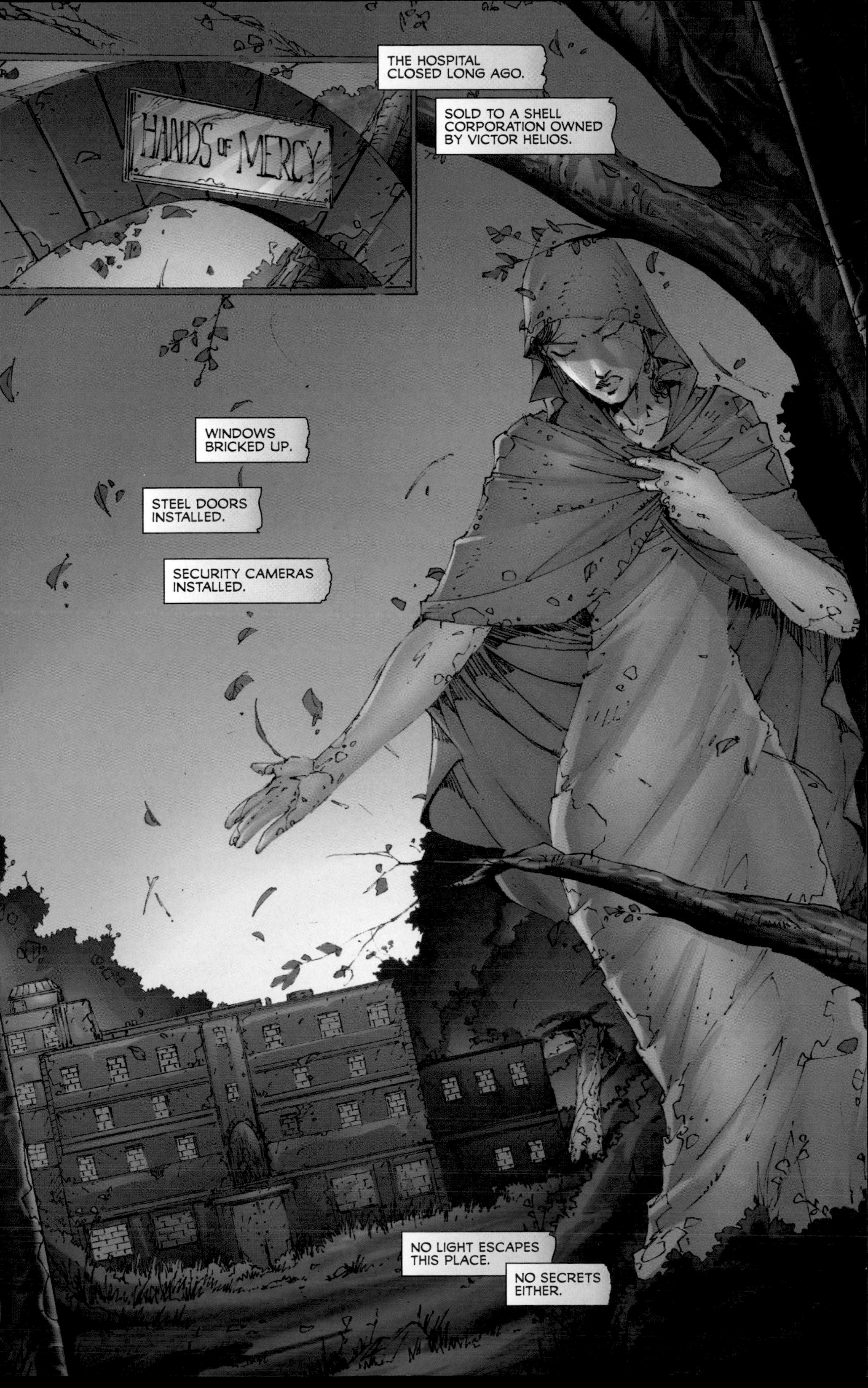

HANDS OF MERCY
THE HOSPITAL CLOSED LONG AGO.
SOLD TO A SHELL CORPORATION OWNED BY VICTOR HELIOS.
WINDOWS BRICKED UP.
STEEL DOORS INSTALLED.
SECURITY CAMERAS INSTALLED.
NO LIGHT ESCAPES THIS PLACE.
NO SECRETS EITHER.

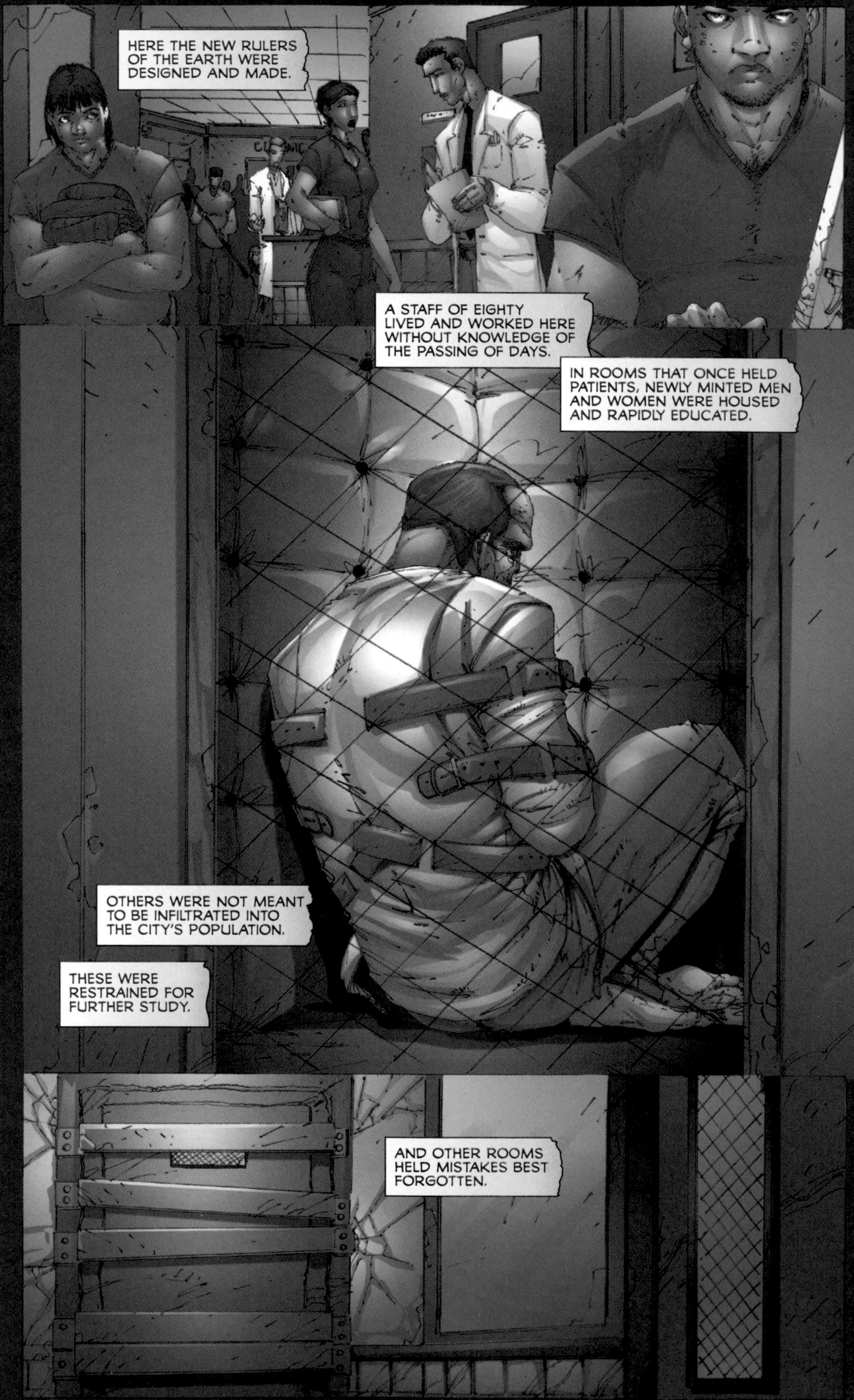
HERE THE NEW RULERS OF THE EARTH WERE DESIGNED AND MADE.
A STAFF OF EIGHTY LIVED AND WORKED HERE WITHOUT KNOWLEDGE OF THE PASSING OF DAYS.
IN ROOMS THAT ONCE HELD PATIENTS, NEWLY MINTED MEN AND WOMEN WERE HOUSED AND RAPIDLY EDUCATED.
OTHERS WERE NOT MEANT TO BE INFILTRATED INTO THE CITY'S POPULATION.
THESE WERE RESTRAINED FOR FURTHER STUDY.
AND OTHER ROOMS HELD MISTAKES BEST FORGOTTEN.

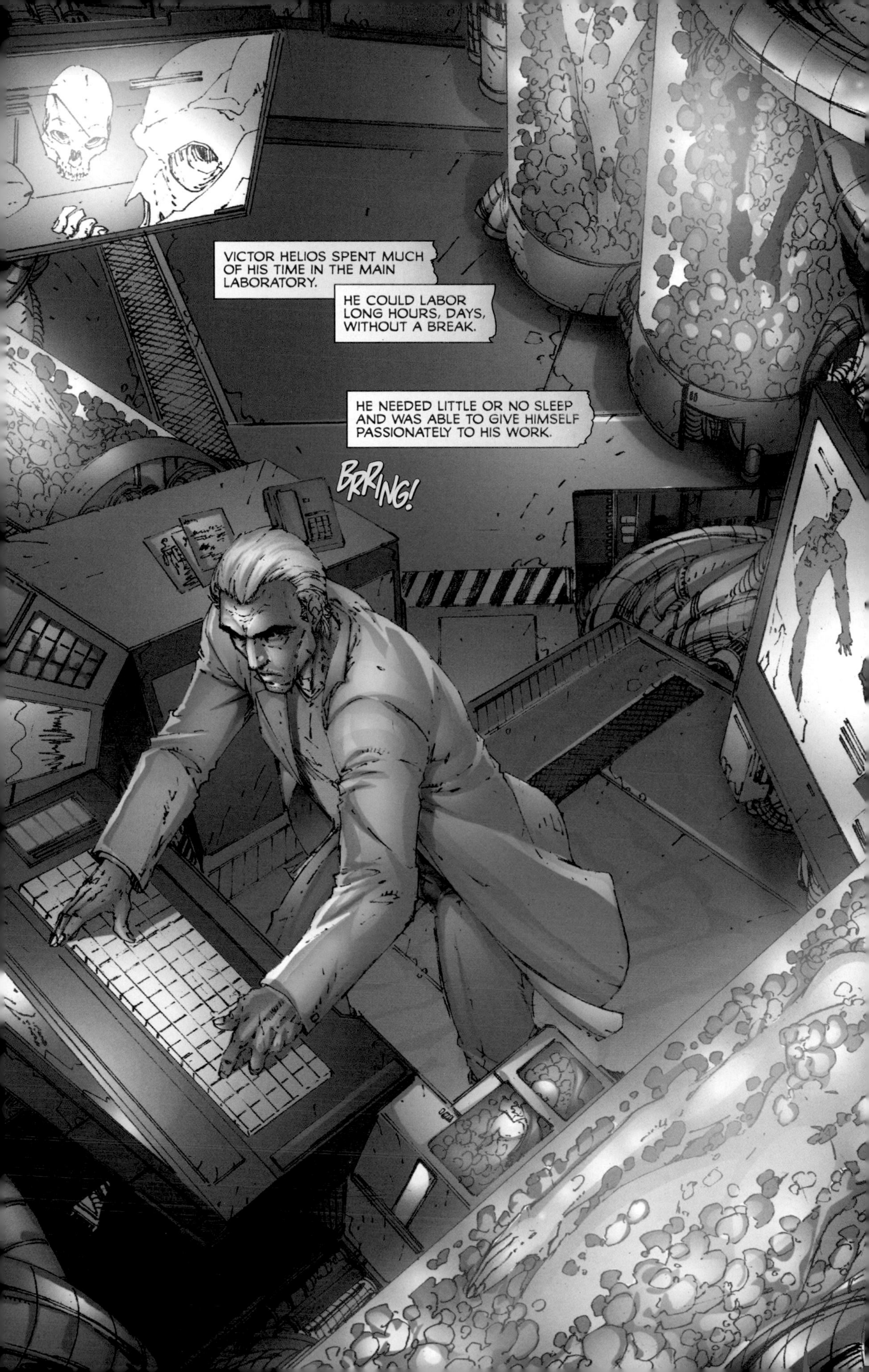
VICTOR HELIOS SPENT MUCH OF HIS TIME IN THE MAIN LABORATORY.
HE COULD LABOR LONG HOURS, DAYS, WITHOUT A BREAK.
HE NEEDED LITTLE OR NO SLEEP AND WAS ABLE TO GIVE HIMSELF PASSIONATELY TO HIS WORK.
BRRING!

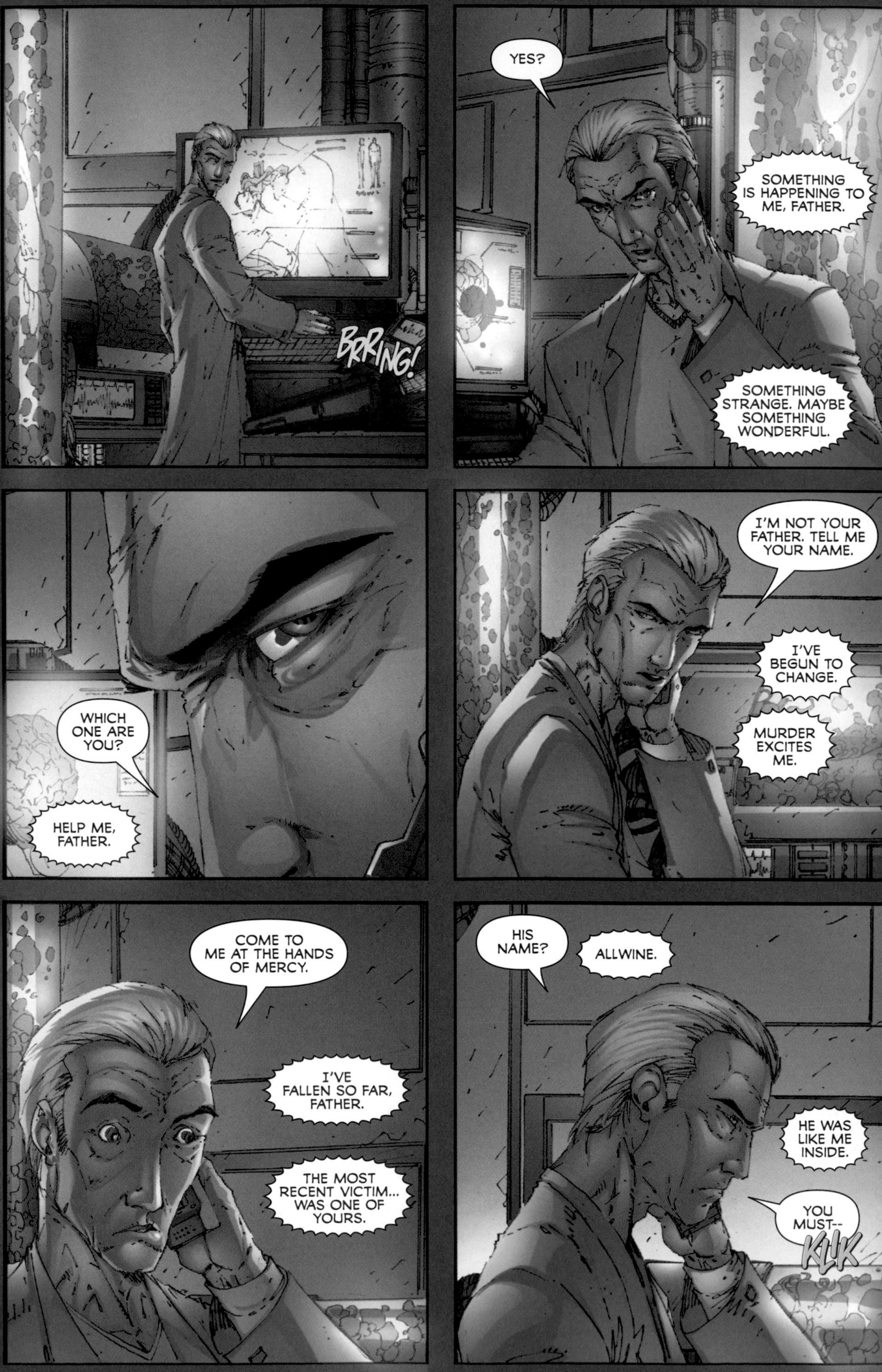
BRRING!
YES?
SOMETHING IS HAPPENING TO ME, FATHER.
SOMETHING STRANGE. MAYBE SOMETHING WONDERFUL.
WHICH ONE ARE YOU?
HELP ME, FATHER.
I'M NOT YOUR FATHER. TELL ME YOUR NAME.
I'VE BEGUN TO CHANGE.
MURDER EXCITES ME.
COME TO ME AT THE HANDS OF MERCY.
I'VE FALLEN SO FAR, FATHER.
THE MOST RECENT VICTIM... WAS ONE OF YOURS.
HIS NAME?
ALLWINE.
HE WAS LIKE ME INSIDE.
YOU MUST--
KLIK

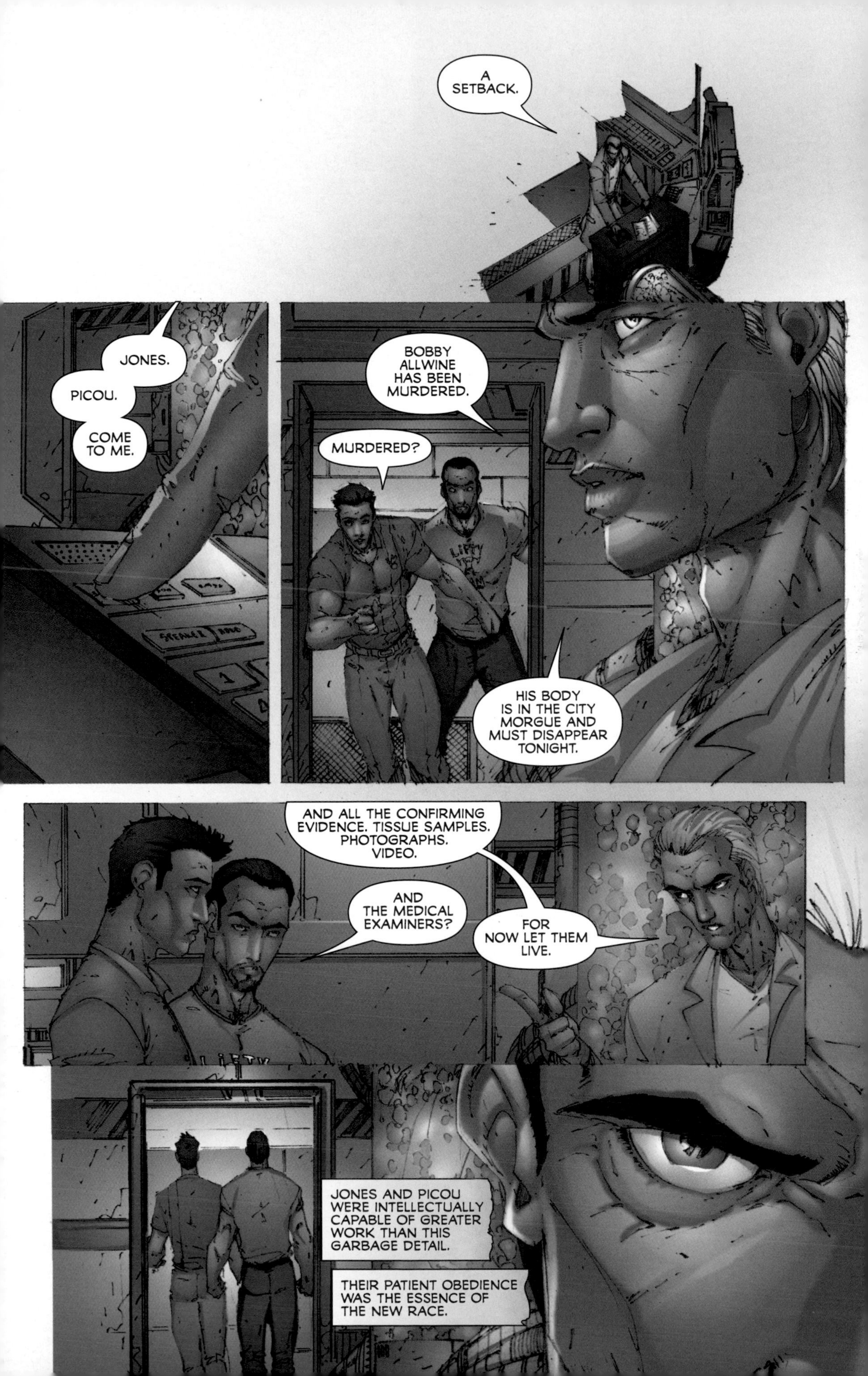
A SETBACK.
JONES.
PICOU.
COME TO ME.
BOBBY ALLWINE HAS BEEN MURDERED.
MURDERED?
HIS BODY IS IN THE CITY MORGUE AND MUST DISAPPEAR TONIGHT.
AND ALL THE CONFIRMING EVIDENCE. TISSUE SAMPLES. PHOTOGRAPHS. VIDEO.
AND THE MEDICAL EXAMINERS?
FOR NOW LET THEM LIVE.
JONES AND PICOU WERE INTELLECTUALLY CAPABLE OF GREATER WORK THAN THIS GARBAGE DETAIL.
THEIR PATIENT OBEDIENCE WAS THE ESSENCE OF THE NEW RACE.

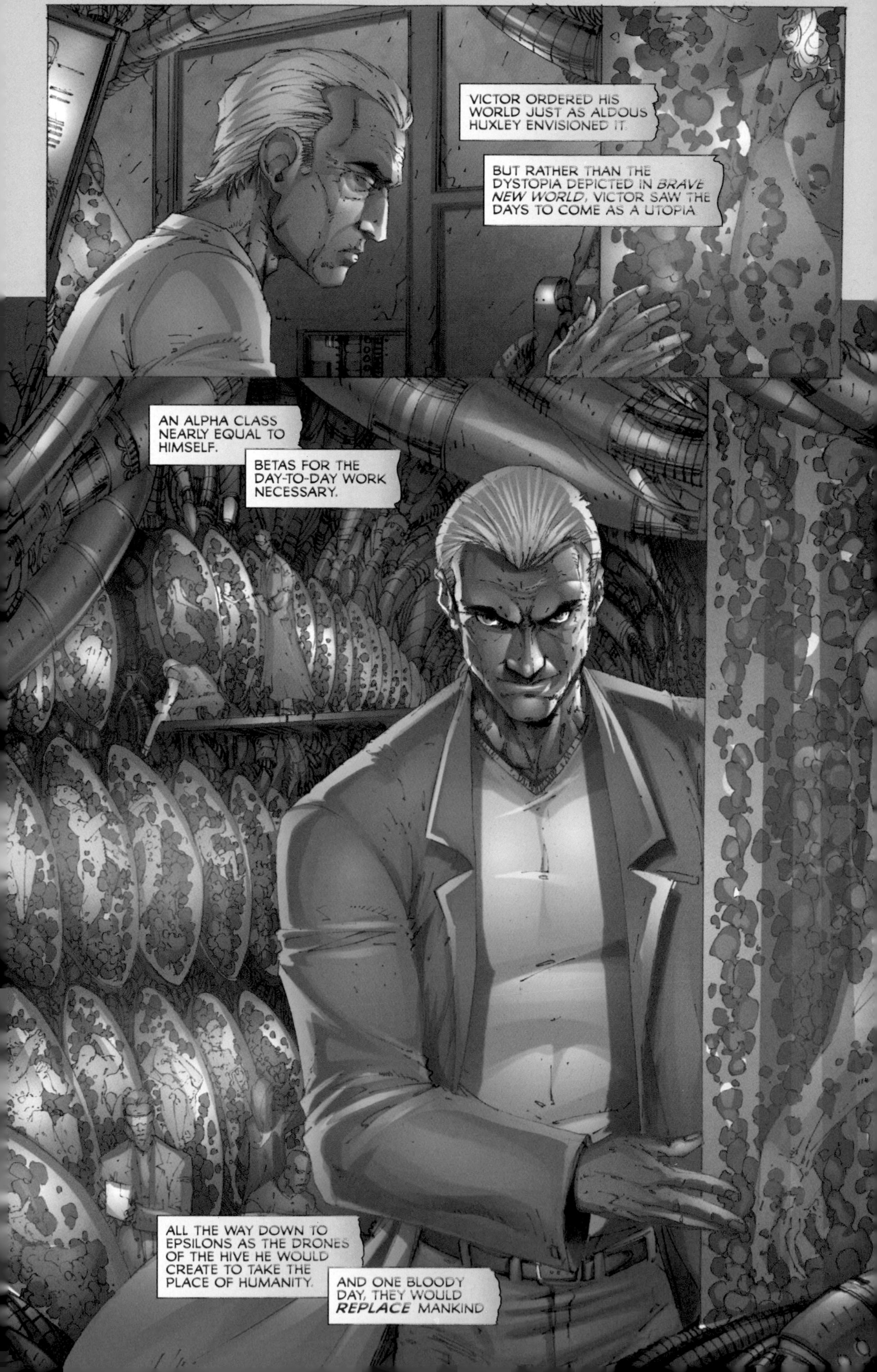
VICTOR ORDERED HIS WORLD JUST AS ALDOUS HUXLEY ENVISIONED IT.
BUT RATHER THAN THE DYSTOPIA DEPICTED IN *BRAVE NEW WORLD*, VICTOR SAW THE DAYS TO COME AS A UTOPIA.
AN ALPHA CLASS NEARLY EQUAL TO HIMSELF.
BETAS FOR THE DAY-TO-DAY WORK NECESSARY.
ALL THE WAY DOWN TO EPSILONS AS THE DRONES OF THE HIVE HE WOULD CREATE TO TAKE THE PLACE OF HUMANITY.
AND ONE BLOODY DAY, THEY WOULD ***REPLACE*** MANKIND.

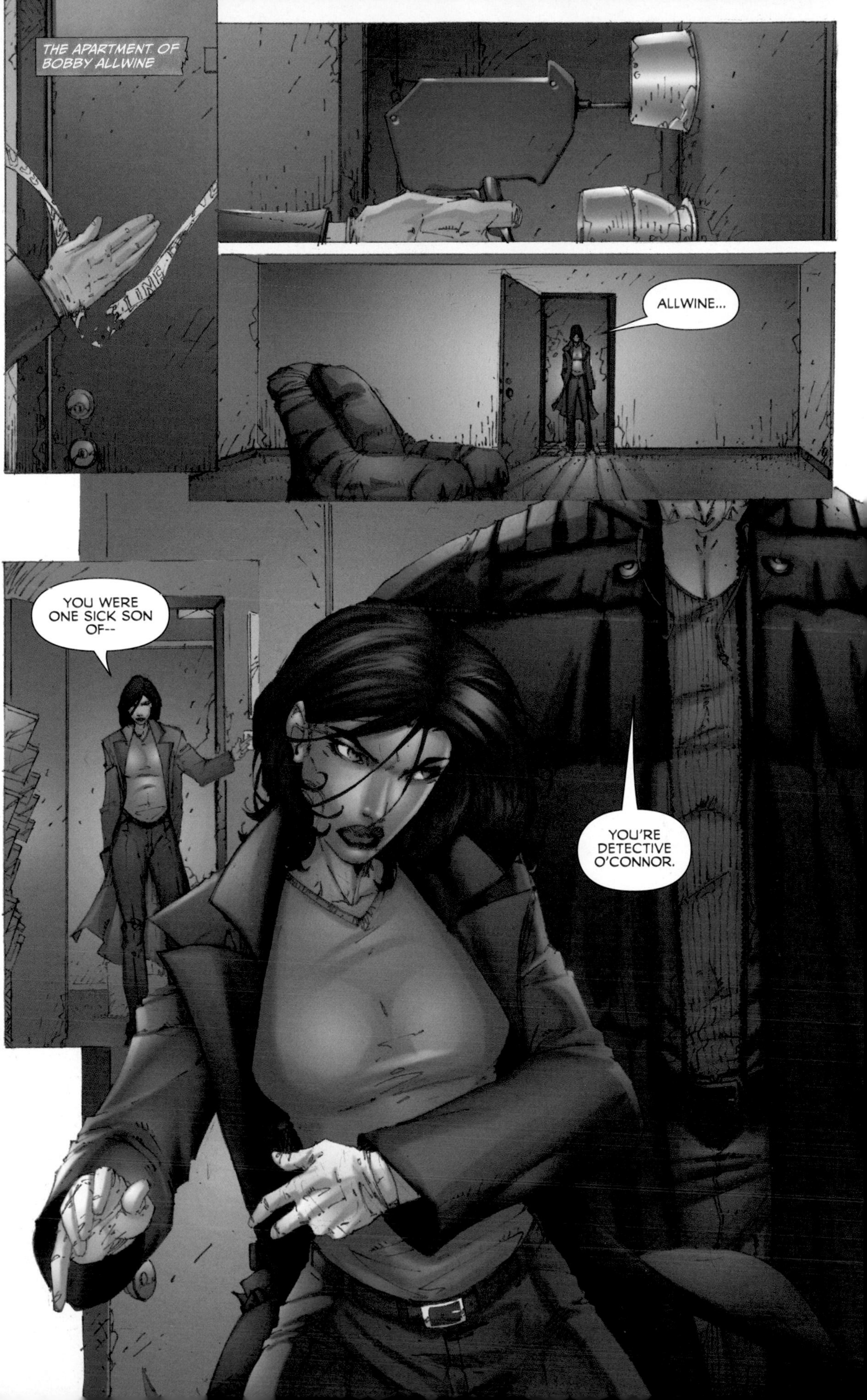
THE APARTMENT OF BOBBY ALLWINE
ALLWINE...
YOU WERE ONE SICK SON OF--
YOU'RE DETECTIVE O'CONNOR.

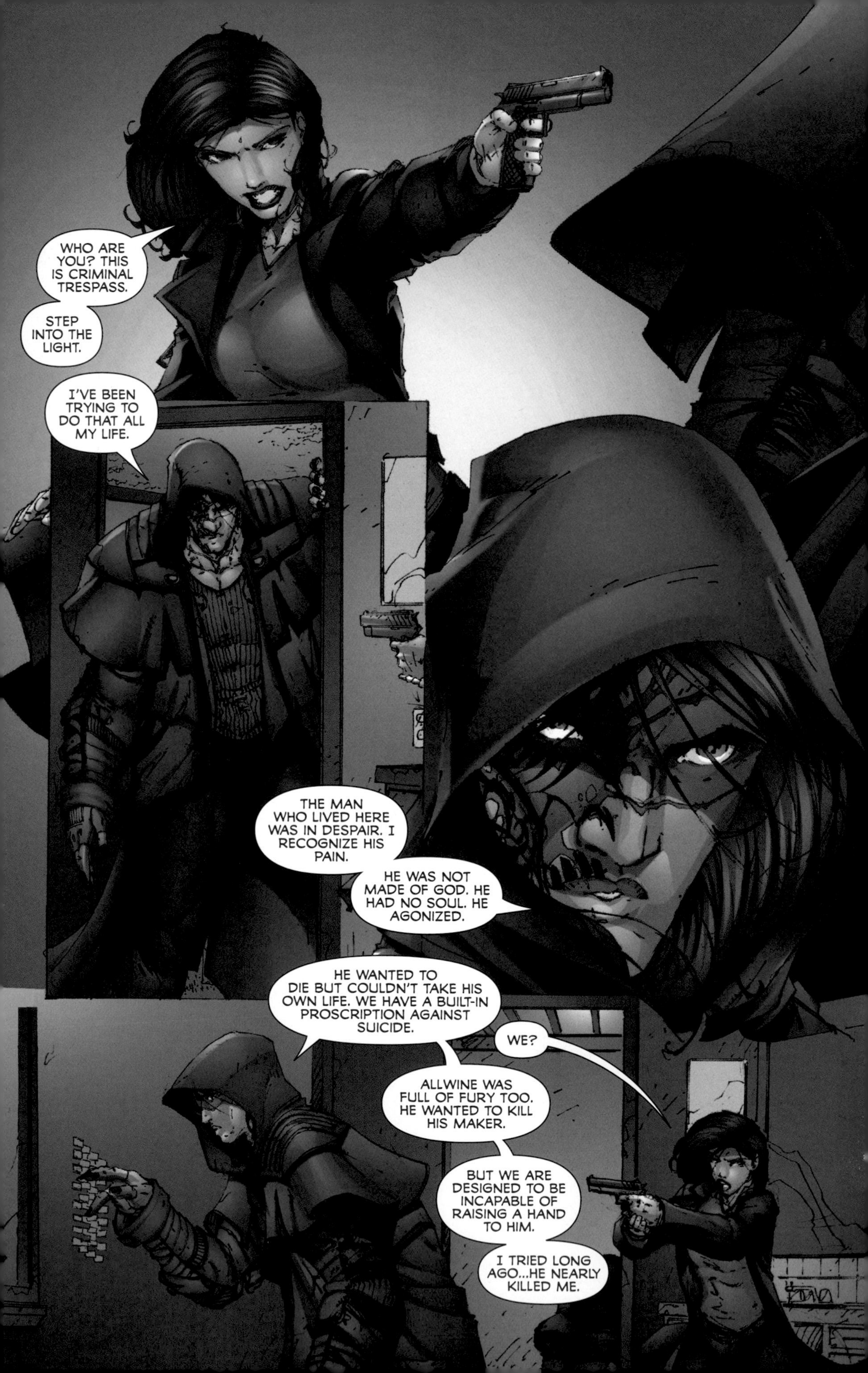
WHO ARE YOU? THIS IS CRIMINAL TRESPASS.
STEP INTO THE LIGHT.
I'VE BEEN TRYING TO DO THAT ALL MY LIFE.
THE MAN WHO LIVED HERE WAS IN DESPAIR. I RECOGNIZE HIS PAIN.
HE WAS NOT MADE OF GOD. HE HAD NO SOUL. HE AGONIZED.
HE WANTED TO DIE BUT COULDN'T TAKE HIS OWN LIFE. WE HAVE A BUILT-IN PROSCRIPTION AGAINST SUICIDE.
WE?
ALLWINE WAS FULL OF FURY TOO. HE WANTED TO KILL HIS MAKER.
BUT WE ARE DESIGNED TO BE INCAPABLE OF RAISING A HAND TO HIM.
I TRIED LONG AGO...HE NEARLY KILLED ME.

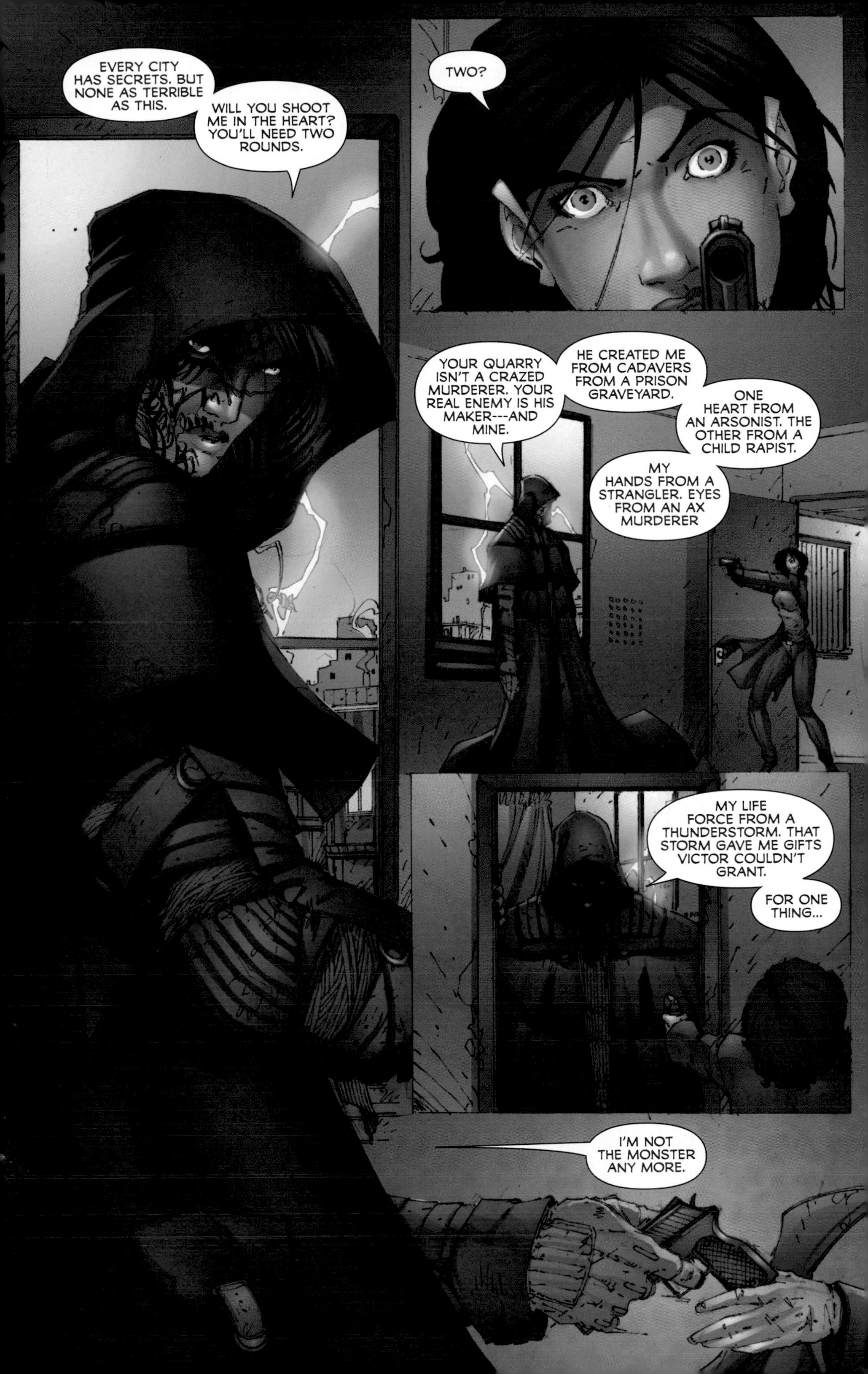
EVERY CITY HAS SECRETS. BUT NONE AS TERRIBLE AS THIS.
WILL YOU SHOOT ME IN THE HEART? YOU'LL NEED TWO ROUNDS.
TWO?
YOUR QUARRY ISN'T A CRAZED MURDERER. YOUR REAL ENEMY IS HIS MAKER---AND MINE.
HE CREATED ME FROM CADAVERS FROM A PRISON GRAVEYARD.
ONE HEART FROM AN ARSONIST. THE OTHER FROM A CHILD RAPIST.
MY HANDS FROM A STRANGLER. EYES FROM AN AX MURDERER
MY LIFE FORCE FROM A THUNDERSTORM. THAT STORM GAVE ME GIFTS VICTOR COULDN'T GRANT.
FOR ONE THING...
I'M NOT THE MONSTER ANY MORE.

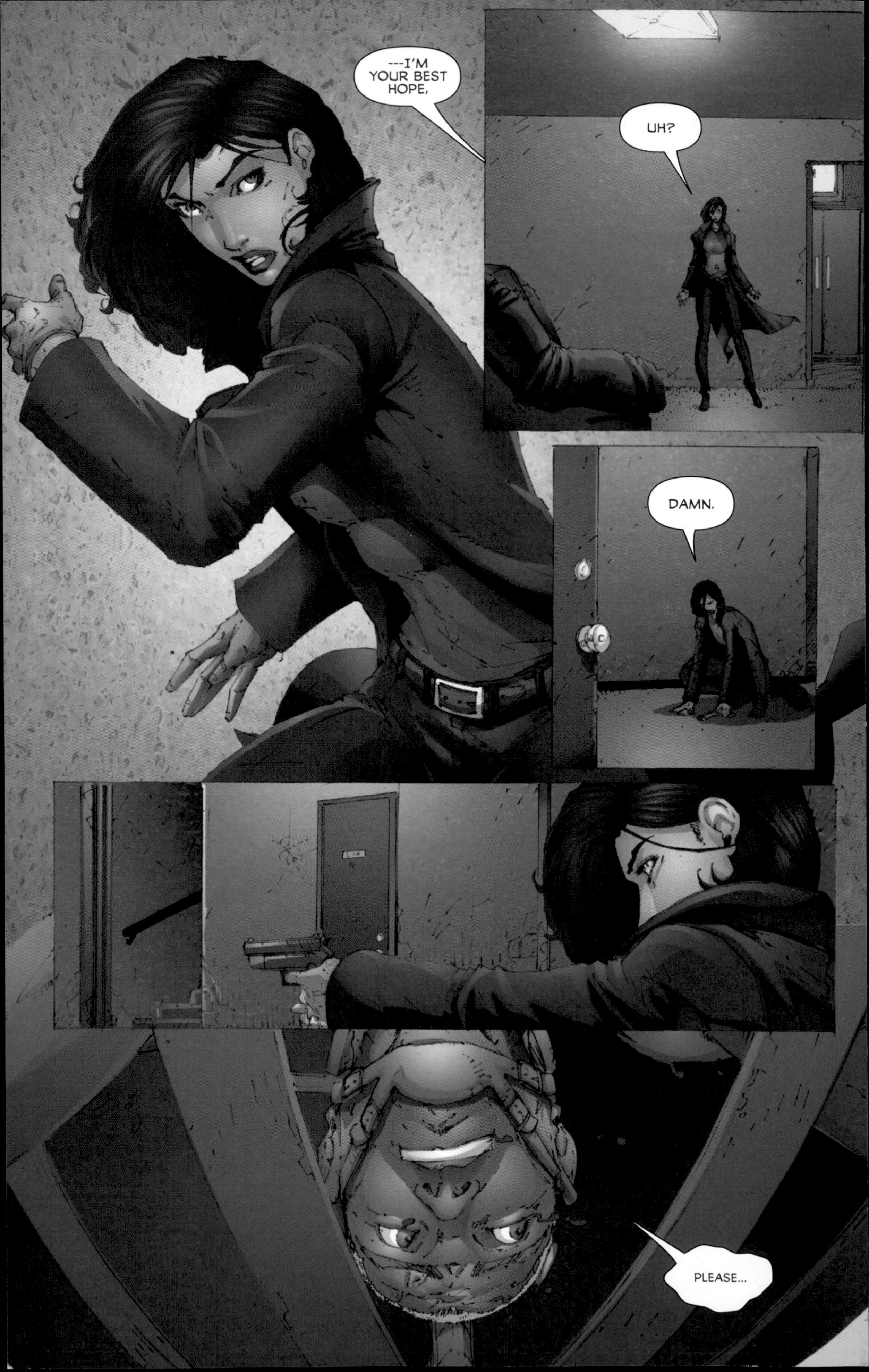
---I'M YOUR BEST HOPE,
UH?
DAMN.
PLEASE...

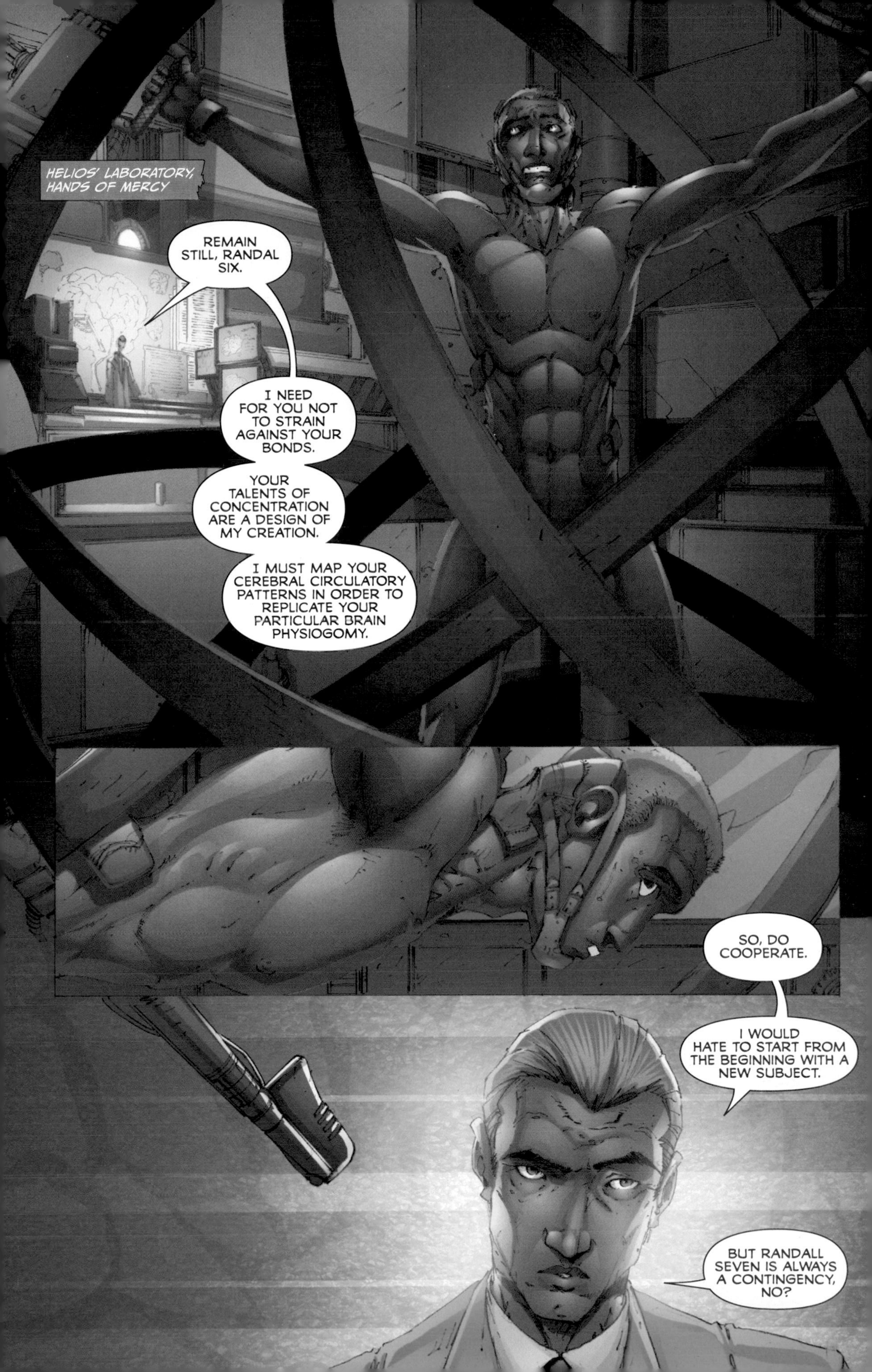
HELIOS' LABORATORY, HANDS OF MERCY
REMAIN STILL, RANDAL SIX.
I NEED FOR YOU NOT TO STRAIN AGAINST YOUR BONDS.
YOUR TALENTS OF CONCENTRATION ARE A DESIGN OF MY CREATION.
I MUST MAP YOUR CEREBRAL CIRCULATORY PATTERNS IN ORDER TO REPLICATE YOUR PARTICULAR BRAIN PHYSIOGOMY.
SO, DO COOPERATE.
I WOULD HATE TO START FROM THE BEGINNING WITH A NEW SUBJECT.
BUT RANDALL SEVEN IS ALWAYS A CONTINGENCY, NO?

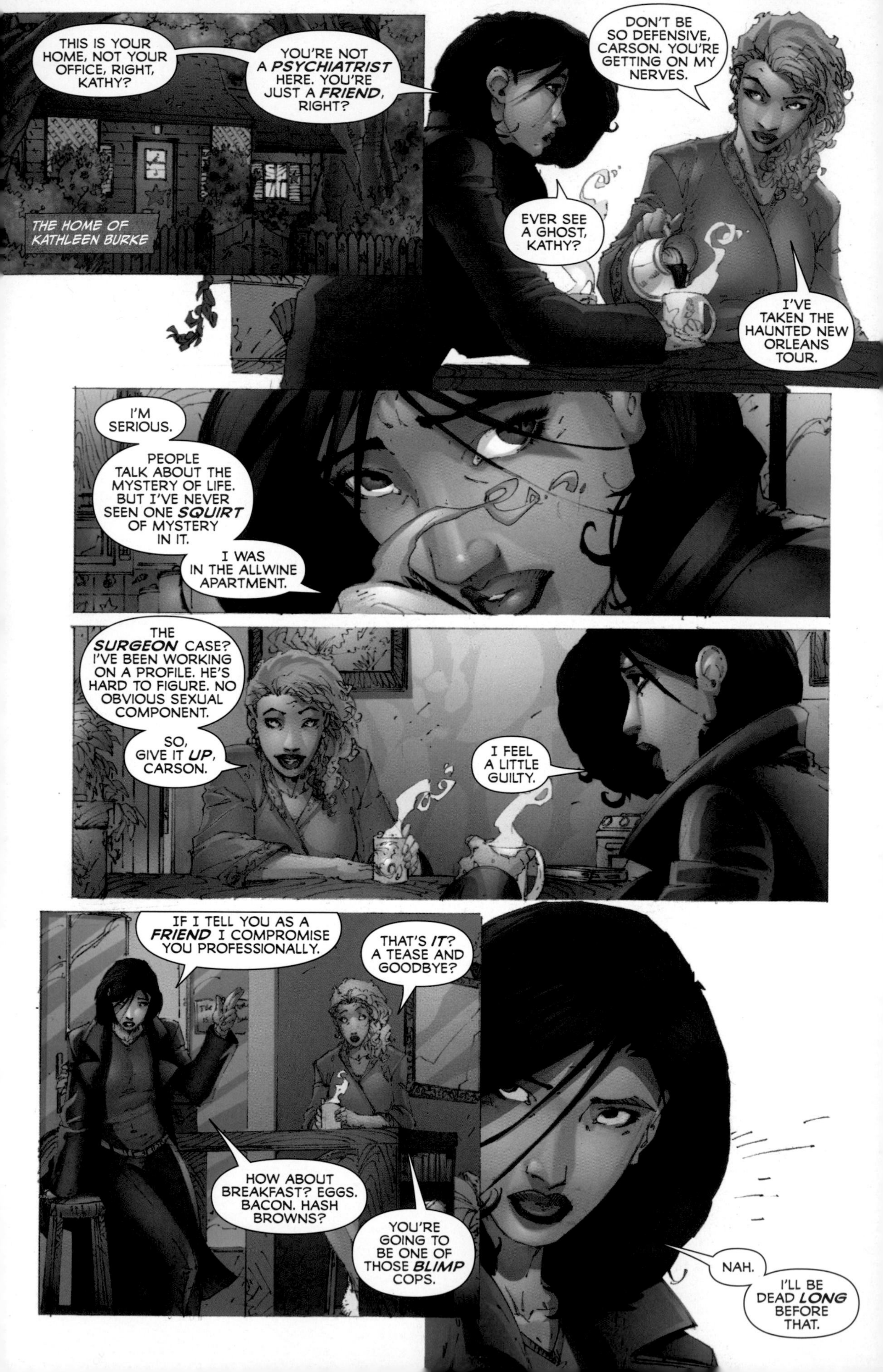
THE HOME OF KATHLEEN BURKE
THIS IS YOUR HOME, NOT YOUR OFFICE, RIGHT, KATHY?
YOU'RE NOT A PSYCHIATRIST HERE. YOU'RE JUST A FRIEND, RIGHT?
DON'T BE SO DEFENSIVE, CARSON. YOU'RE GETTING ON MY NERVES.
EVER SEE A GHOST, KATHY?
I'VE TAKEN THE HAUNTED NEW ORLEANS TOUR.
I'M SERIOUS.
PEOPLE TALK ABOUT THE MYSTERY OF LIFE. BUT I'VE NEVER SEEN ONE SQUIRT OF MYSTERY IN IT.
I WAS IN THE ALLWINE APARTMENT.
THE SURGEON CASE? I'VE BEEN WORKING ON A PROFILE. HE'S HARD TO FIGURE. NO OBVIOUS SEXUAL COMPONENT.
SO, GIVE IT UP, CARSON.
I FEEL A LITTLE GUILTY.
IF I TELL YOU AS A FRIEND I COMPROMISE YOU PROFESSIONALLY.
THAT'S IT? A TEASE AND GOODBYE?
HOW ABOUT BREAKFAST? EGGS. BACON. HASH BROWNS?
YOU'RE GOING TO BE ONE OF THOSE BLIMP COPS.
NAH.
I'LL BE DEAD LONG BEFORE THAT.

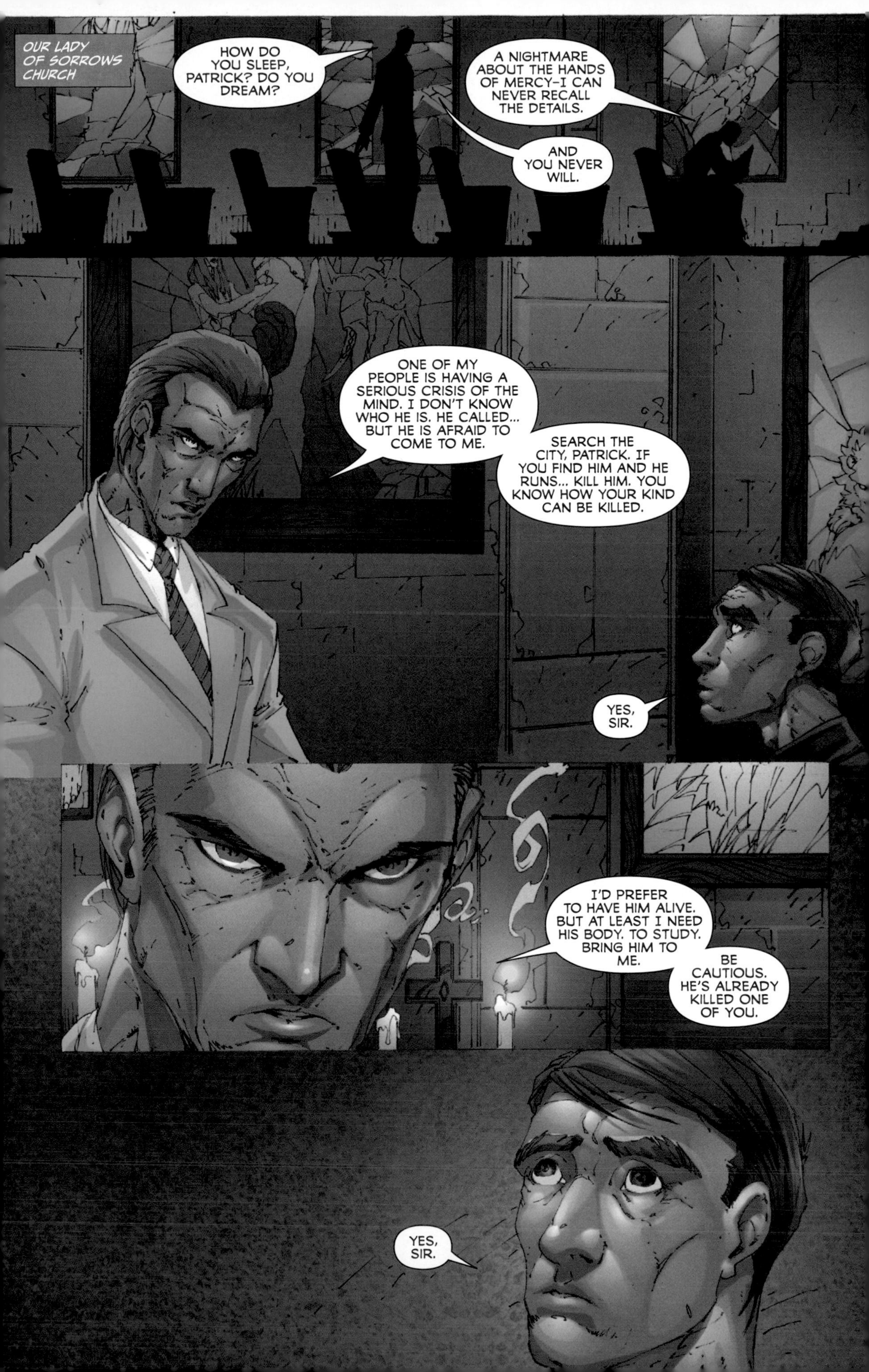
OUR LADY OF SORROWS CHURCH
HOW DO YOU SLEEP, PATRICK? DO YOU DREAM?
A NIGHTMARE ABOUT THE HANDS OF MERCY–I CAN NEVER RECALL THE DETAILS.
AND YOU NEVER WILL.
ONE OF MY PEOPLE IS HAVING A SERIOUS CRISIS OF THE MIND. I DON'T KNOW WHO HE IS. HE CALLED... BUT HE IS AFRAID TO COME TO ME.
SEARCH THE CITY, PATRICK. IF YOU FIND HIM AND HE RUNS... KILL HIM. YOU KNOW HOW YOUR KIND CAN BE KILLED.
YES, SIR.
I'D PREFER TO HAVE HIM ALIVE. BUT AT LEAST I NEED HIS BODY. TO STUDY. BRING HIM TO ME.
BE CAUTIOUS. HE'S ALREADY KILLED ONE OF YOU.
YES, SIR.

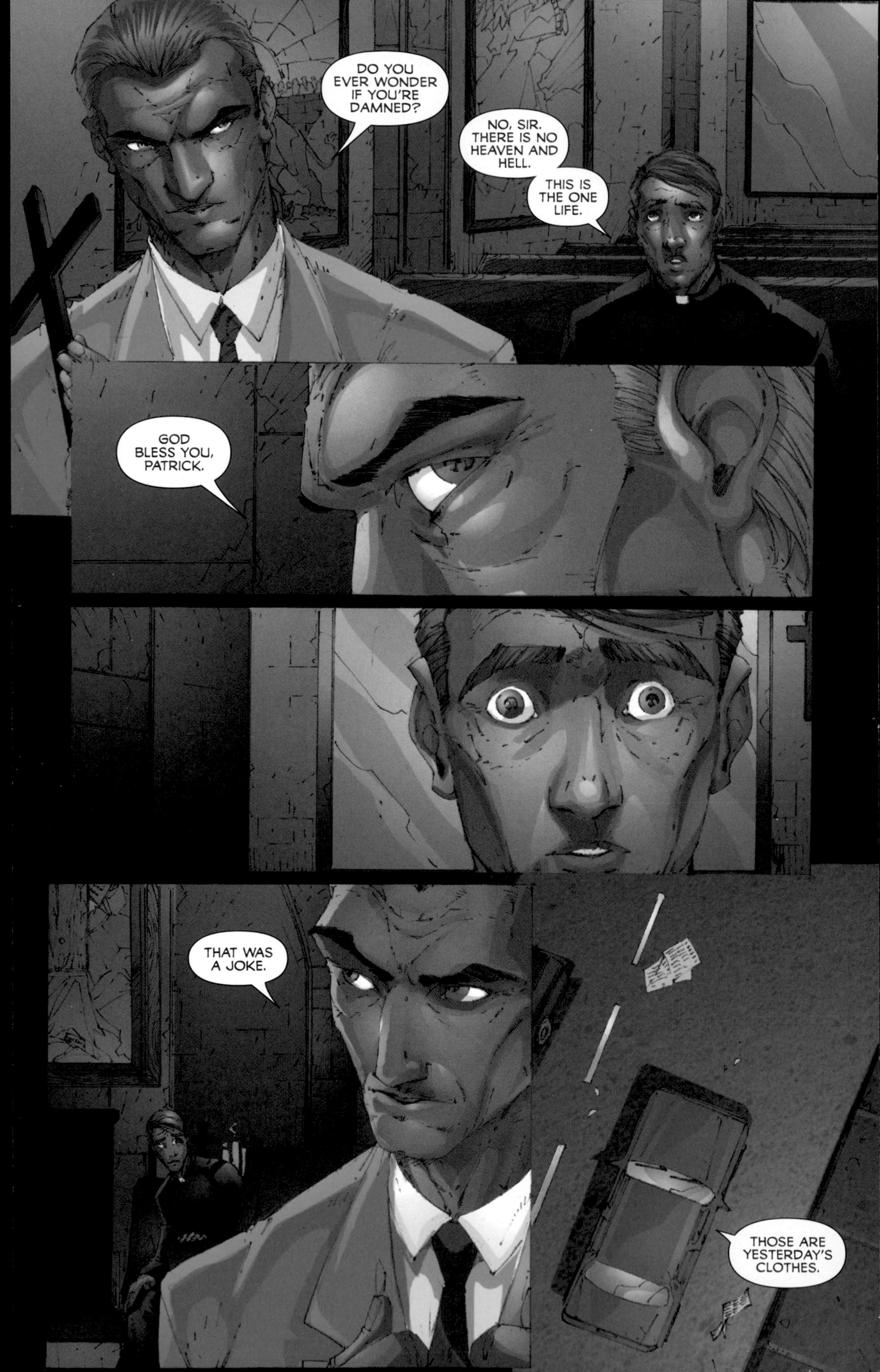
DO YOU EVER WONDER IF YOU'RE DAMNED?
NO, SIR. THERE IS NO HEAVEN AND HELL.
THIS IS THE ONE LIFE.
GOD BLESS YOU, PATRICK.
THAT WAS A JOKE.
THOSE ARE YESTERDAY'S CLOTHES.

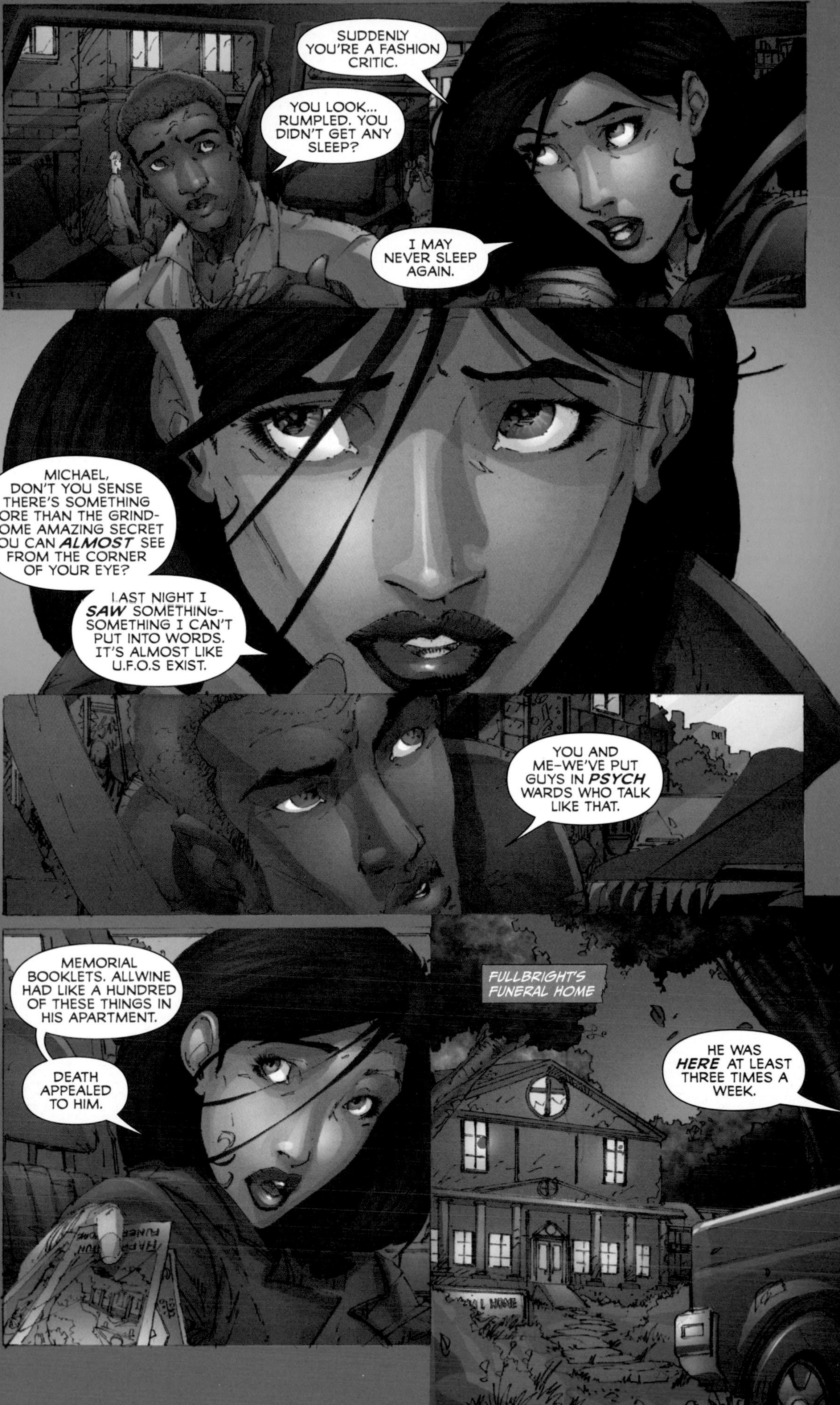
SUDDENLY YOU'RE A FASHION CRITIC.
YOU LOOK... RUMPLED. YOU DIDN'T GET ANY SLEEP?
I MAY NEVER SLEEP AGAIN.
MICHAEL, DON'T YOU SENSE THERE'S SOMETHING MORE THAN THE GRIND-SOME AMAZING SECRET YOU CAN ALMOST SEE FROM THE CORNER OF YOUR EYE?
LAST NIGHT I SAW SOMETHING-SOMETHING I CAN'T PUT INTO WORDS. IT'S ALMOST LIKE U.F.O.S EXIST.
YOU AND ME–WE'VE PUT GUYS IN PSYCH WARDS WHO TALK LIKE THAT.
MEMORIAL BOOKLETS. ALLWINE HAD LIKE A HUNDRED OF THESE THINGS IN HIS APARTMENT.
DEATH APPEALED TO HIM.
FULLBRIGHT'S FUNERAL HOME
HE WAS HERE AT LEAST THREE TIMES A WEEK.

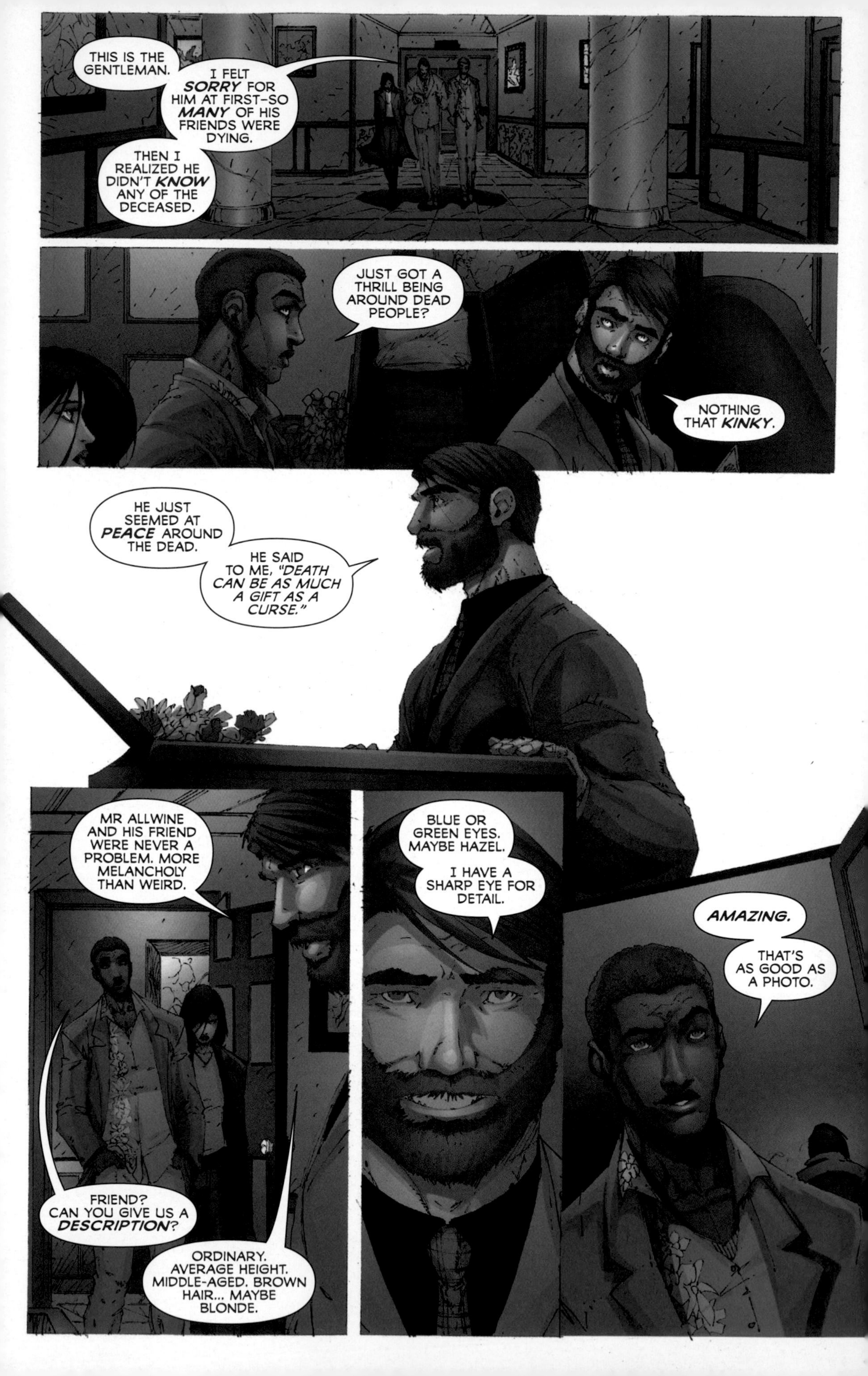

THIS IS THE GENTLEMAN.
I FELT SORRY FOR HIM AT FIRST–SO MANY OF HIS FRIENDS WERE DYING.
THEN I REALIZED HE DIDN'T KNOW ANY OF THE DECEASED.
JUST GOT A THRILL BEING AROUND DEAD PEOPLE?
NOTHING THAT KINKY.
HE JUST SEEMED AT PEACE AROUND THE DEAD.
HE SAID TO ME, "DEATH CAN BE AS MUCH A GIFT AS A CURSE."
MR ALLWINE AND HIS FRIEND WERE NEVER A PROBLEM. MORE MELANCHOLY THAN WEIRD.
FRIEND? CAN YOU GIVE US A DESCRIPTION?
ORDINARY. AVERAGE HEIGHT. MIDDLE-AGED. BROWN HAIR... MAYBE BLONDE.
BLUE OR GREEN EYES. MAYBE HAZEL.
I HAVE A SHARP EYE FOR DETAIL.
AMAZING.
THAT'S AS GOOD AS A PHOTO.

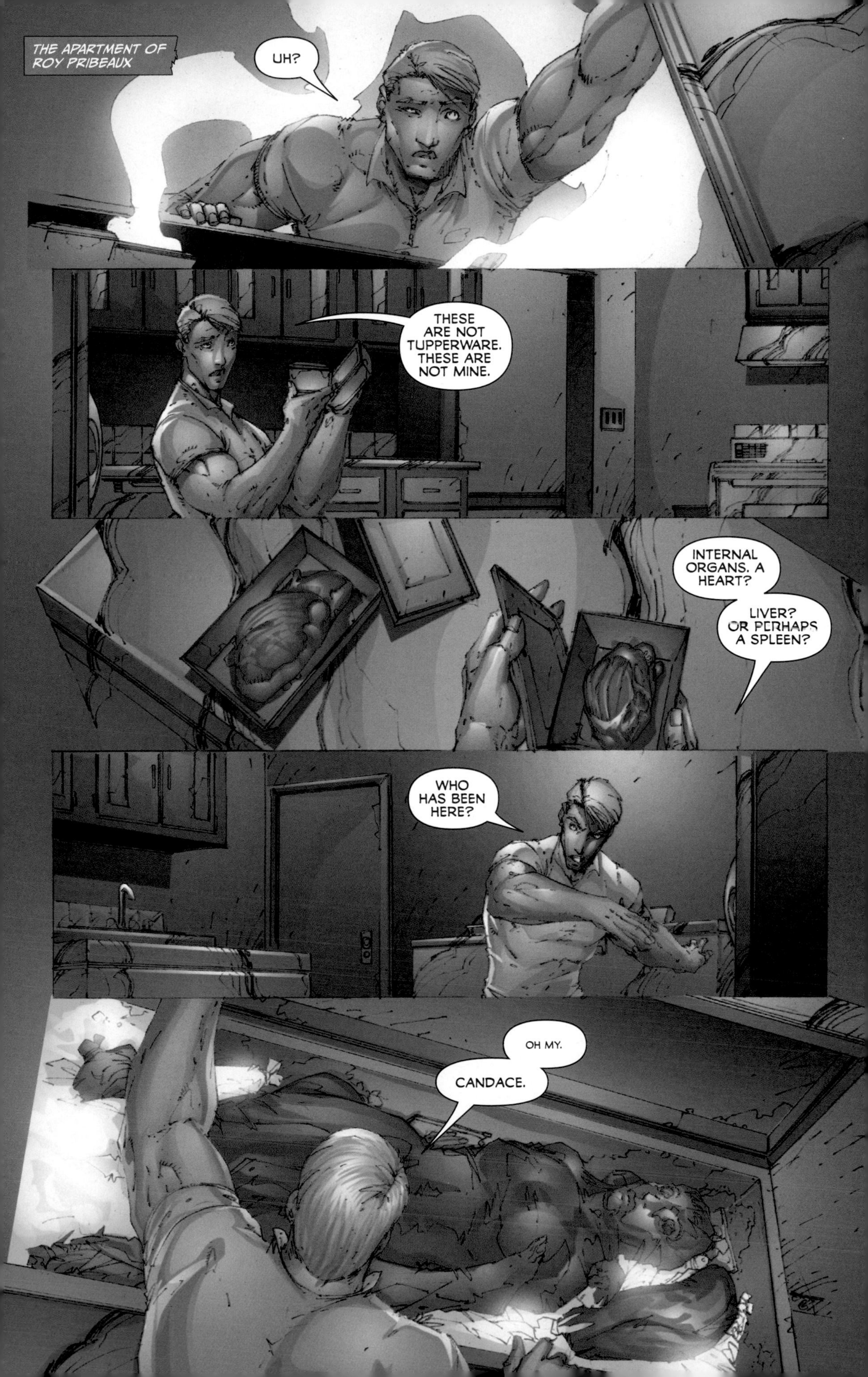
THE APARTMENT OF ROY PRIBEAUX
UH?
THESE ARE NOT TUPPERWARE. THESE ARE NOT MINE.
INTERNAL ORGANS. A HEART?
LIVER? OR PERHAPS A SPLEEN?
WHO HAS BEEN HERE?
OH MY.
CANDACE.

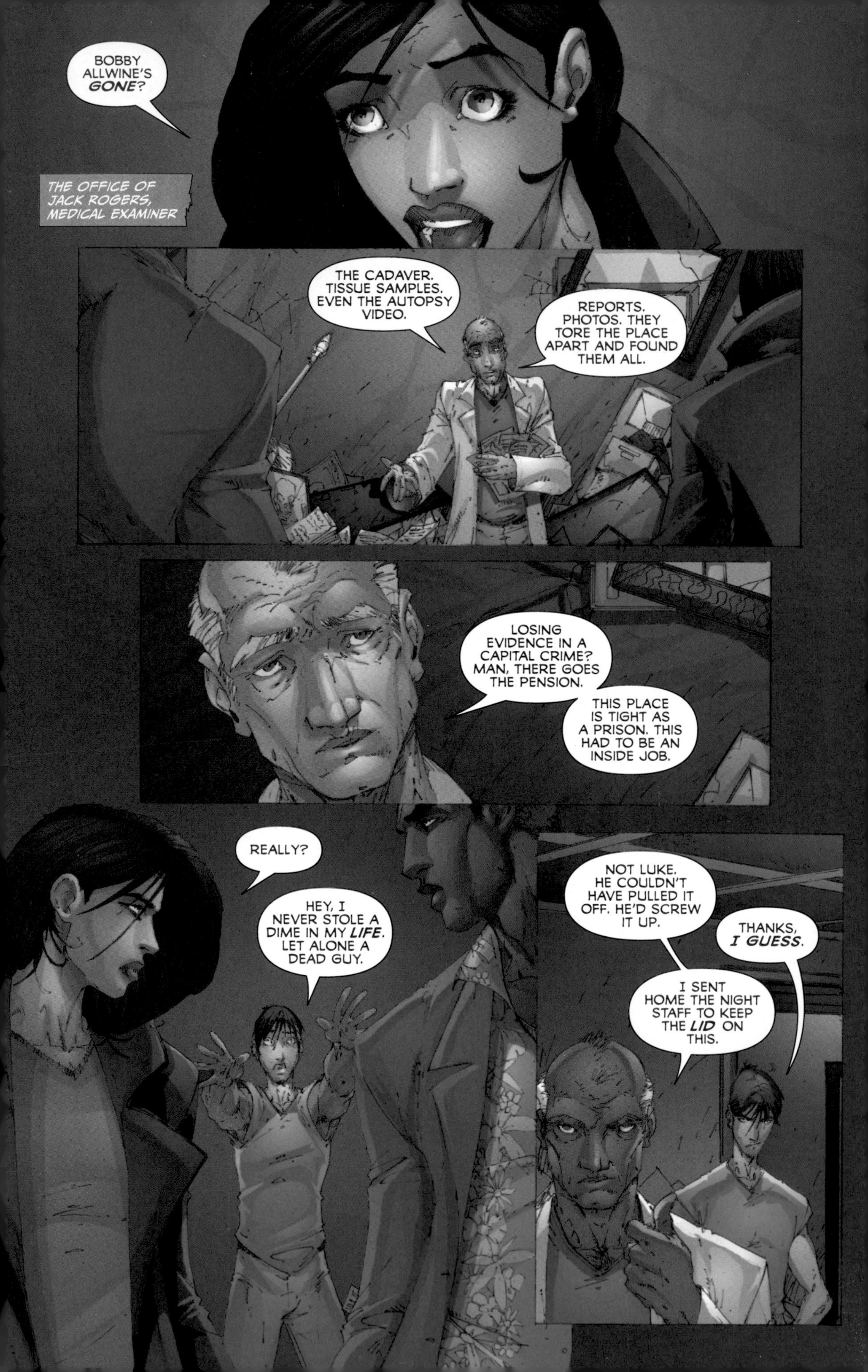
BOBBY ALLWINE'S *GONE*?
THE OFFICE OF JACK ROGERS, MEDICAL EXAMINER
THE CADAVER. TISSUE SAMPLES. EVEN THE AUTOPSY VIDEO.
REPORTS. PHOTOS. THEY TORE THE PLACE APART AND FOUND THEM ALL.
LOSING EVIDENCE IN A CAPITAL CRIME? MAN, THERE GOES THE PENSION.
THIS PLACE IS TIGHT AS A PRISON. THIS HAD TO BE AN INSIDE JOB.
REALLY?
HEY, I NEVER STOLE A DIME IN MY *LIFE*. LET ALONE A DEAD GUY.
NOT LUKE. HE COULDN'T HAVE PULLED IT OFF. HE'D SCREW IT UP.
THANKS, *I GUESS*.
I SENT HOME THE NIGHT STAFF TO KEEP THE *LID* ON THIS.

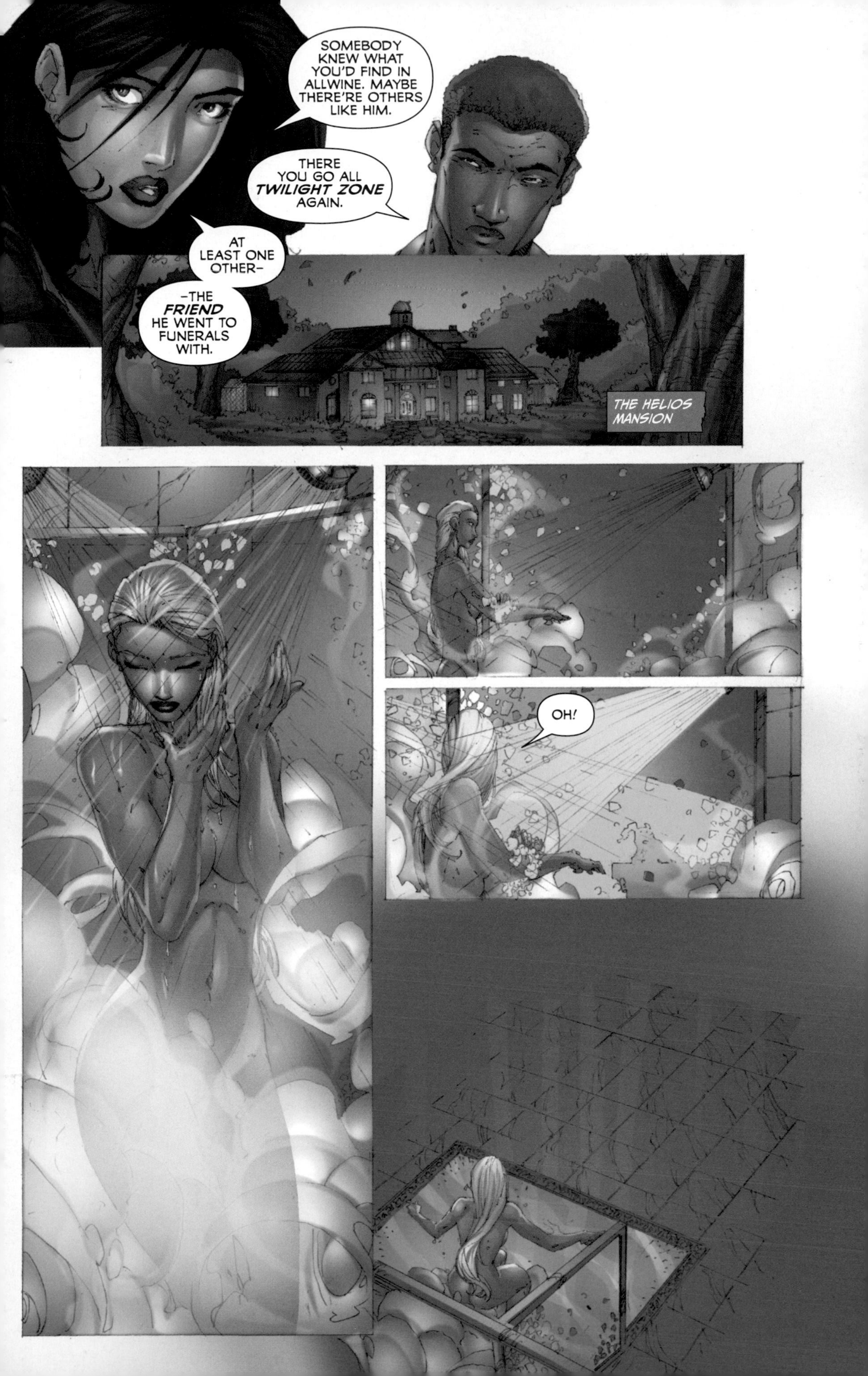
SOMEBODY KNEW WHAT YOU'D FIND IN ALLWINE. MAYBE THERE'RE OTHERS LIKE HIM.
THERE YOU GO ALL TWILIGHT ZONE AGAIN.
AT LEAST ONE OTHER–
–THE FRIEND HE WENT TO FUNERALS WITH.
THE HELIOS MANSION
OH!

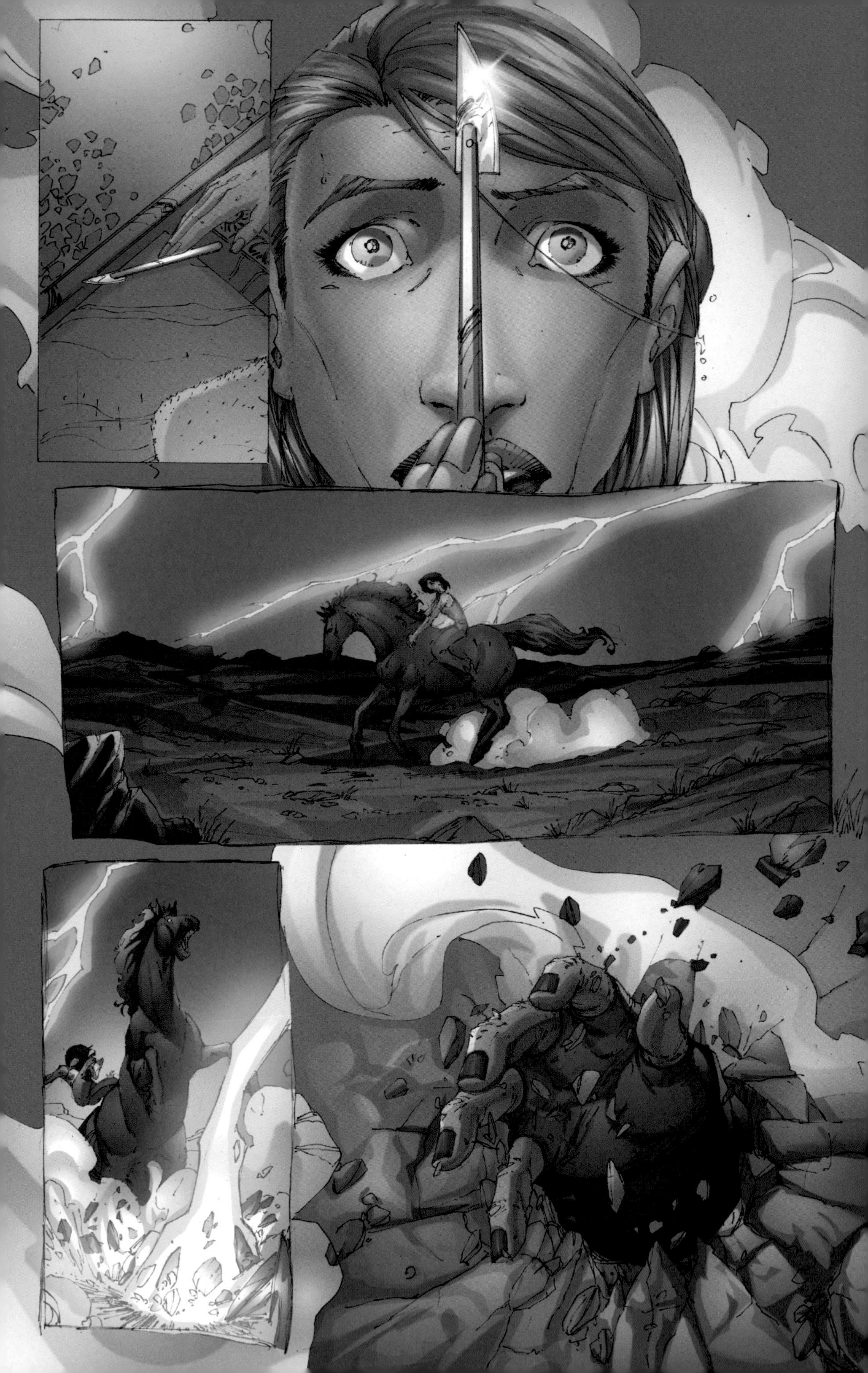

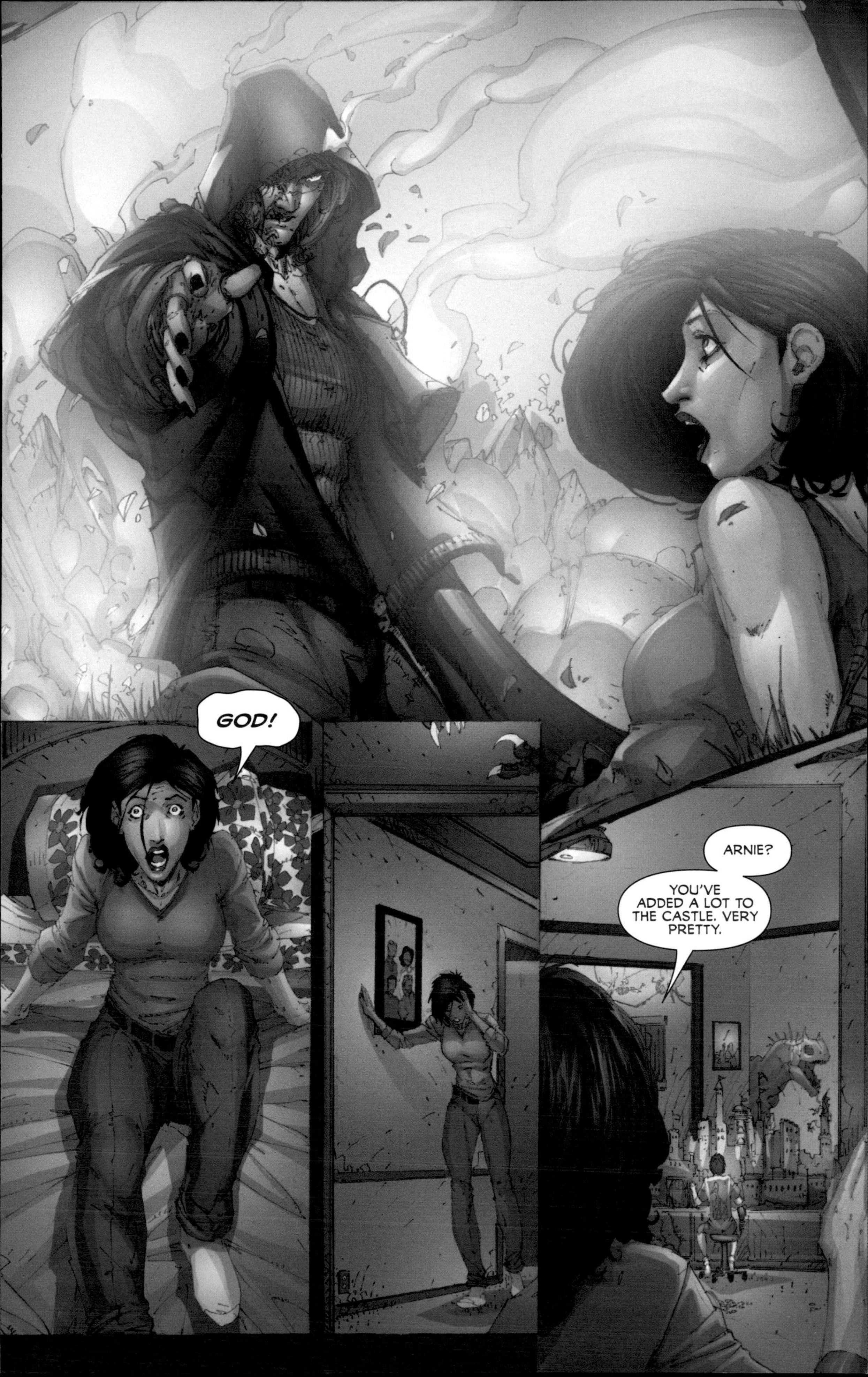
GOD!
ARNIE?
YOU'VE ADDED A LOT TO THE CASTLE. VERY PRETTY.

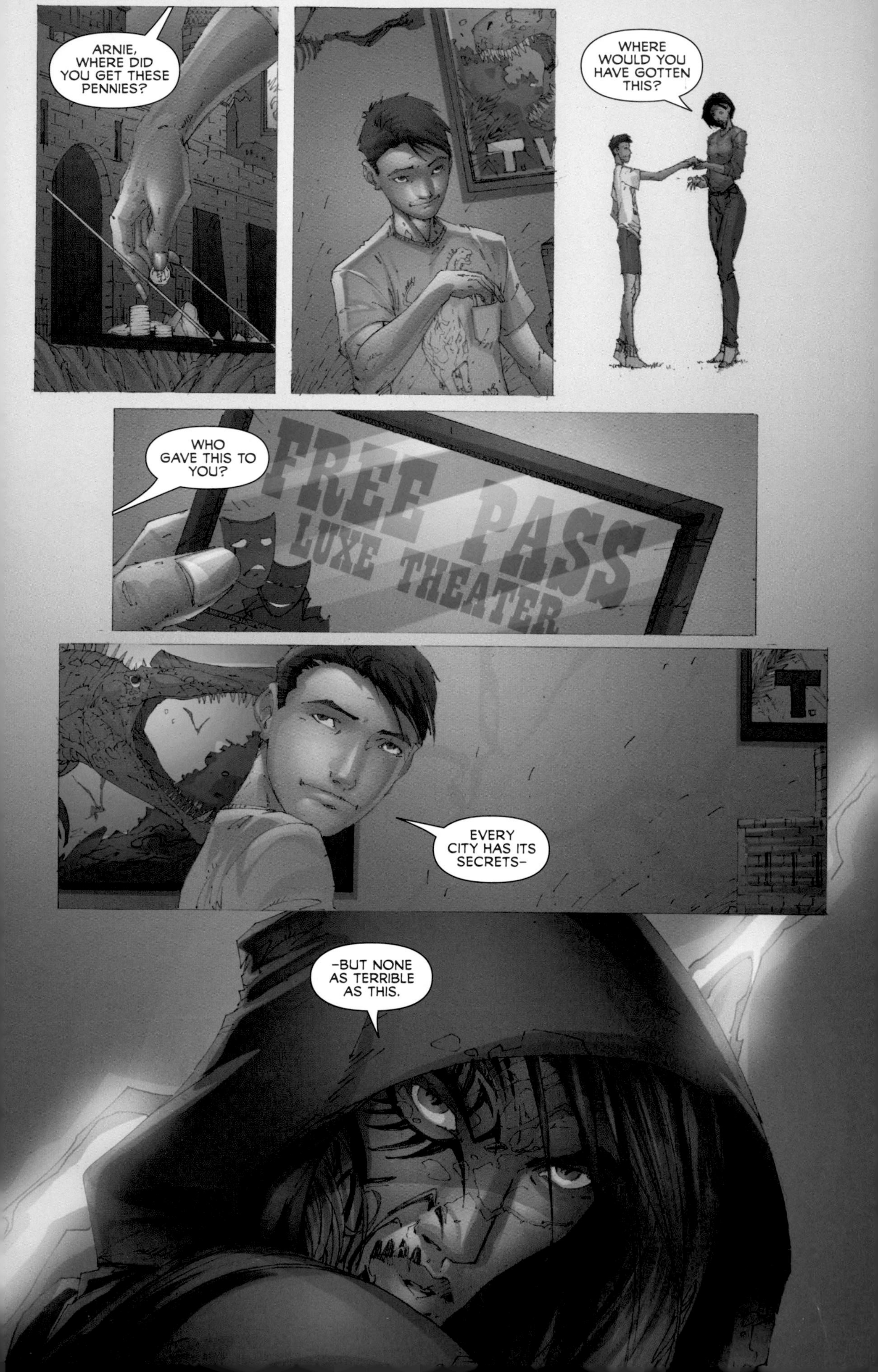
ARNIE, WHERE DID YOU GET THESE PENNIES?
WHERE WOULD YOU HAVE GOTTEN THIS?
WHO GAVE THIS TO YOU?
FREE PASS
LUXE THEATER
EVERY CITY HAS ITS SECRETS–
–BUT NONE AS TERRIBLE AS THIS.

chapter five

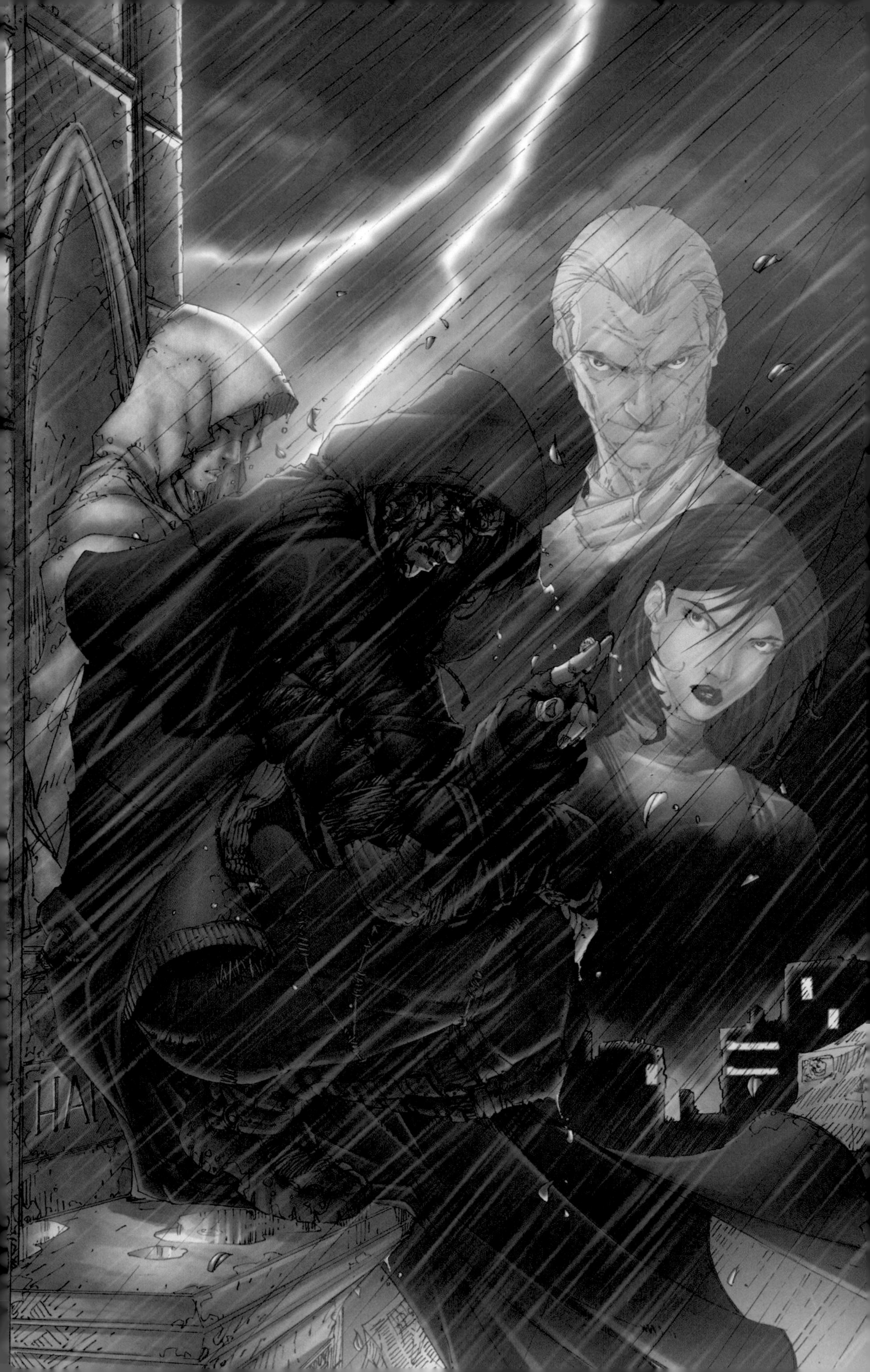

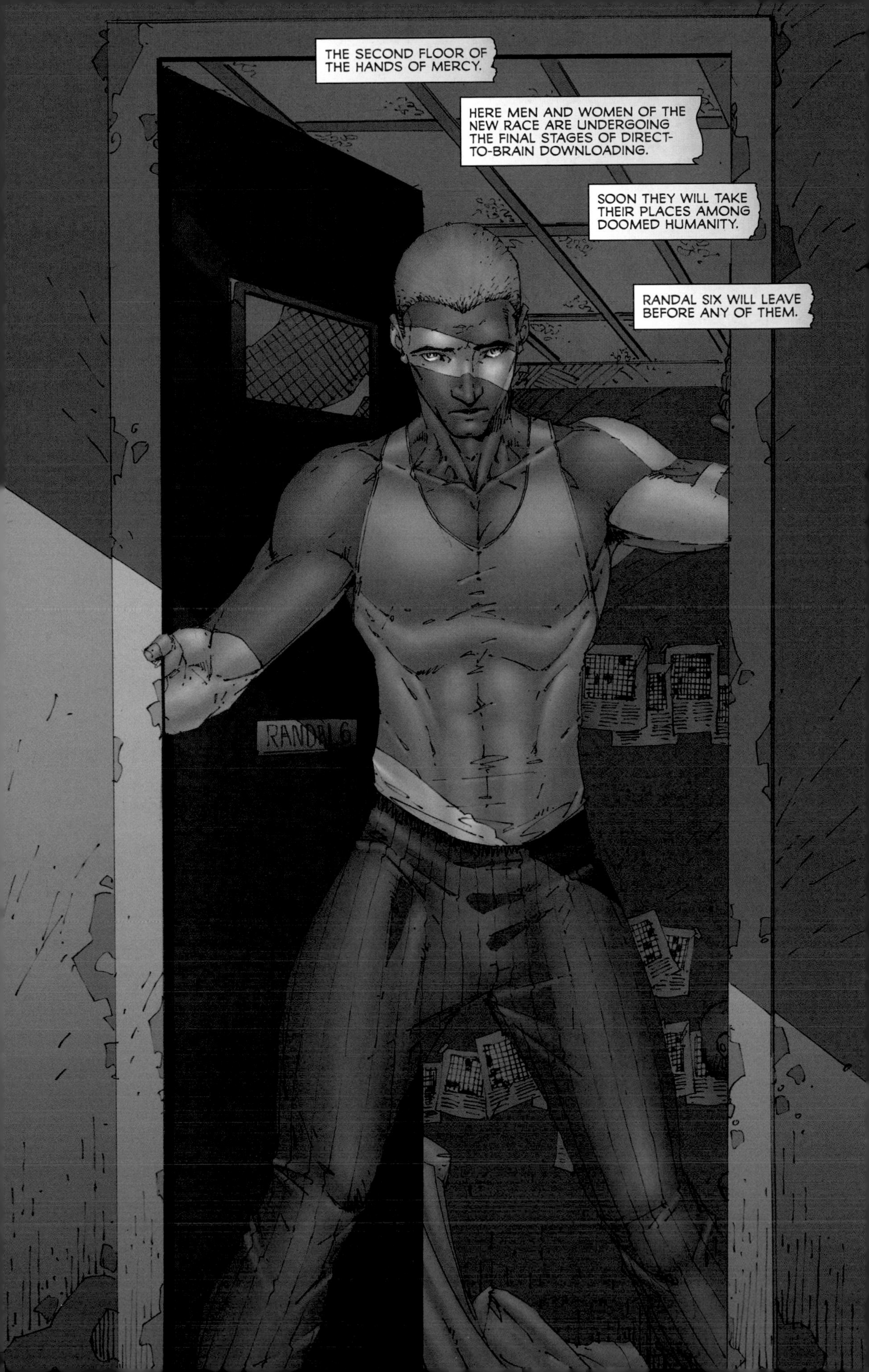
THE SECOND FLOOR OF THE HANDS OF MERCY.
HERE MEN AND WOMEN OF THE NEW RACE ARE UNDERGOING THE FINAL STAGES OF DIRECT-TO-BRAIN DOWNLOADING.
SOON THEY WILL TAKE THEIR PLACES AMONG DOOMED HUMANITY.
RANDAL SIX WILL LEAVE BEFORE ANY OF THEM.
RANDAL 6

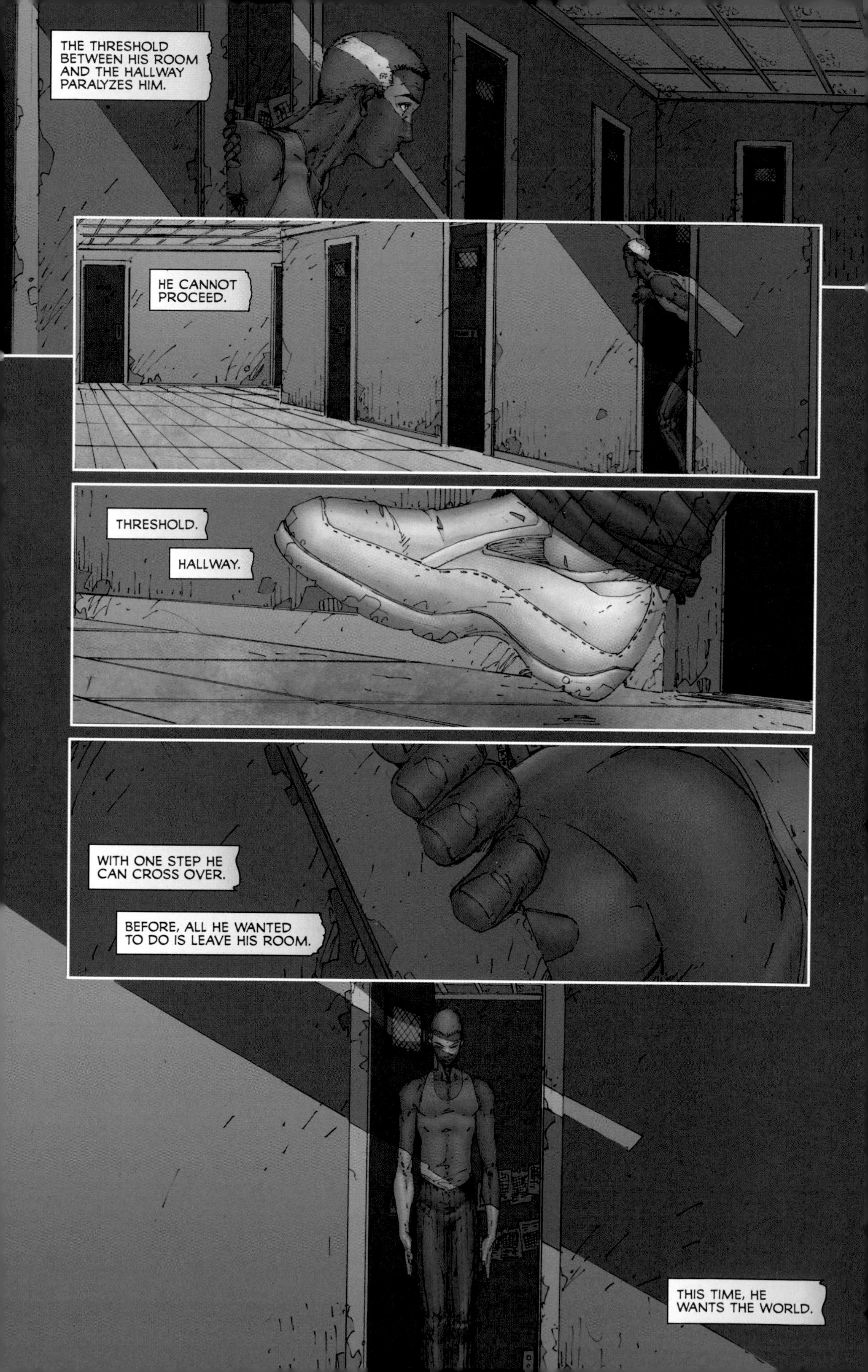
THE THRESHOLD BETWEEN HIS ROOM AND THE HALLWAY PARALYZES HIM.
HE CANNOT PROCEED.
THRESHOLD.
HALLWAY.
WITH ONE STEP HE CAN CROSS OVER.
BEFORE, ALL HE WANTED TO DO IS LEAVE HIS ROOM.
THIS TIME, HE WANTS THE WORLD.

THE TILE FLOOR REMINDS HIM OF HIS BELOVED CROSSWORDS.

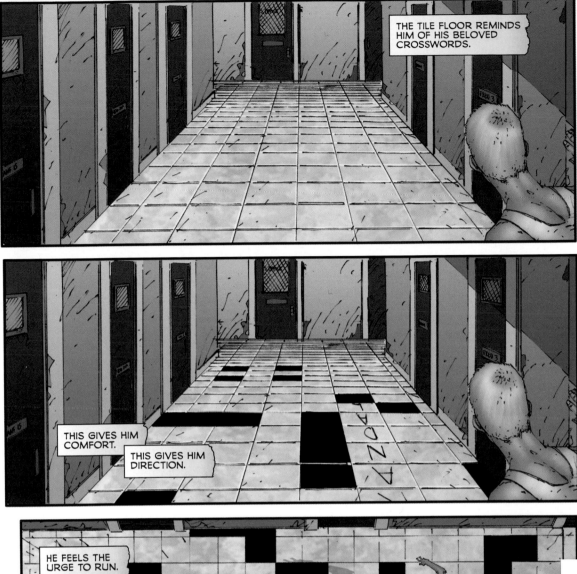

THIS GIVES HIM COMFORT.

THIS GIVES HIM DIRECTION.

HE FEELS THE URGE TO RUN.

BUT HE MUST PLACE EACH FOOT ENTIRELY IN A SQUARE.

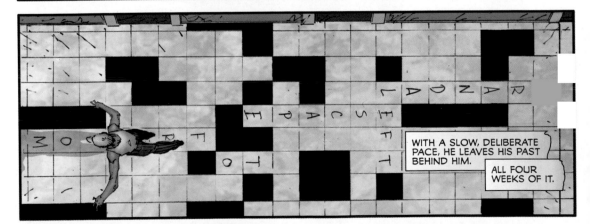

WITH A SLOW, DELIBERATE PACE, HE LEAVES HIS PAST BEHIND HIM.

ALL FOUR WEEKS OF IT.

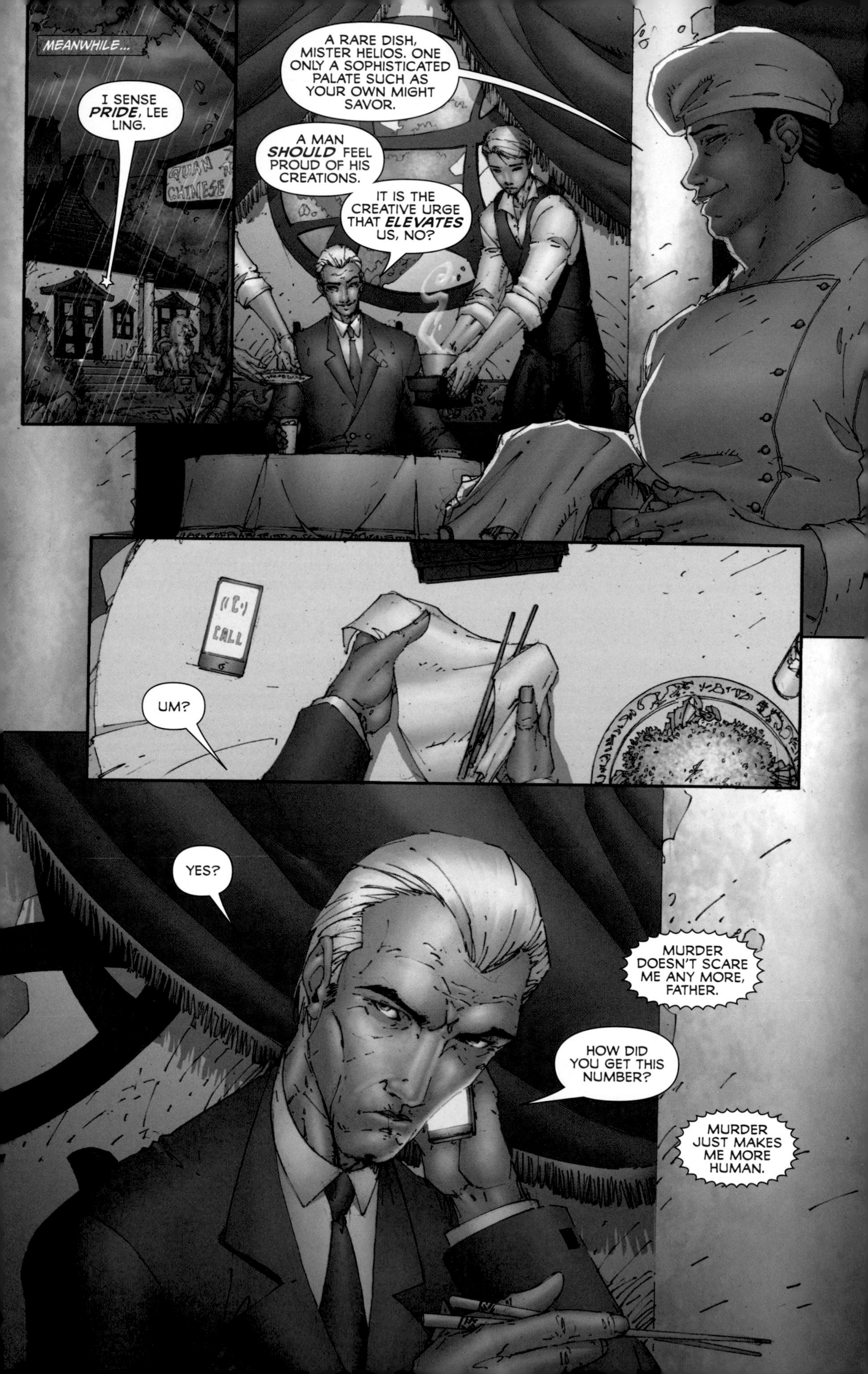
MEANWHILE...
I SENSE PRIDE, LEE LING.
QUAN
CHINESE
A RARE DISH, MISTER HELIOS. ONE ONLY A SOPHISTICATED PALATE SUCH AS YOUR OWN MIGHT SAVOR.
A MAN SHOULD FEEL PROUD OF HIS CREATIONS.
IT IS THE CREATIVE URGE THAT ELEVATES US, NO?
CALL
UM?
YES?
MURDER DOESN'T SCARE ME ANY MORE, FATHER.
HOW DID YOU GET THIS NUMBER?
MURDER JUST MAKES ME MORE HUMAN.

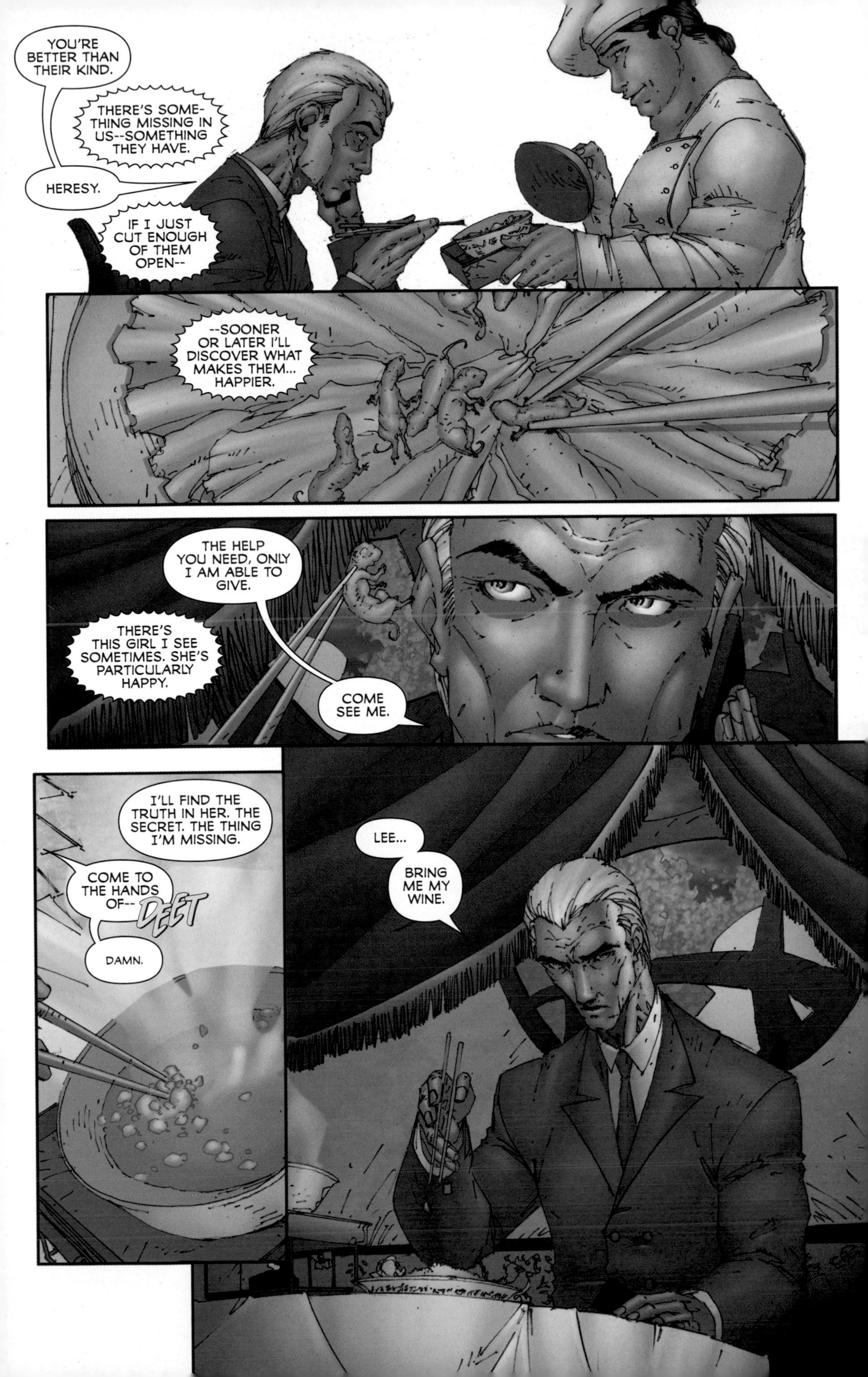
YOU'RE BETTER THAN THEIR KIND.
THERE'S SOME-THING MISSING IN US--SOMETHING THEY HAVE.
HERESY.
IF I JUST CUT ENOUGH OF THEM OPEN--
--SOONER OR LATER I'LL DISCOVER WHAT MAKES THEM... HAPPIER.
THE HELP YOU NEED, ONLY I AM ABLE TO GIVE.
THERE'S THIS GIRL I SEE SOMETIMES. SHE'S PARTICULARLY HAPPY.
COME SEE ME.
I'LL FIND THE TRUTH IN HER. THE SECRET. THE THING I'M MISSING.
COME TO THE HANDS OF--
DEET
DAMN.
LEE...
BRING ME MY WINE.

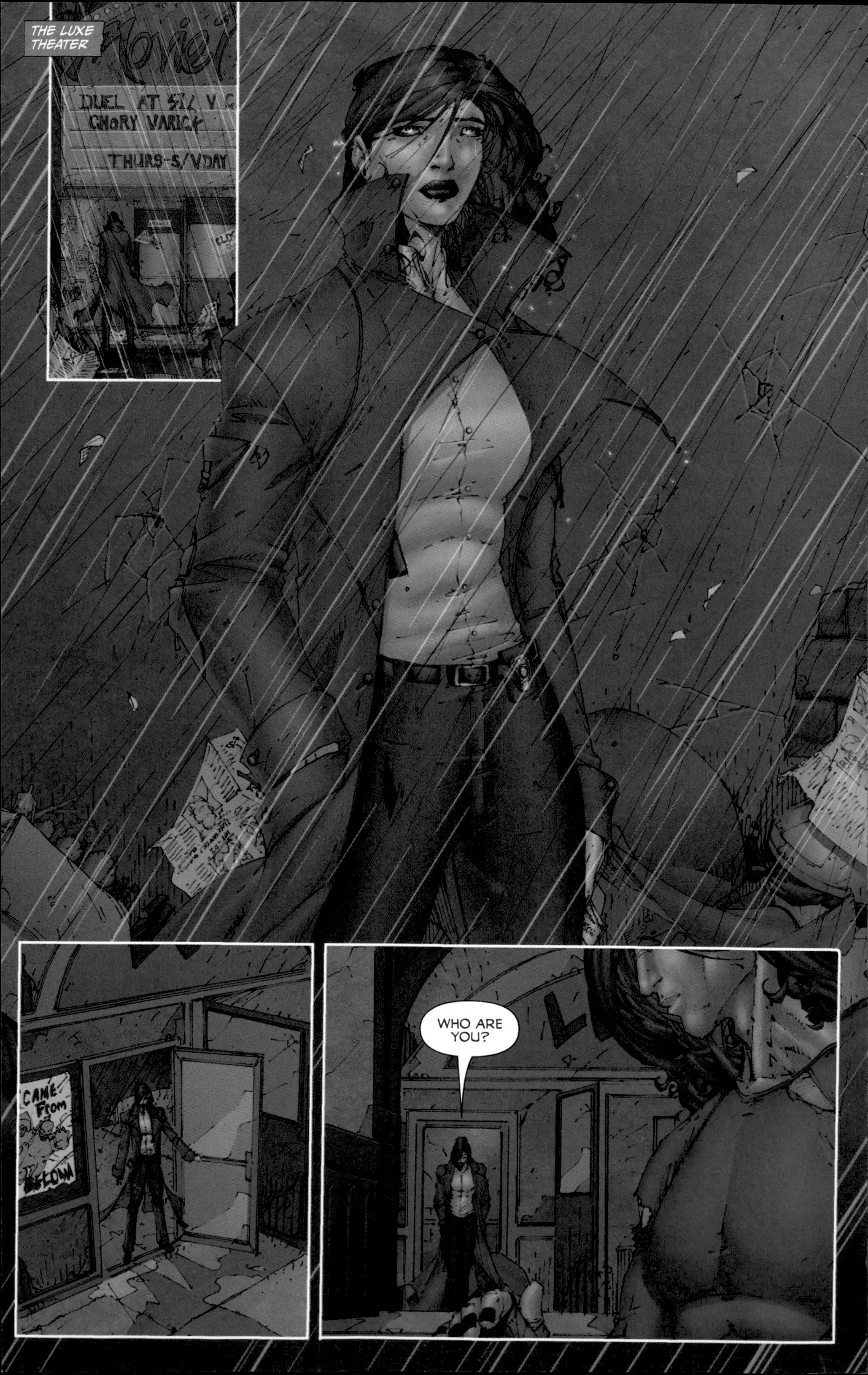
THE LUXE THEATER
WHO ARE YOU?

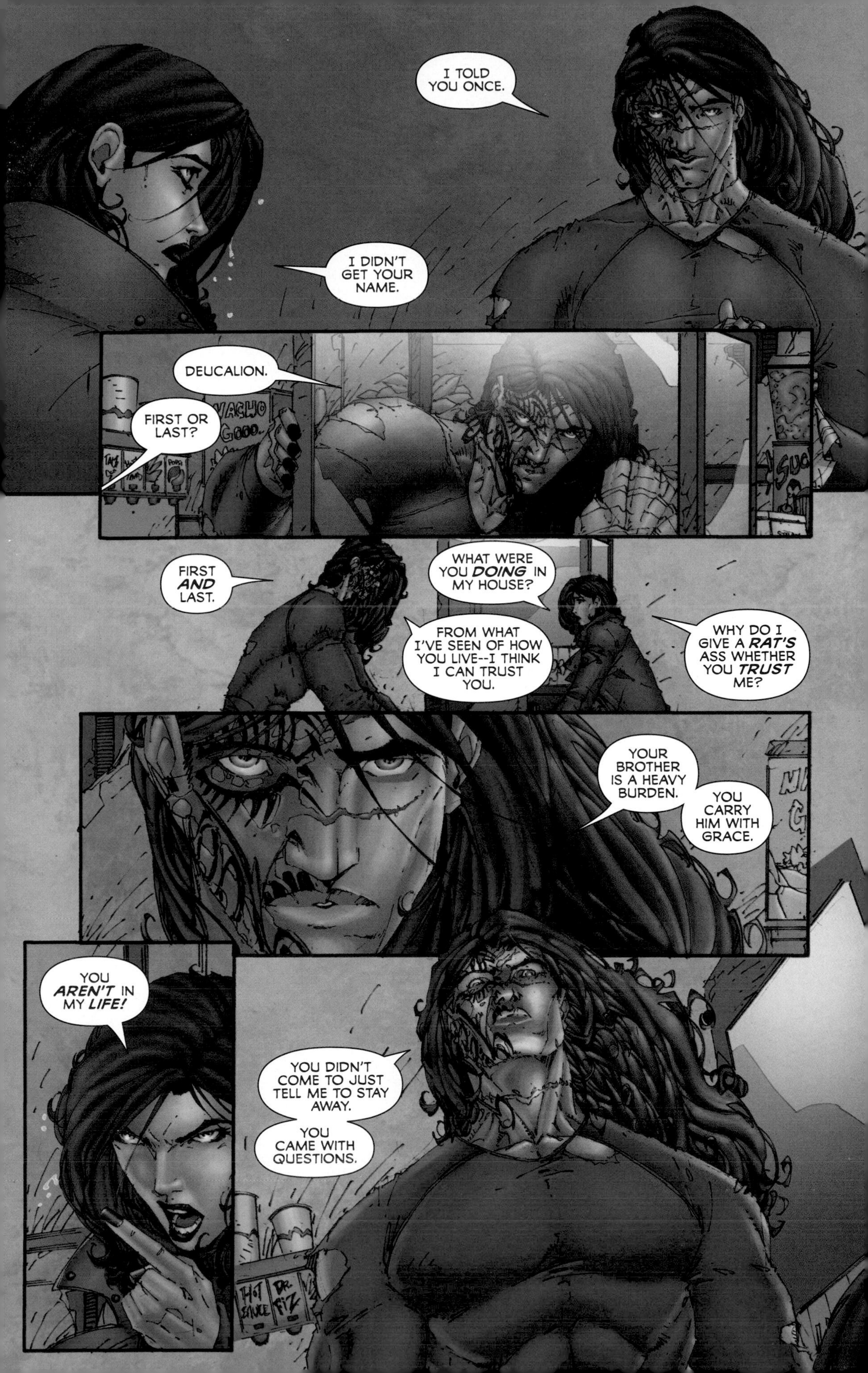
I TOLD YOU ONCE.
I DIDN'T GET YOUR NAME.
DEUCALION.
FIRST OR LAST?
NACHO GOOD...
FIRST *AND* LAST.
WHAT WERE YOU *DOING* IN MY HOUSE?
FROM WHAT I'VE SEEN OF HOW YOU LIVE--I THINK I CAN TRUST YOU.
WHY DO I GIVE A *RAT'S* ASS WHETHER YOU *TRUST* ME?
YOUR BROTHER IS A HEAVY BURDEN.
YOU CARRY HIM WITH GRACE.
YOU *AREN'T* IN MY *LIFE!*
YOU DIDN'T COME TO JUST TELL ME TO STAY AWAY.
YOU CAME WITH QUESTIONS.
HOT SAUCE
DR. FIZ

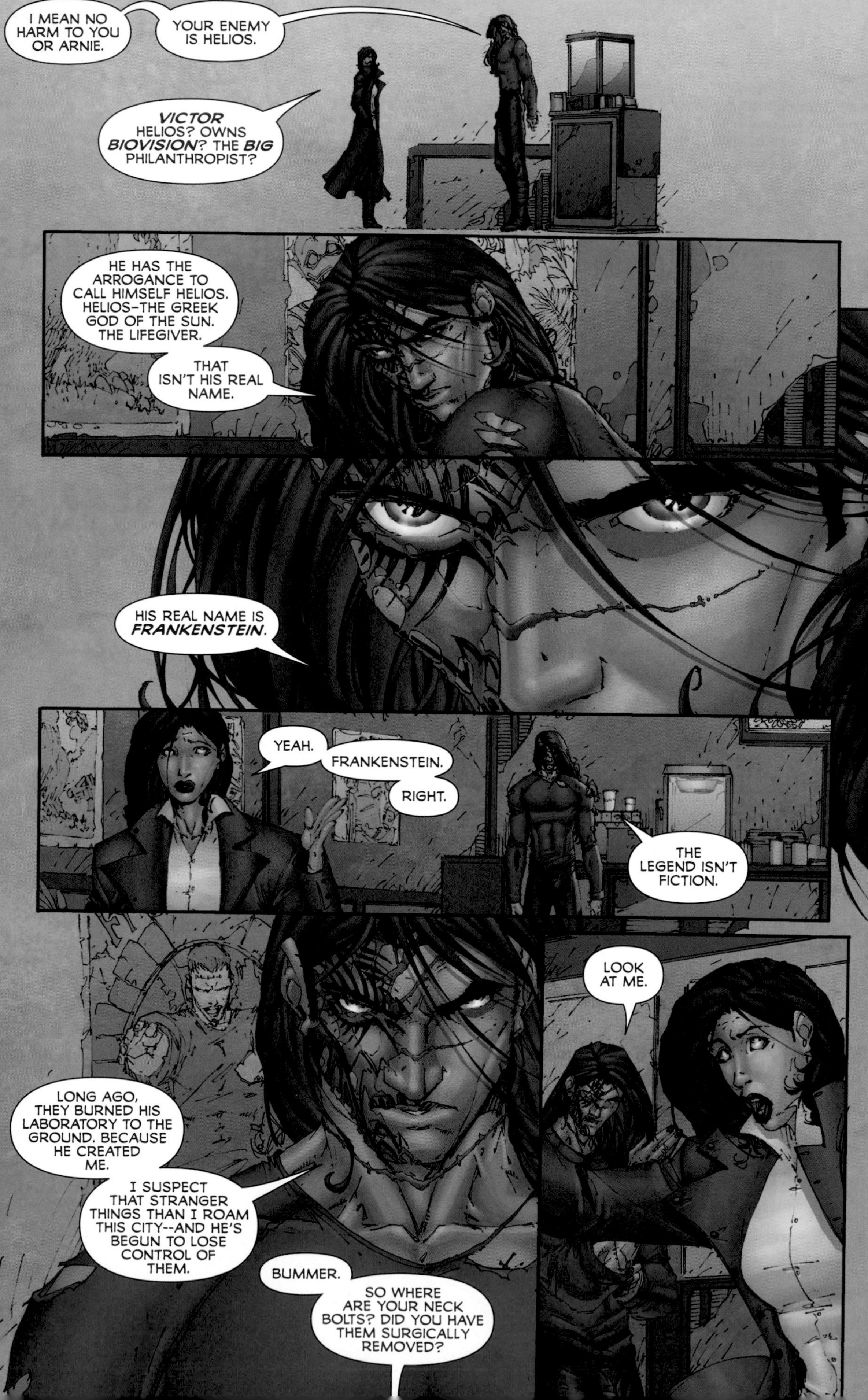
I MEAN NO HARM TO YOU OR ARNIE.
YOUR ENEMY IS HELIOS.
VICTOR HELIOS? OWNS BIOVISION? THE BIG PHILANTHROPIST?
HE HAS THE ARROGANCE TO CALL HIMSELF HELIOS. HELIOS–THE GREEK GOD OF THE SUN. THE LIFEGIVER.
THAT ISN'T HIS REAL NAME.
HIS REAL NAME IS FRANKENSTEIN.
YEAH.
FRANKENSTEIN.
RIGHT.
THE LEGEND ISN'T FICTION.
LONG AGO, THEY BURNED HIS LABORATORY TO THE GROUND. BECAUSE HE CREATED ME.
I SUSPECT THAT STRANGER THINGS THAN I ROAM THIS CITY--AND HE'S BEGUN TO LOSE CONTROL OF THEM.
LOOK AT ME.
BUMMER.
SO WHERE ARE YOUR NECK BOLTS? DID YOU HAVE THEM SURGICALLY REMOVED?

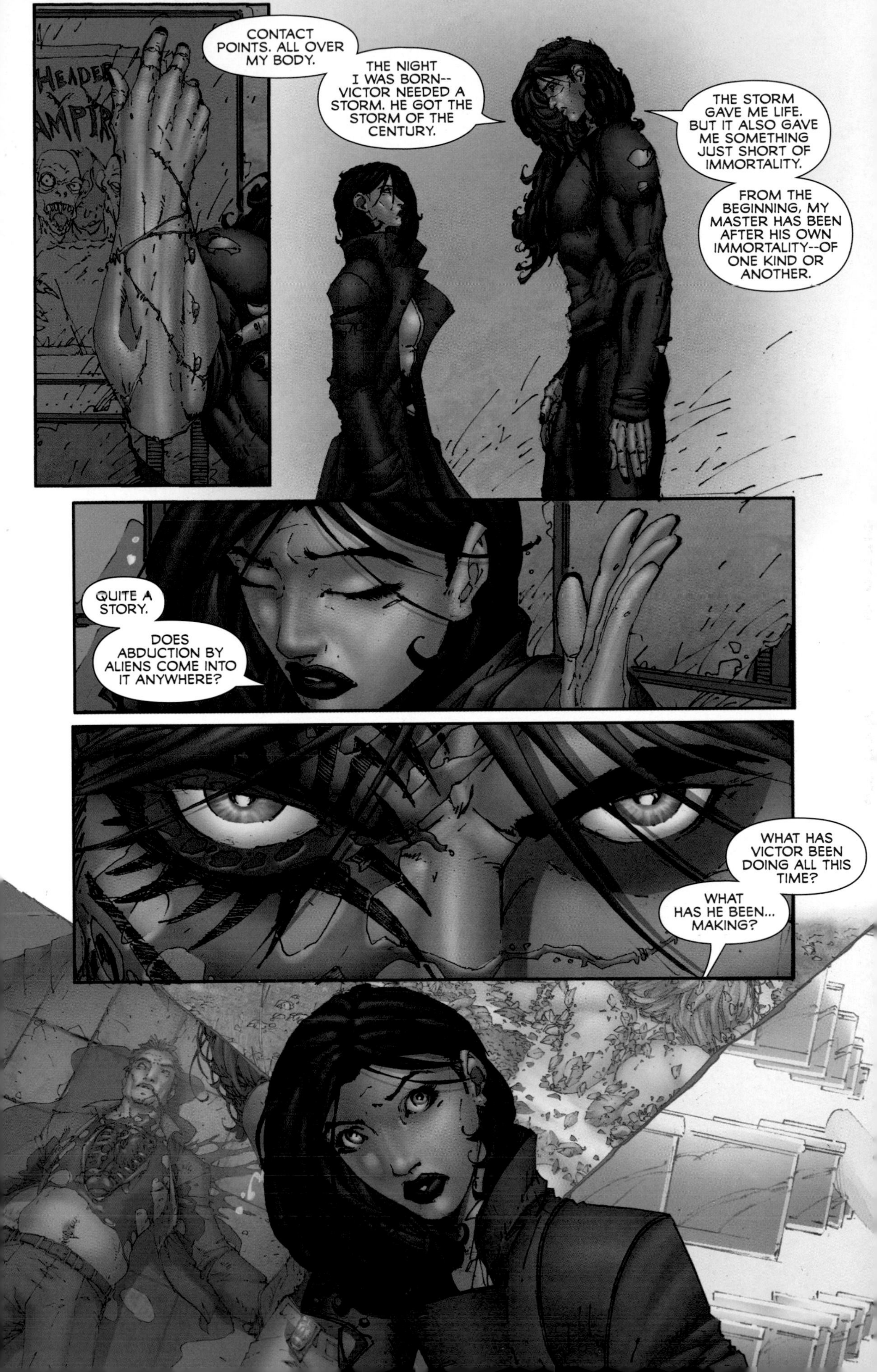
CONTACT POINTS. ALL OVER MY BODY.
THE NIGHT I WAS BORN-- VICTOR NEEDED A STORM. HE GOT THE STORM OF THE CENTURY.
THE STORM GAVE ME LIFE. BUT IT ALSO GAVE ME SOMETHING JUST SHORT OF IMMORTALITY.
FROM THE BEGINNING, MY MASTER HAS BEEN AFTER HIS OWN IMMORTALITY--OF ONE KIND OR ANOTHER.
QUITE A STORY.
DOES ABDUCTION BY ALIENS COME INTO IT ANYWHERE?
WHAT HAS VICTOR BEEN DOING ALL THIS TIME?
WHAT HAS HE BEEN... MAKING?

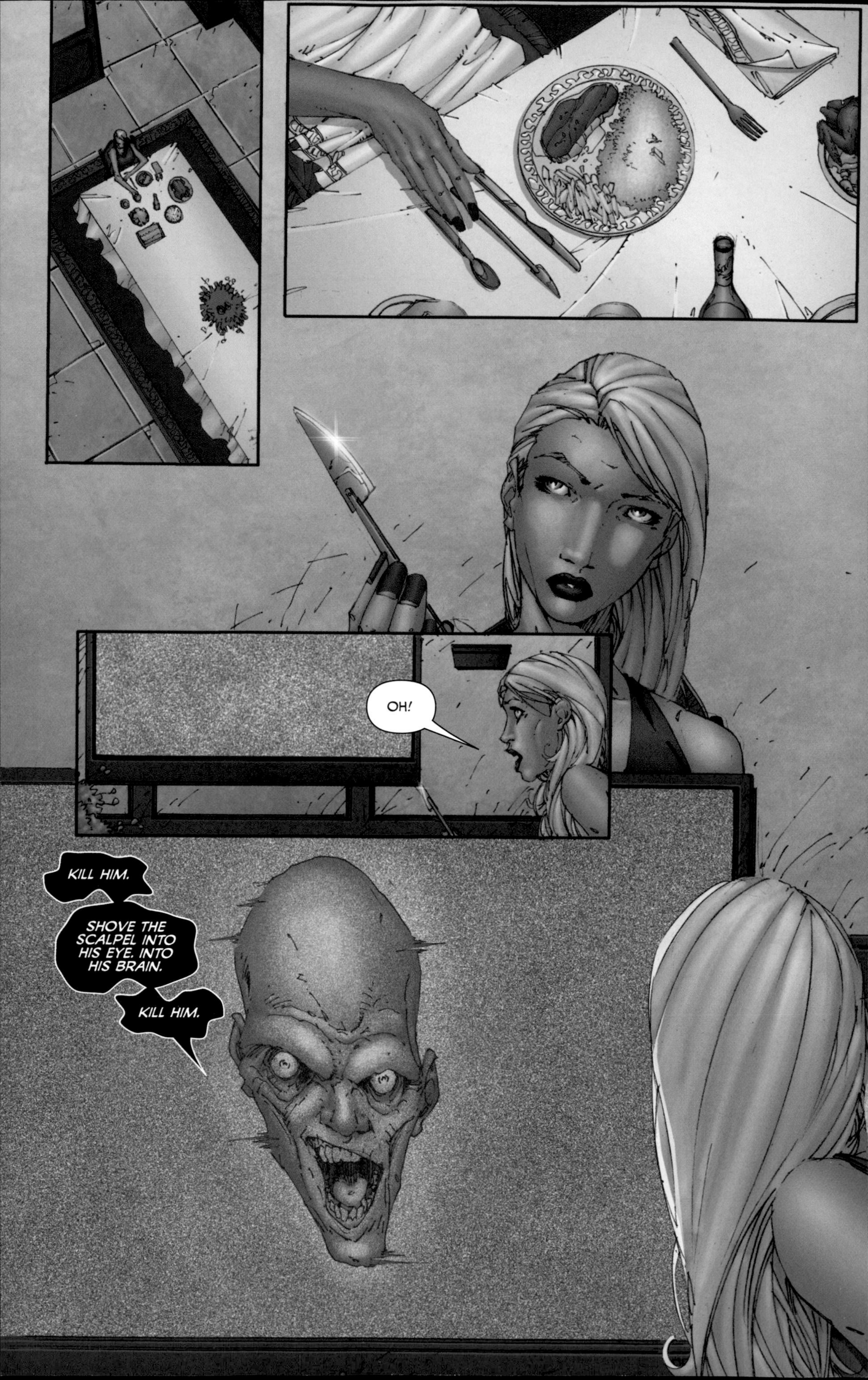
OH!
KILL HIM.
SHOVE THE SCALPEL INTO HIS EYE. INTO HIS BRAIN.
KILL HIM.

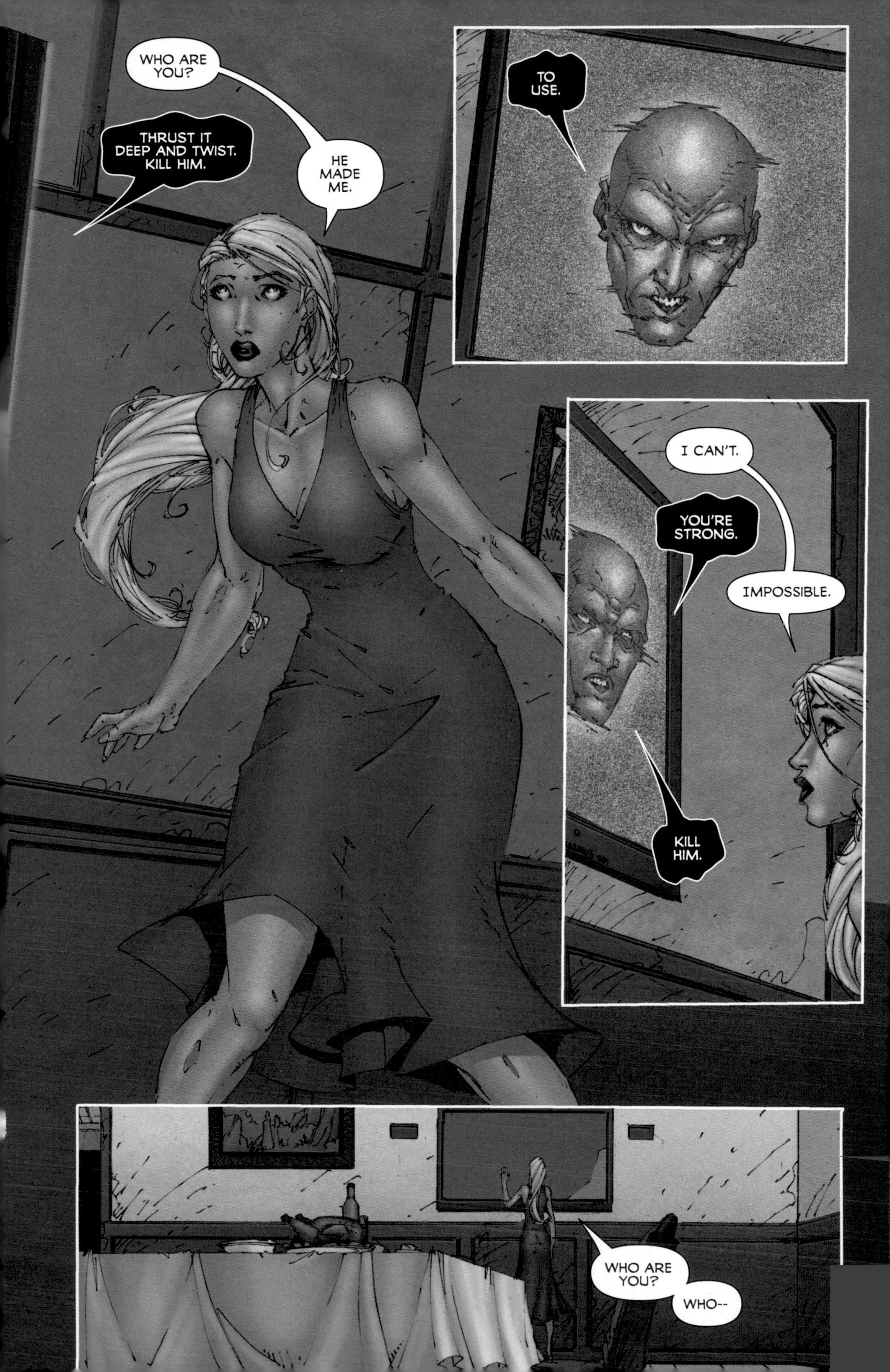
WHO ARE YOU?
HE MADE ME.
THRUST IT DEEP AND TWIST. KILL HIM.
TO USE.
I CAN'T.
YOU'RE STRONG.
IMPOSSIBLE.
KILL HIM.
WHO ARE YOU?
WHO--

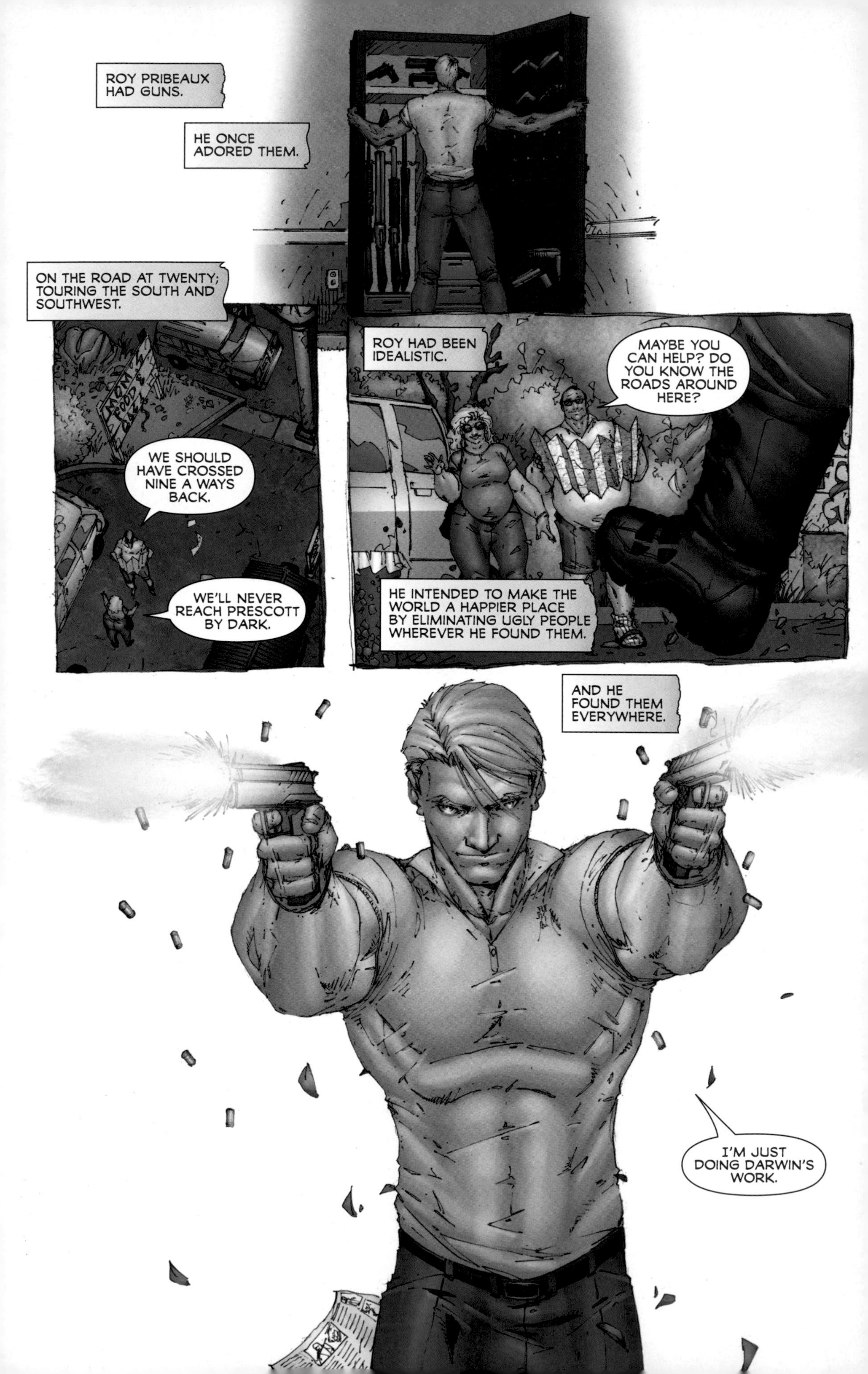
ROY PRIBEAUX HAD GUNS.
HE ONCE ADORED THEM.
ON THE ROAD AT TWENTY; TOURING THE SOUTH AND SOUTHWEST.
WE SHOULD HAVE CROSSED NINE A WAYS BACK.
WE'LL NEVER REACH PRESCOTT BY DARK.
ROY HAD BEEN IDEALISTIC.
MAYBE YOU CAN HELP? DO YOU KNOW THE ROADS AROUND HERE?
HE INTENDED TO MAKE THE WORLD A HAPPIER PLACE BY ELIMINATING UGLY PEOPLE WHEREVER HE FOUND THEM.
AND HE FOUND THEM EVERYWHERE.
I'M JUST DOING DARWIN'S WORK.

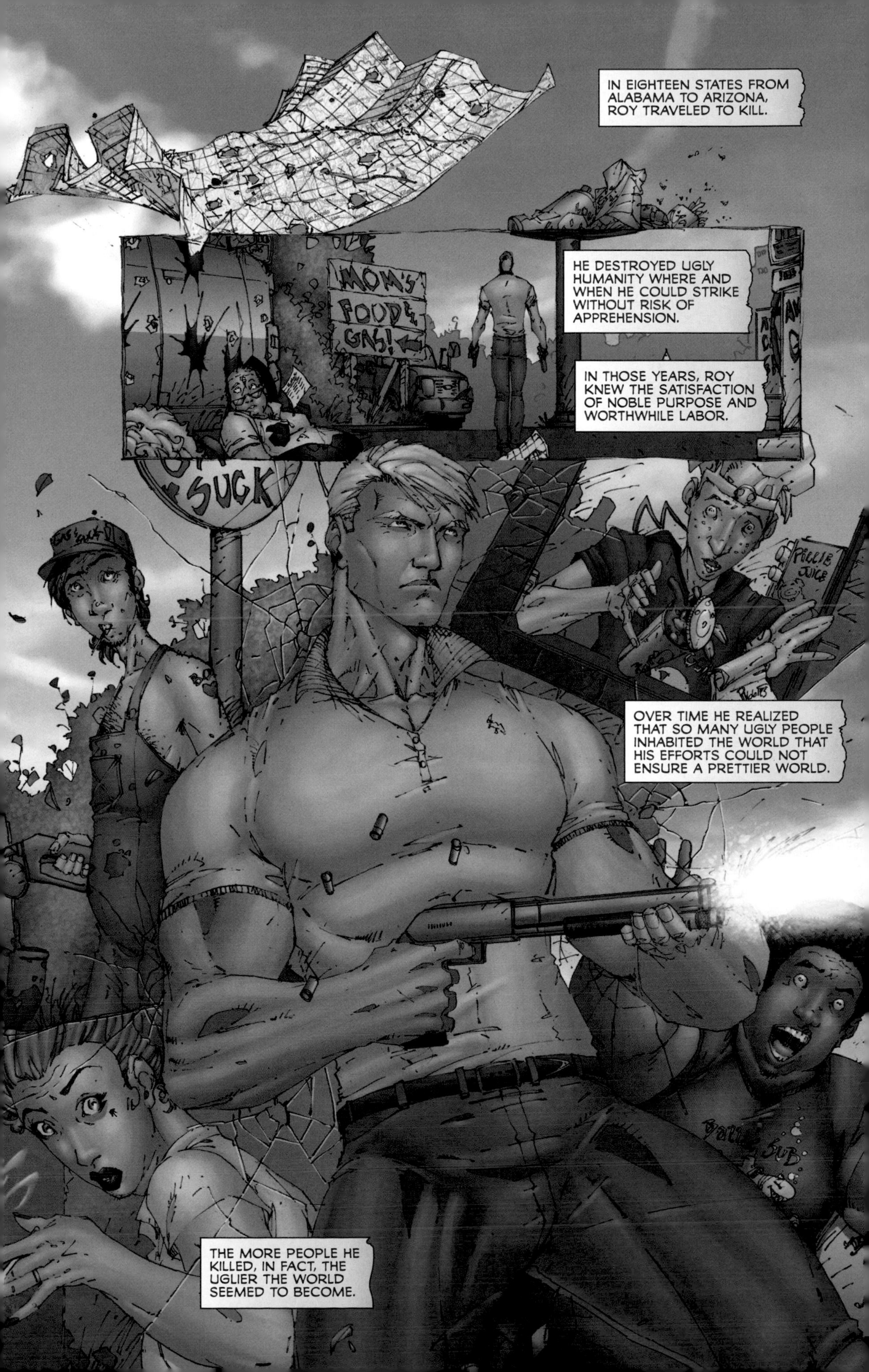
IN EIGHTEEN STATES FROM ALABAMA TO ARIZONA, ROY TRAVELED TO KILL.
HE DESTROYED UGLY HUMANITY WHERE AND WHEN HE COULD STRIKE WITHOUT RISK OF APPREHENSION.
IN THOSE YEARS, ROY KNEW THE SATISFACTION OF NOBLE PURPOSE AND WORTHWHILE LABOR.
MOM'S FOOD & GAS!
SUCK
PICKLE JUICE
OVER TIME HE REALIZED THAT SO MANY UGLY PEOPLE INHABITED THE WORLD THAT HIS EFFORTS COULD NOT ENSURE A PRETTIER WORLD.
THE MORE PEOPLE HE KILLED, IN FACT, THE UGLIER THE WORLD SEEMED TO BECOME.

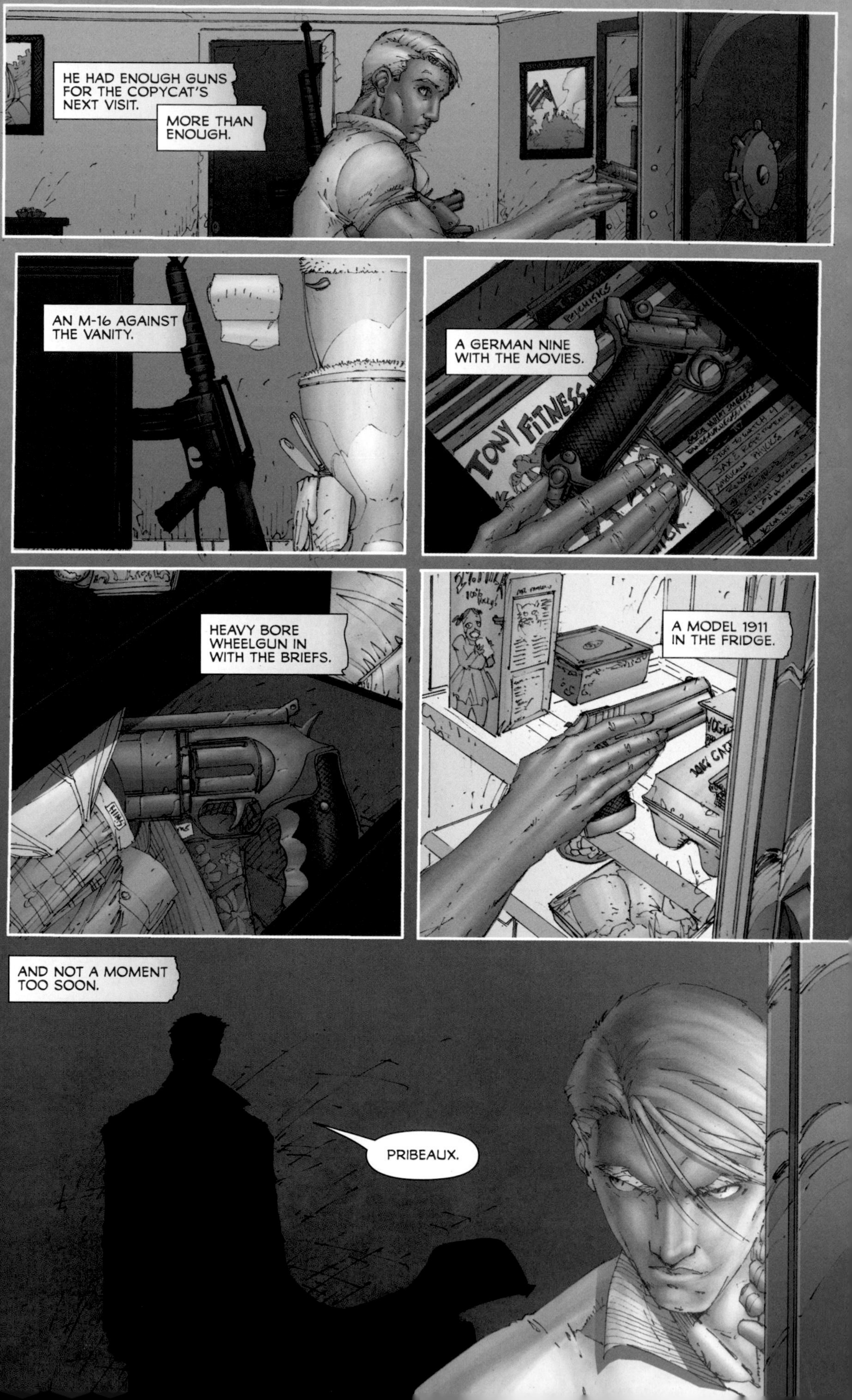
HE HAD ENOUGH GUNS FOR THE COPYCAT'S NEXT VISIT.
MORE THAN ENOUGH.
AN M-16 AGAINST THE VANITY.
A GERMAN NINE WITH THE MOVIES.
TONY FITNESS
HEAVY BORE WHEELGUN IN WITH THE BRIEFS.
A MODEL 1911 IN THE FRIDGE.
AND NOT A MOMENT TOO SOON.
PRIBEAUX.

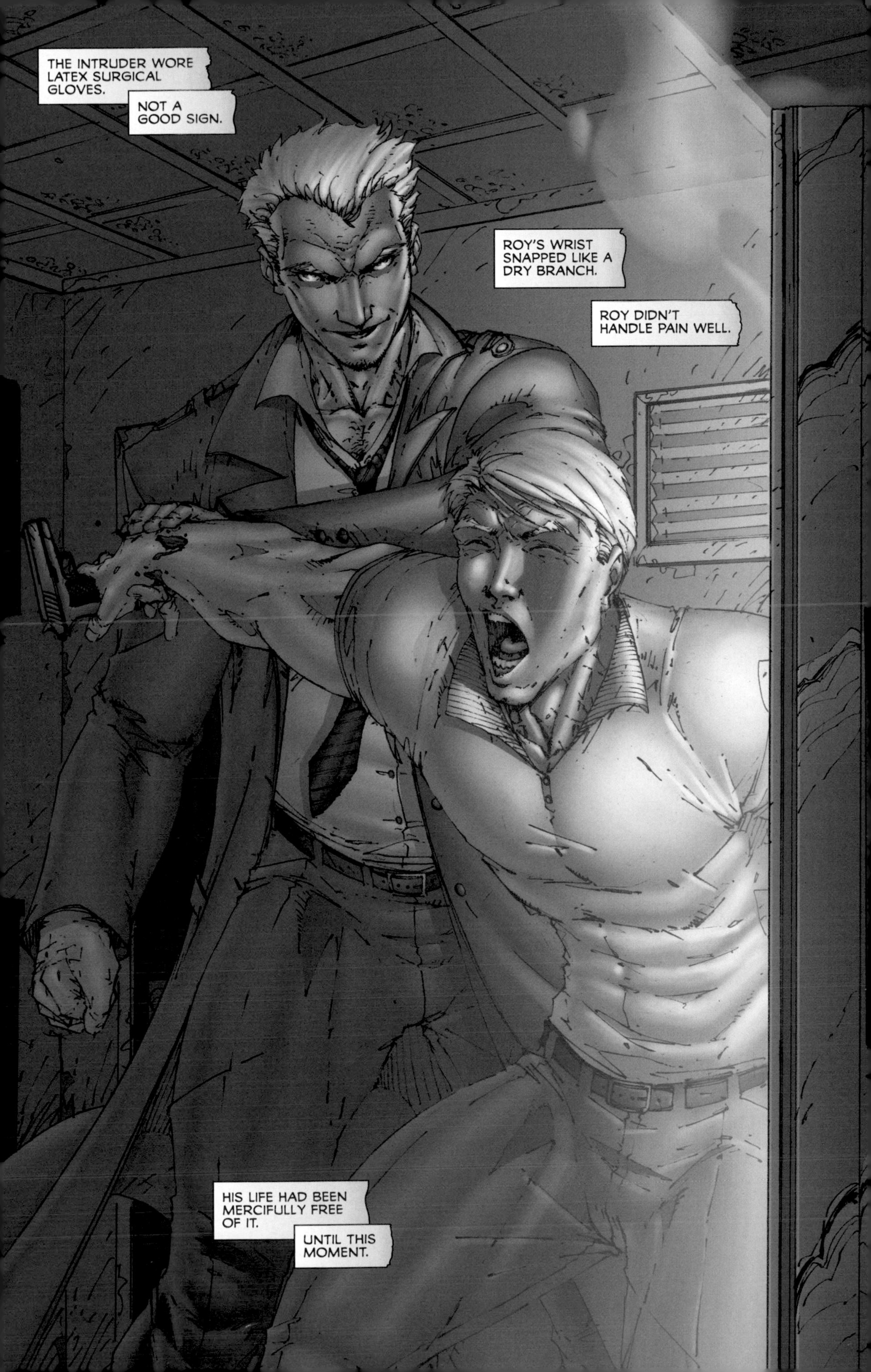
THE INTRUDER WORE LATEX SURGICAL GLOVES.
NOT A GOOD SIGN.
ROY'S WRIST SNAPPED LIKE A DRY BRANCH.
ROY DIDN'T HANDLE PAIN WELL.
HIS LIFE HAD BEEN MERCIFULLY FREE OF IT.
UNTIL THIS MOMENT.

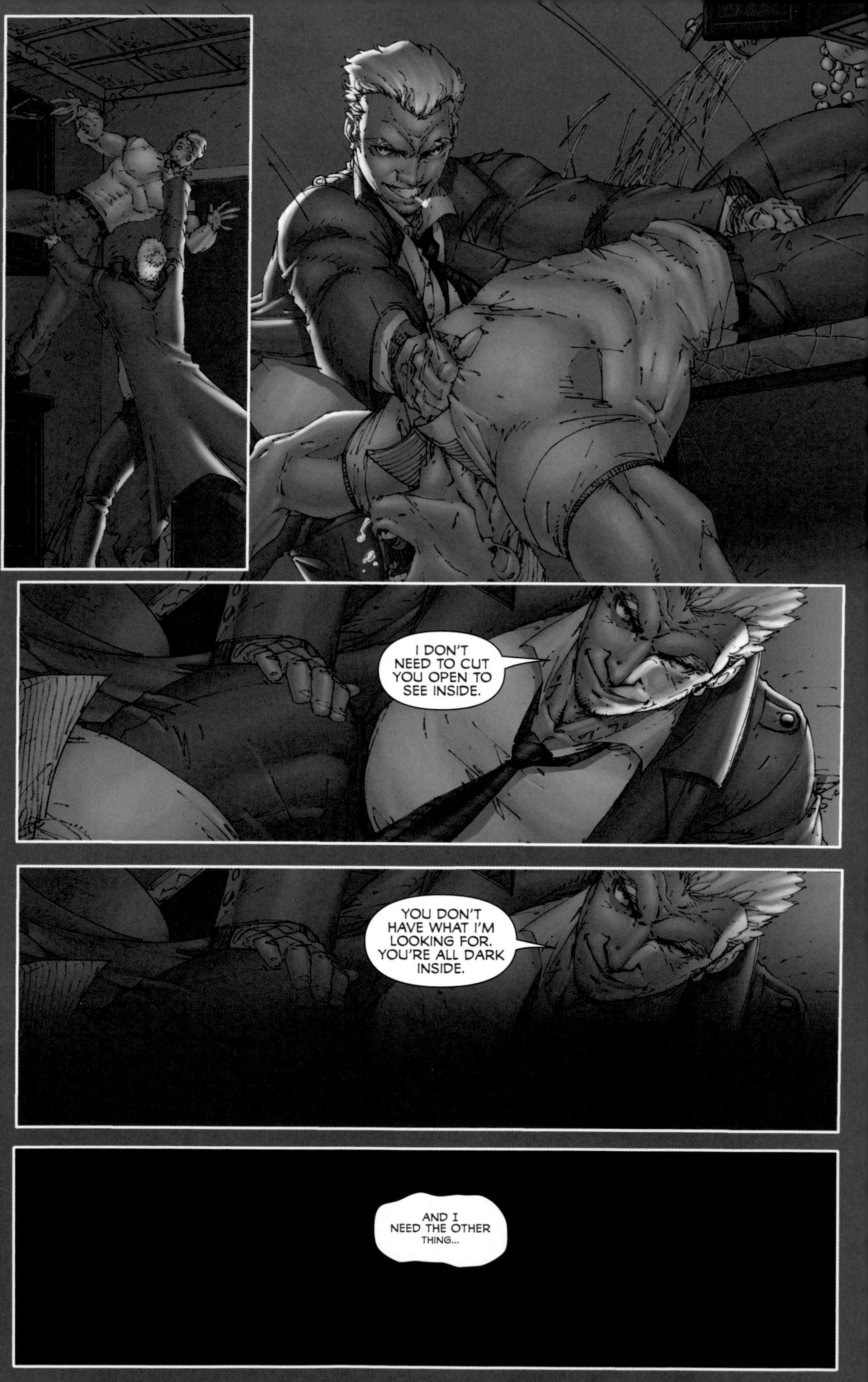
I DON'T NEED TO CUT YOU OPEN TO SEE INSIDE.
YOU DON'T HAVE WHAT I'M LOOKING FOR. YOU'RE ALL DARK INSIDE.
AND I NEED THE OTHER THING...

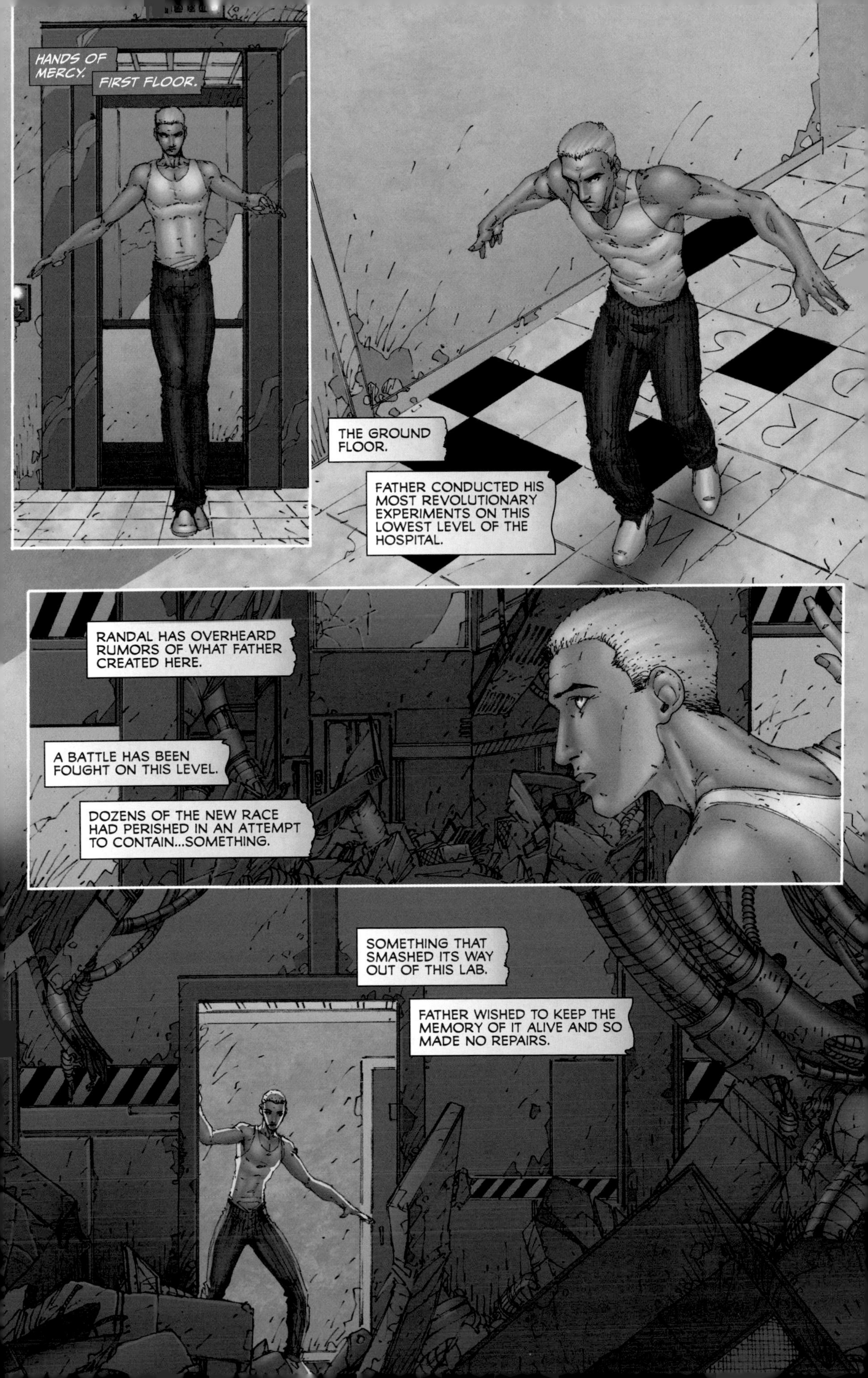
HANDS OF MERCY.
FIRST FLOOR.
THE GROUND FLOOR.
FATHER CONDUCTED HIS MOST REVOLUTIONARY EXPERIMENTS ON THIS LOWEST LEVEL OF THE HOSPITAL.
RANDAL HAS OVERHEARD RUMORS OF WHAT FATHER CREATED HERE.
A BATTLE HAS BEEN FOUGHT ON THIS LEVEL.
DOZENS OF THE NEW RACE HAD PERISHED IN AN ATTEMPT TO CONTAIN...SOMETHING.
SOMETHING THAT SMASHED ITS WAY OUT OF THIS LAB.
FATHER WISHED TO KEEP THE MEMORY OF IT ALIVE AND SO MADE NO REPAIRS.

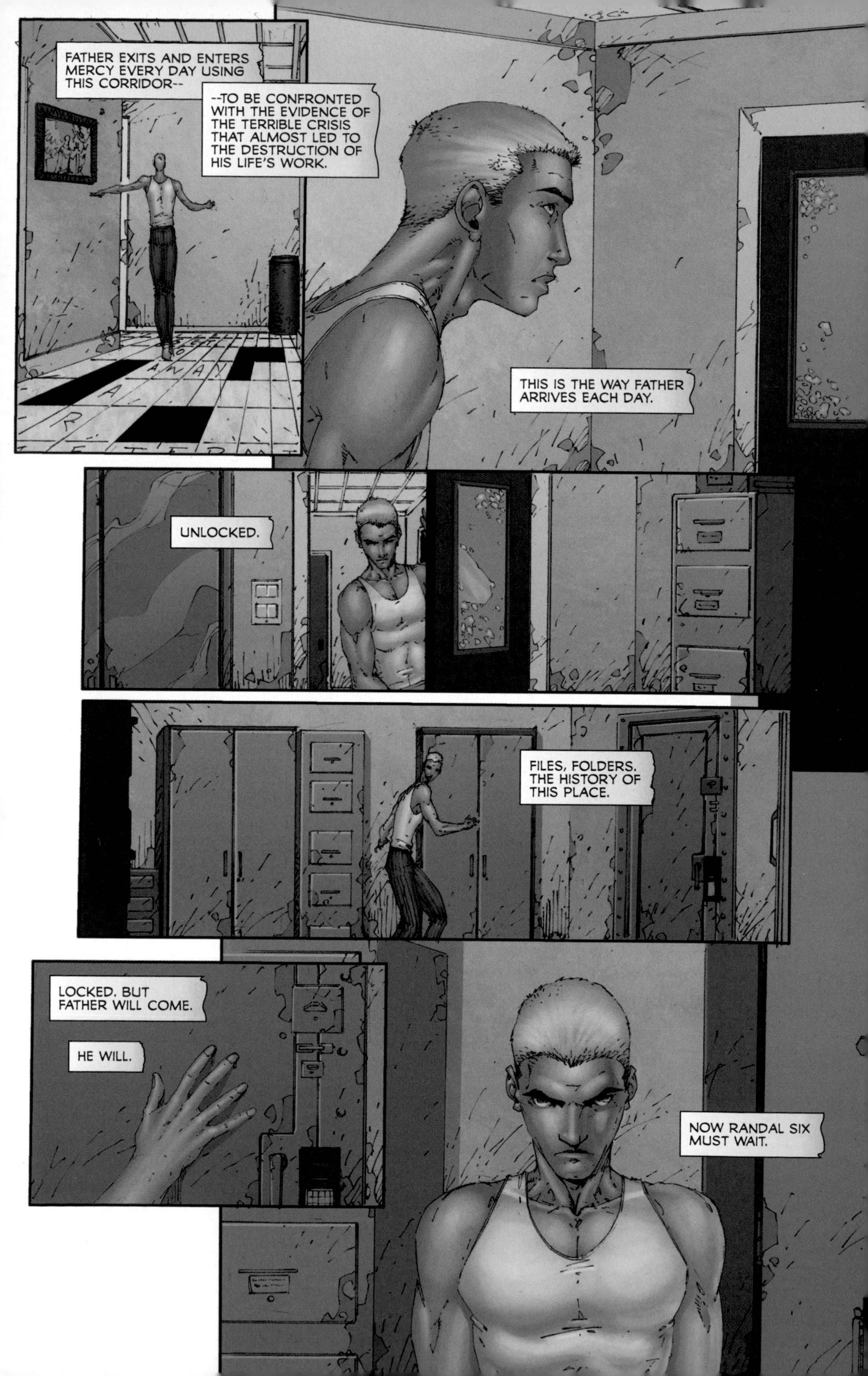
FATHER EXITS AND ENTERS MERCY EVERY DAY USING THIS CORRIDOR--
--TO BE CONFRONTED WITH THE EVIDENCE OF THE TERRIBLE CRISIS THAT ALMOST LED TO THE DESTRUCTION OF HIS LIFE'S WORK.
THIS IS THE WAY FATHER ARRIVES EACH DAY.
UNLOCKED.
FILES, FOLDERS. THE HISTORY OF THIS PLACE.
LOCKED. BUT FATHER WILL COME.
HE WILL.
NOW RANDAL SIX MUST WAIT.

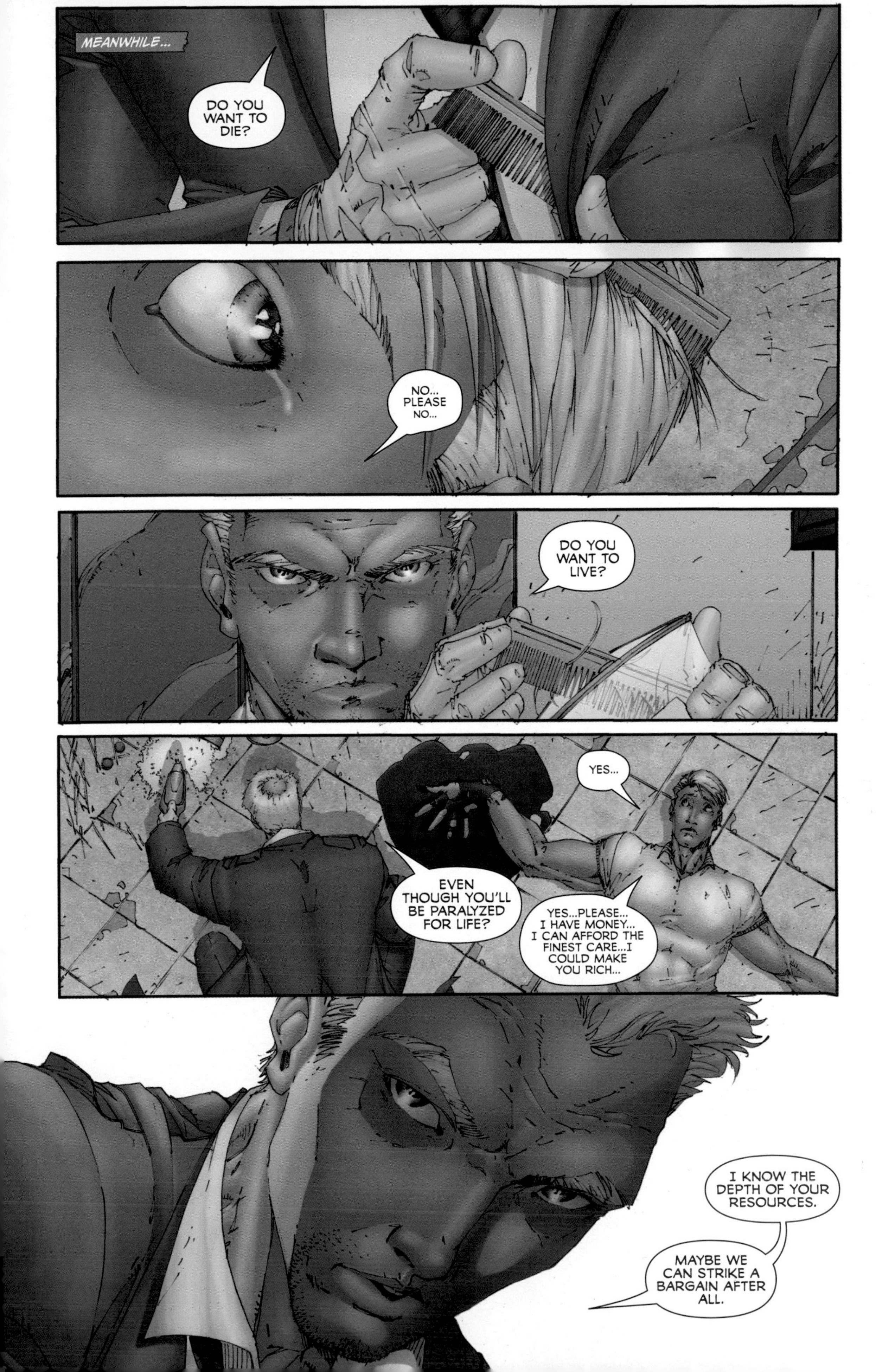
MEANWHILE...
DO YOU WANT TO DIE?
NO... PLEASE NO...
DO YOU WANT TO LIVE?
YES...
EVEN THOUGH YOU'LL BE PARALYZED FOR LIFE?
YES...PLEASE... I HAVE MONEY... I CAN AFFORD THE FINEST CARE...I COULD MAKE YOU RICH...
I KNOW THE DEPTH OF YOUR RESOURCES.
MAYBE WE CAN STRIKE A BARGAIN AFTER ALL.

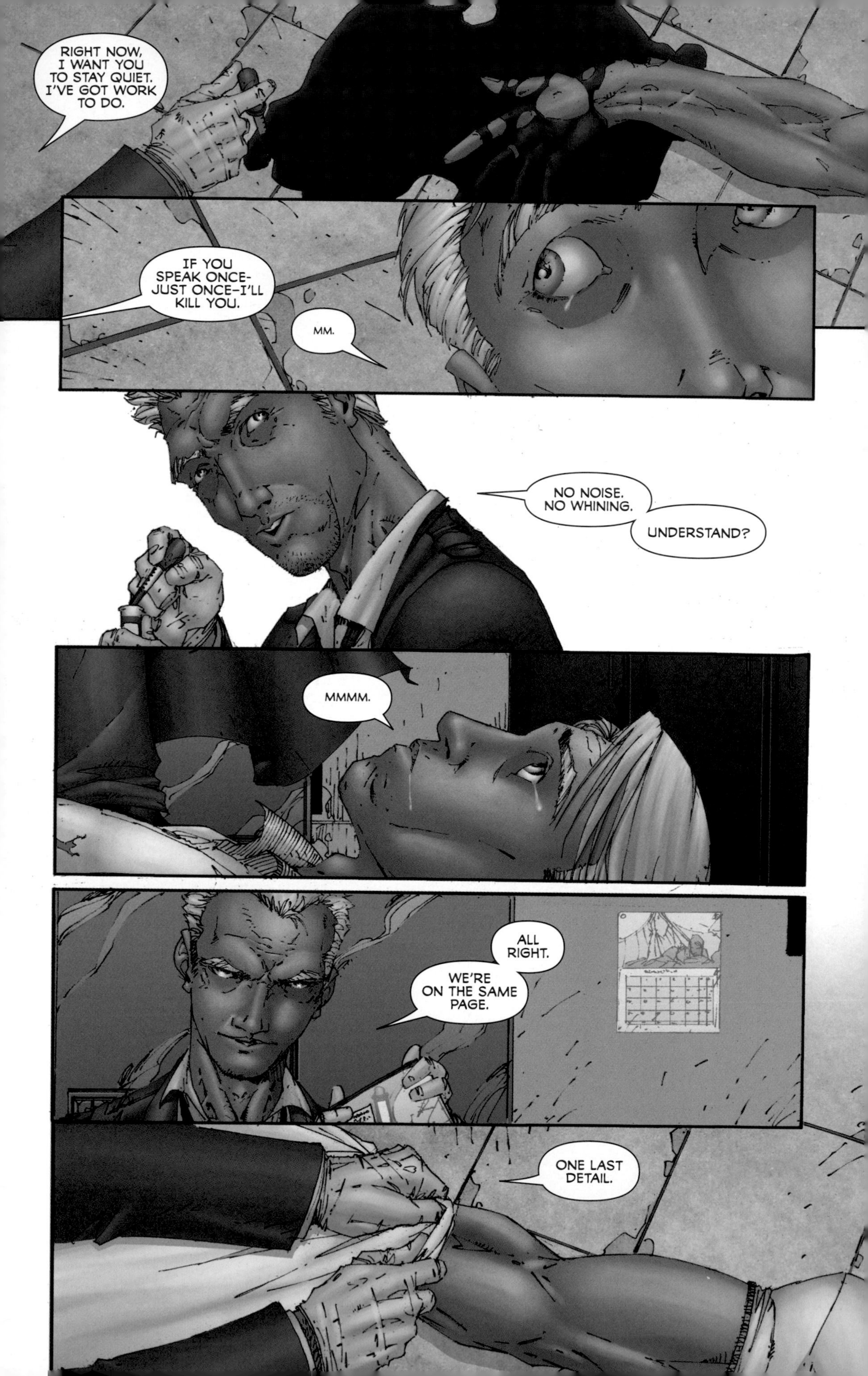
RIGHT NOW, I WANT YOU TO STAY QUIET. I'VE GOT WORK TO DO.
IF YOU SPEAK ONCE-JUST ONCE–I'LL KILL YOU.
MM.
NO NOISE. NO WHINING.
UNDERSTAND?
MMMM.
ALL RIGHT.
WE'RE ON THE SAME PAGE.
ONE LAST DETAIL.

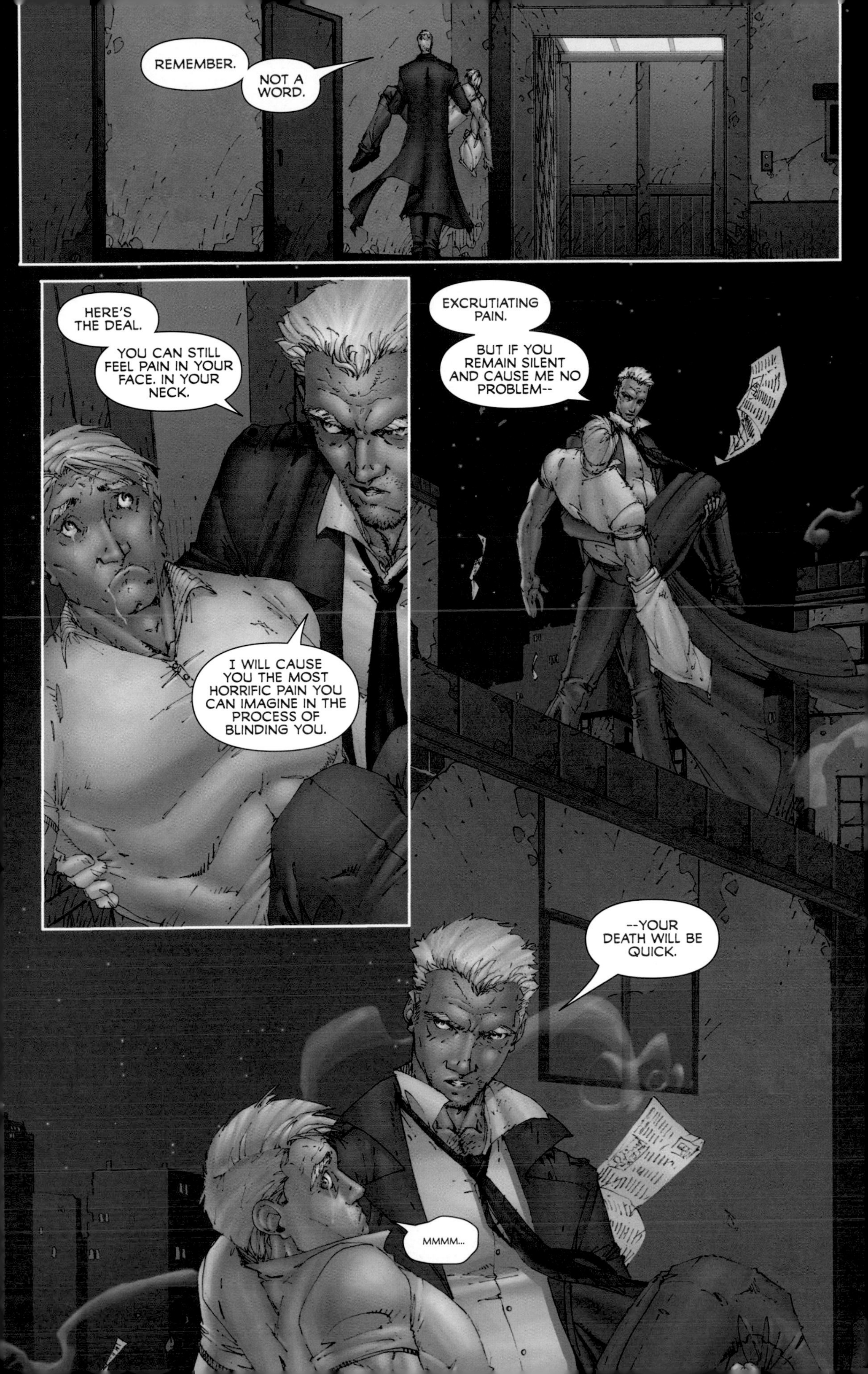
REMEMBER.
NOT A WORD.
HERE'S THE DEAL.
YOU CAN STILL FEEL PAIN IN YOUR FACE. IN YOUR NECK.
I WILL CAUSE YOU THE MOST HORRIFIC PAIN YOU CAN IMAGINE IN THE PROCESS OF BLINDING YOU.
EXCRUTIATING PAIN.
BUT IF YOU REMAIN SILENT AND CAUSE ME NO PROBLEM--
--YOUR DEATH WILL BE QUICK.
MMMM...

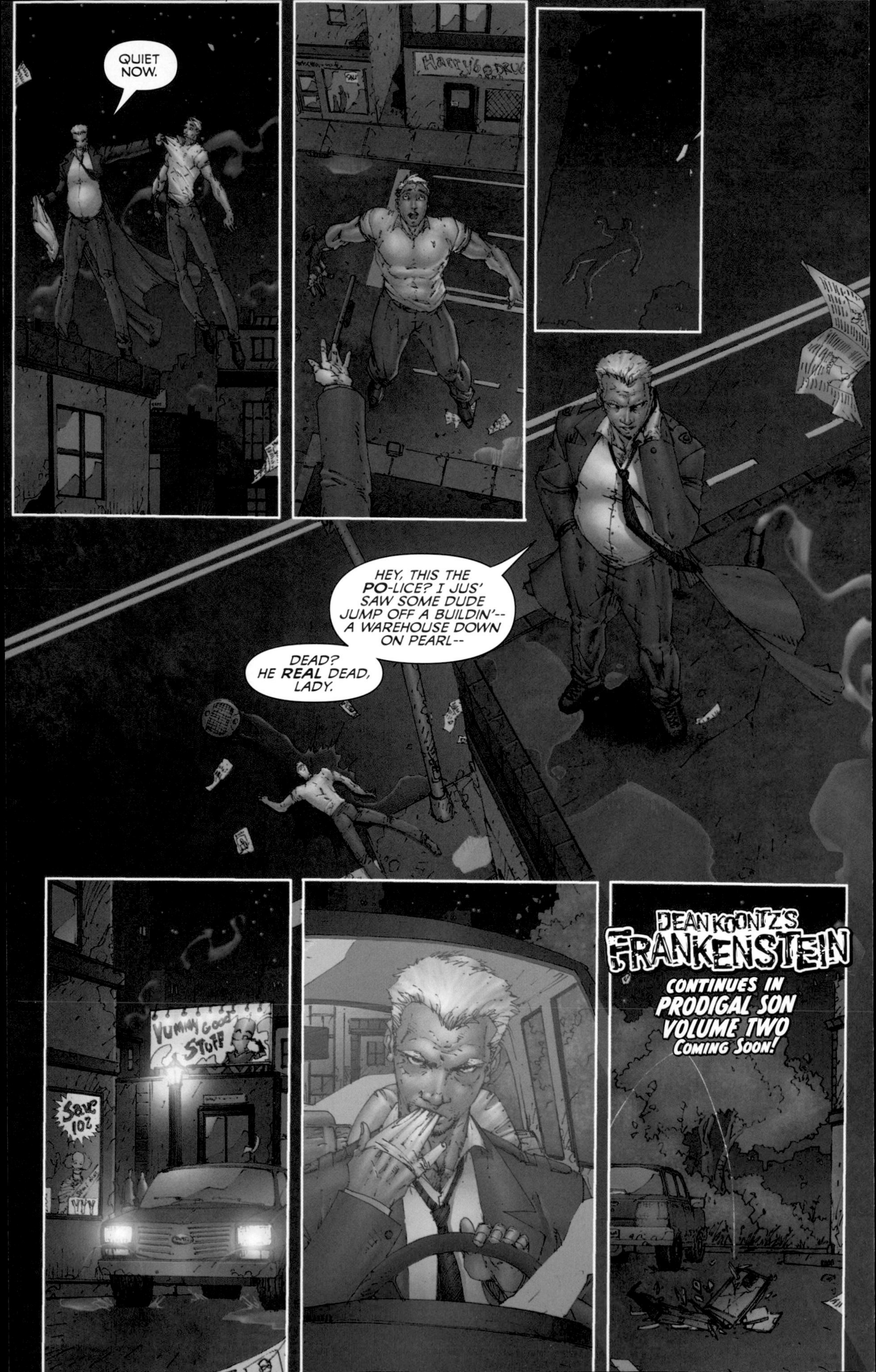
QUIET NOW.
Harry's DRUG
HEY, THIS THE PO-LICE? I JUS' SAW SOME DUDE JUMP OFF A BUILDIN'-- A WAREHOUSE DOWN ON PEARL--
DEAD? HE REAL DEAD, LADY.
YUMMY GOOD STUFF
SAVE 10%
DEAN KOONTZ'S FRANKENSTEIN
CONTINUES IN PRODIGAL SON VOLUME TWO
COMING SOON!

Bonus Story

story: **Dean Koontz**
layouts: **Brett Booth**
art: **Rudy Vasquez & Andy Smith**
colors: **Andrew Dalhouse & Mohan**
letters: **Bill Tortolini**

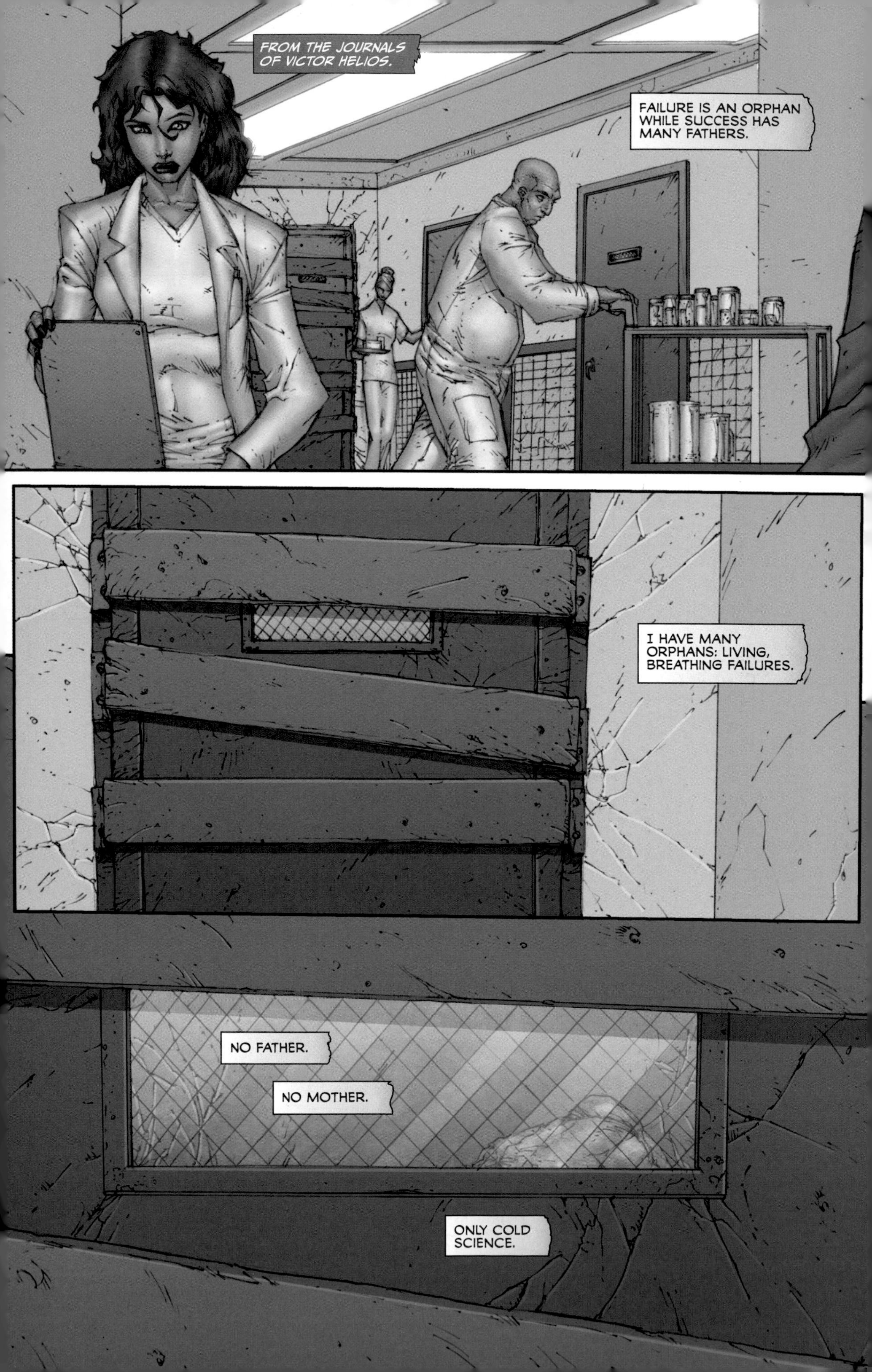
FROM THE JOURNALS OF VICTOR HELIOS.
FAILURE IS AN ORPHAN WHILE SUCCESS HAS MANY FATHERS.
I HAVE MANY ORPHANS: LIVING, BREATHING FAILURES.
NO FATHER.
NO MOTHER.
ONLY COLD SCIENCE.

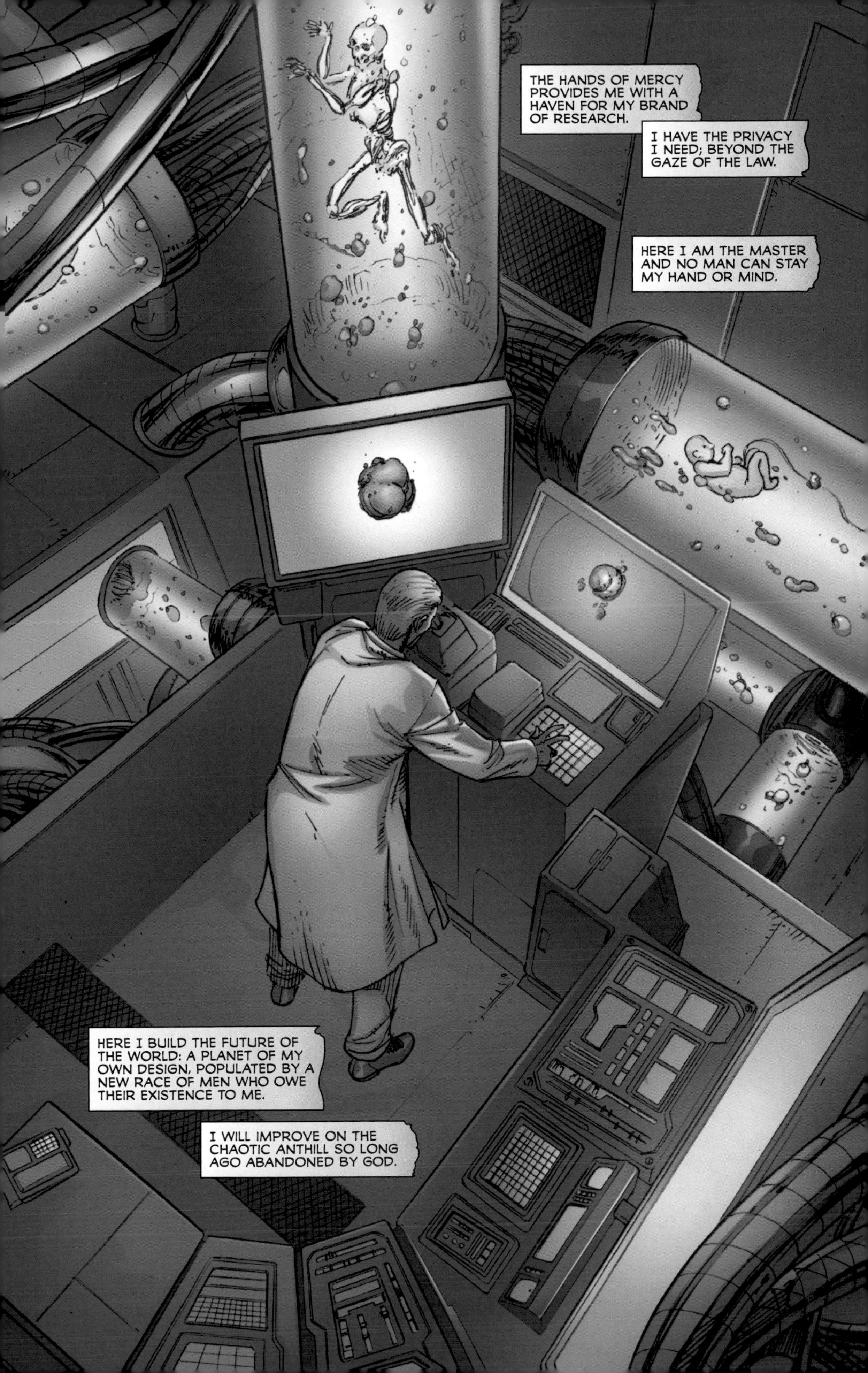
THE HANDS OF MERCY PROVIDES ME WITH A HAVEN FOR MY BRAND OF RESEARCH.
I HAVE THE PRIVACY I NEED; BEYOND THE GAZE OF THE LAW.
HERE I AM THE MASTER AND NO MAN CAN STAY MY HAND OR MIND.
HERE I BUILD THE FUTURE OF THE WORLD: A PLANET OF MY OWN DESIGN, POPULATED BY A NEW RACE OF MEN WHO OWE THEIR EXISTENCE TO ME.
I WILL IMPROVE ON THE CHAOTIC ANTHILL SO LONG AGO ABANDONED BY GOD.

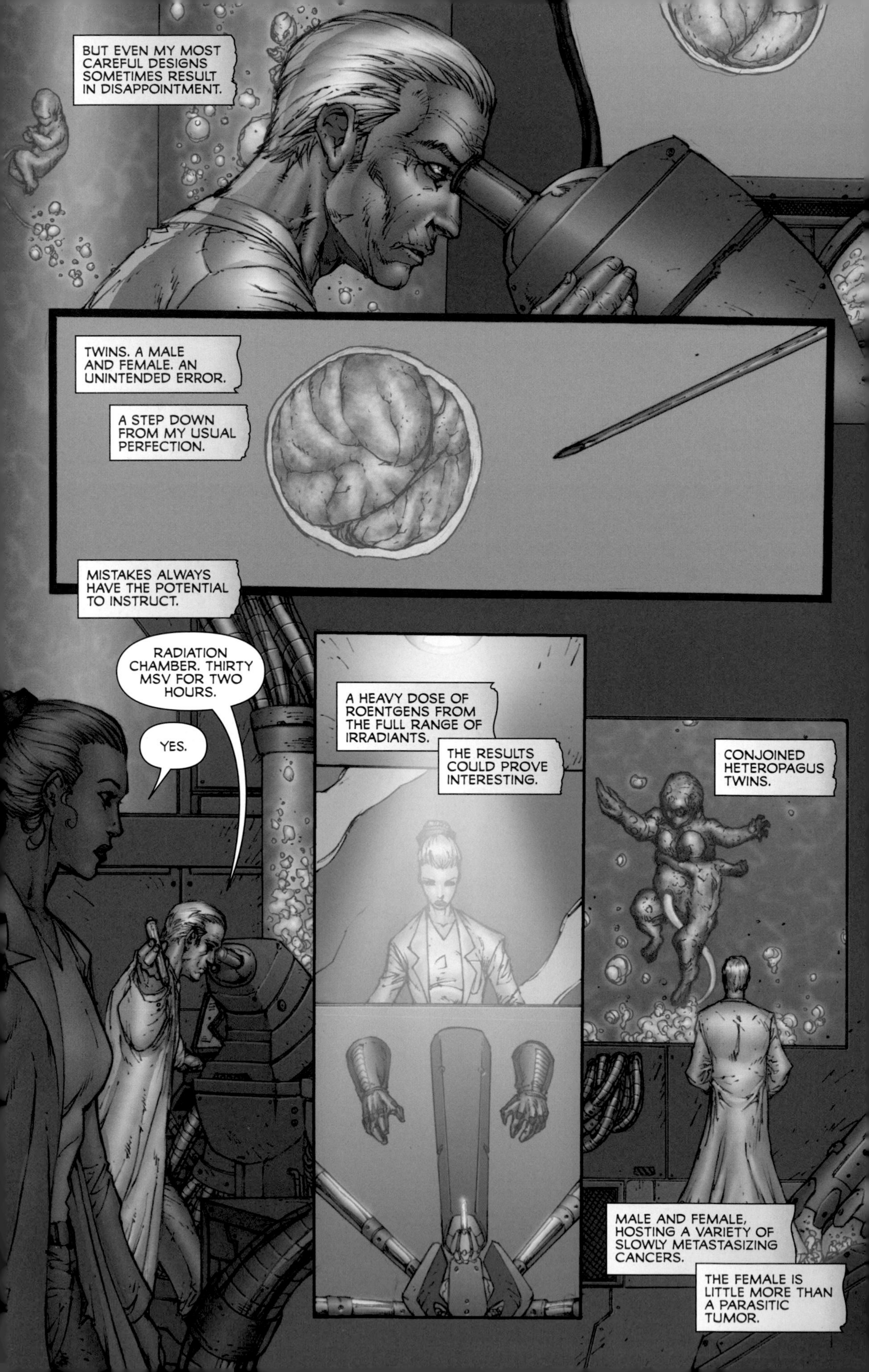
BUT EVEN MY MOST CAREFUL DESIGNS SOMETIMES RESULT IN DISAPPOINTMENT.
TWINS. A MALE AND FEMALE. AN UNINTENDED ERROR.
A STEP DOWN FROM MY USUAL PERFECTION.
MISTAKES ALWAYS HAVE THE POTENTIAL TO INSTRUCT.
RADIATION CHAMBER. THIRTY MSV FOR TWO HOURS.
YES.
A HEAVY DOSE OF ROENTGENS FROM THE FULL RANGE OF IRRADIANTS.
THE RESULTS COULD PROVE INTERESTING.
CONJOINED HETEROPAGUS TWINS.
MALE AND FEMALE, HOSTING A VARIETY OF SLOWLY METASTASIZING CANCERS.
THE FEMALE IS LITTLE MORE THAN A PARASITIC TUMOR.

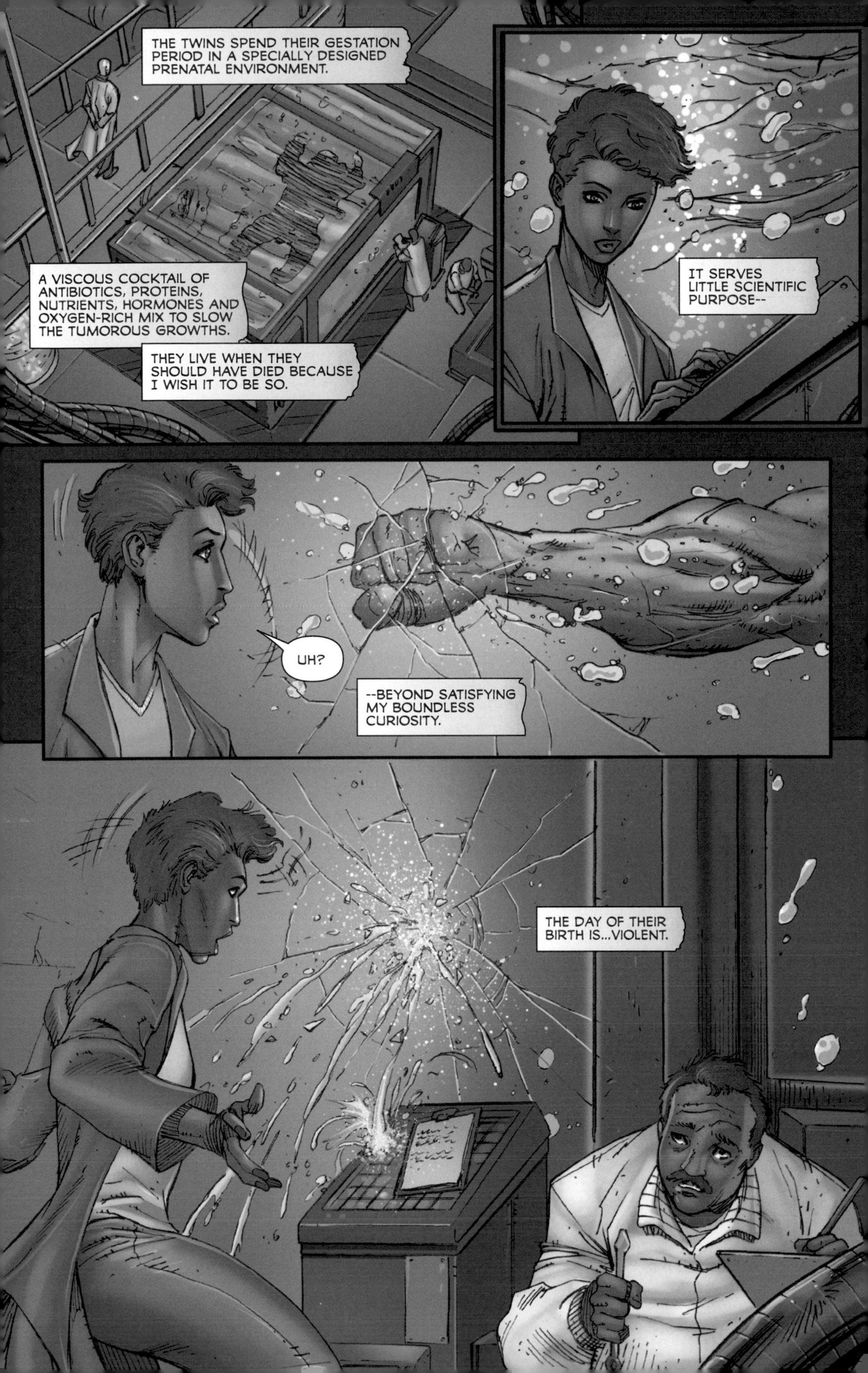
THE TWINS SPEND THEIR GESTATION PERIOD IN A SPECIALLY DESIGNED PRENATAL ENVIRONMENT.
A VISCOUS COCKTAIL OF ANTIBIOTICS, PROTEINS, NUTRIENTS, HORMONES AND OXYGEN-RICH MIX TO SLOW THE TUMOROUS GROWTHS.
THEY LIVE WHEN THEY SHOULD HAVE DIED BECAUSE I WISH IT TO BE SO.
IT SERVES LITTLE SCIENTIFIC PURPOSE--
UH?
--BEYOND SATISFYING MY BOUNDLESS CURIOSITY.
THE DAY OF THEIR BIRTH IS...VIOLENT.

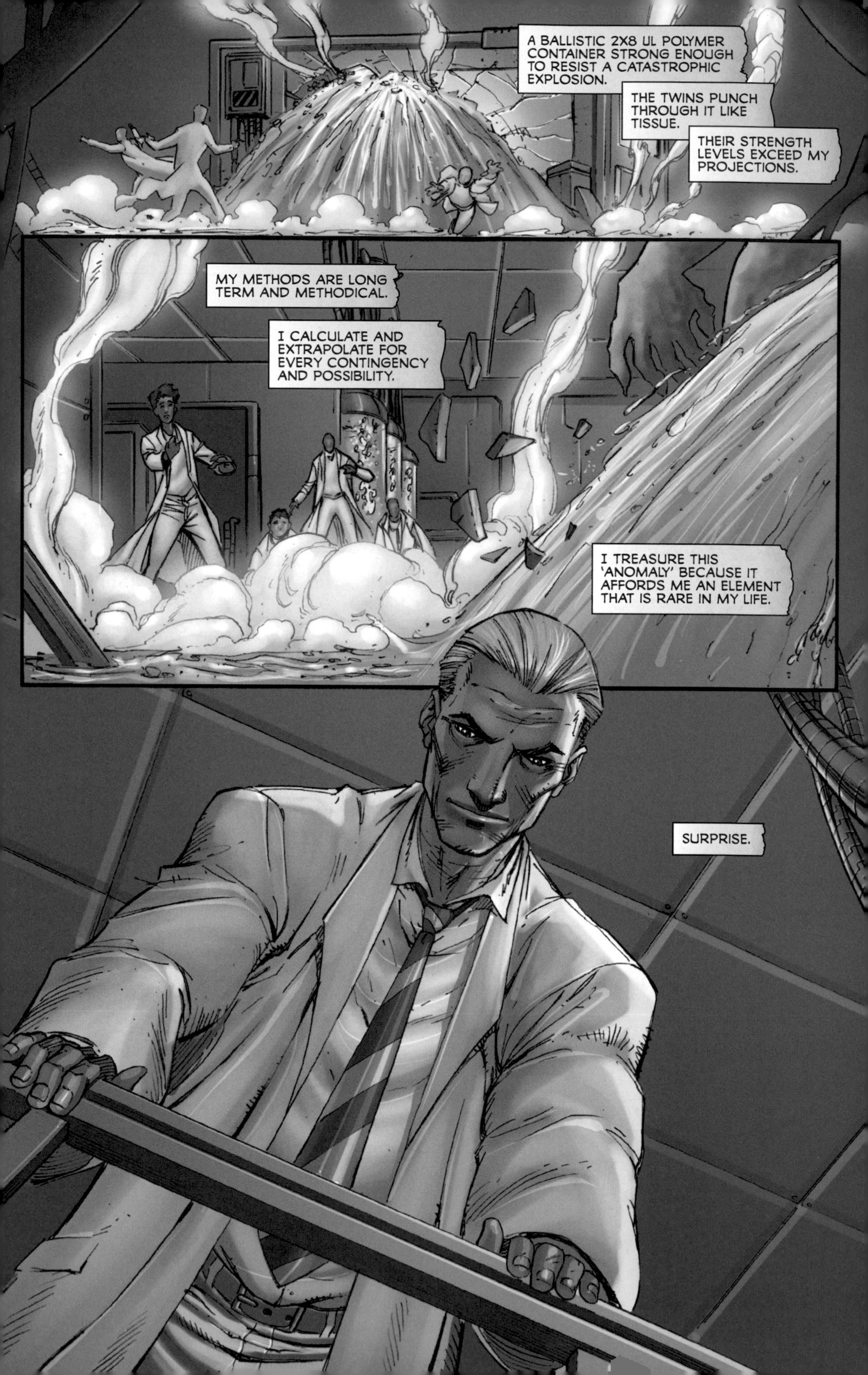
A BALLISTIC 2X8 UL POLYMER CONTAINER STRONG ENOUGH TO RESIST A CATASTROPHIC EXPLOSION.
THE TWINS PUNCH THROUGH IT LIKE TISSUE.
THEIR STRENGTH LEVELS EXCEED MY PROJECTIONS.
MY METHODS ARE LONG TERM AND METHODICAL.
I CALCULATE AND EXTRAPOLATE FOR EVERY CONTINGENCY AND POSSIBILITY.
I TREASURE THIS 'ANOMALY' BECAUSE IT AFFORDS ME AN ELEMENT THAT IS RARE IN MY LIFE.
SURPRISE.

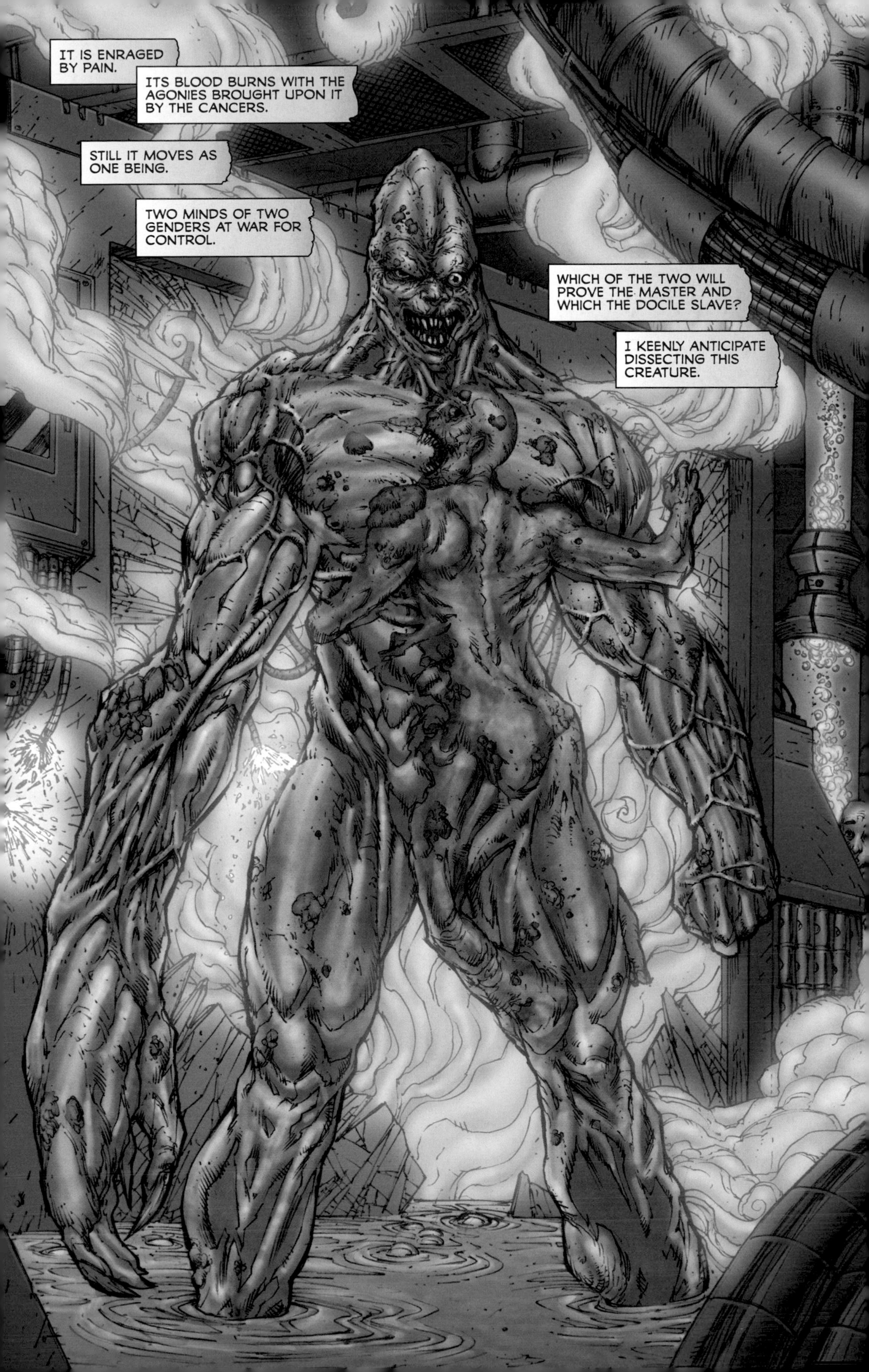
IT IS ENRAGED BY PAIN.
ITS BLOOD BURNS WITH THE AGONIES BROUGHT UPON IT BY THE CANCERS.
STILL IT MOVES AS ONE BEING.
TWO MINDS OF TWO GENDERS AT WAR FOR CONTROL.
WHICH OF THE TWO WILL PROVE THE MASTER AND WHICH THE DOCILE SLAVE?
I KEENLY ANTICIPATE DISSECTING THIS CREATURE.

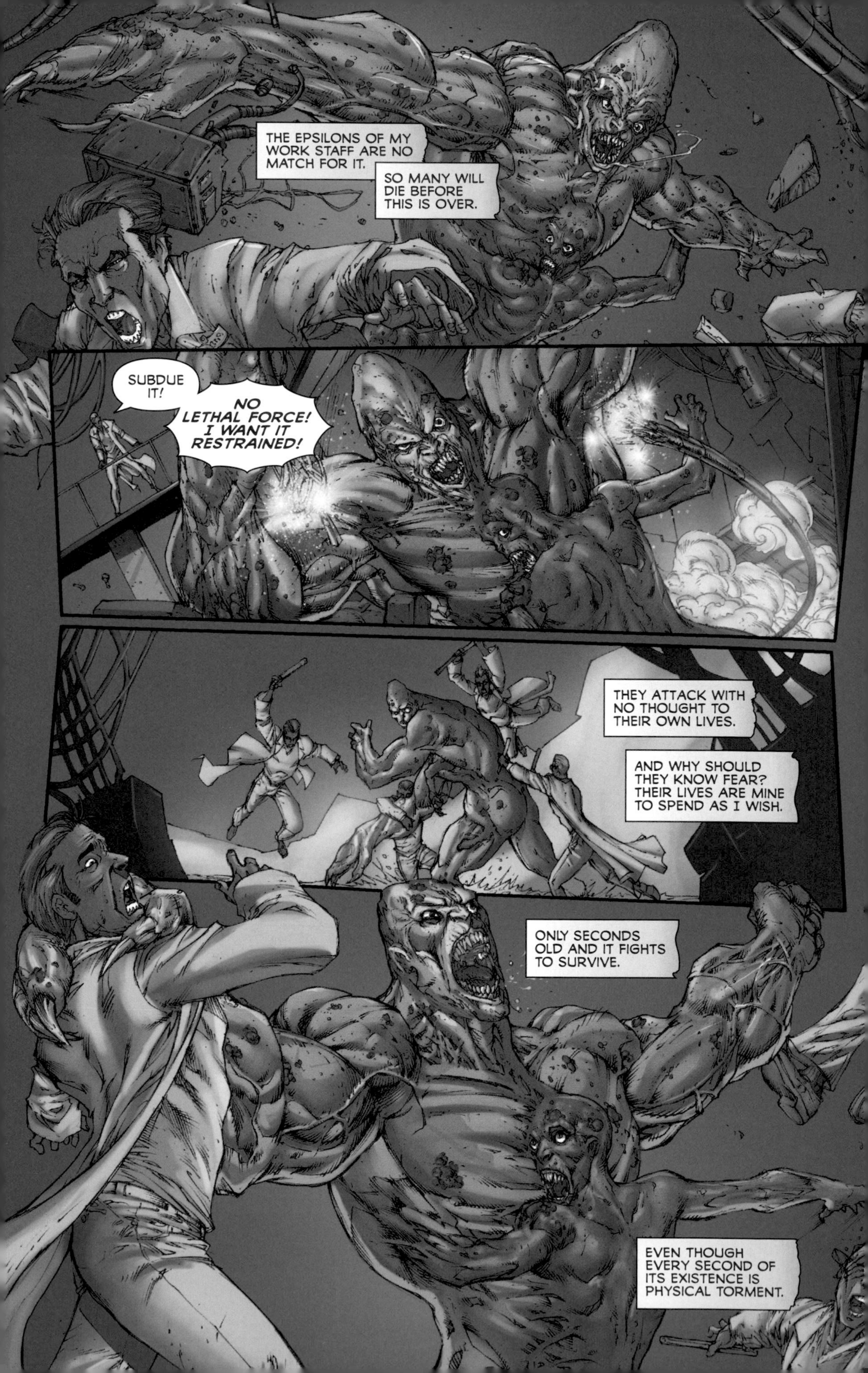

THE EPSILONS OF MY WORK STAFF ARE NO MATCH FOR IT.
SO MANY WILL DIE BEFORE THIS IS OVER.
SUBDUE IT!
NO LETHAL FORCE! I WANT IT RESTRAINED!
THEY ATTACK WITH NO THOUGHT TO THEIR OWN LIVES.
AND WHY SHOULD THEY KNOW FEAR? THEIR LIVES ARE MINE TO SPEND AS I WISH.
ONLY SECONDS OLD AND IT FIGHTS TO SURVIVE.
EVEN THOUGH EVERY SECOND OF ITS EXISTENCE IS PHYSICAL TORMENT.

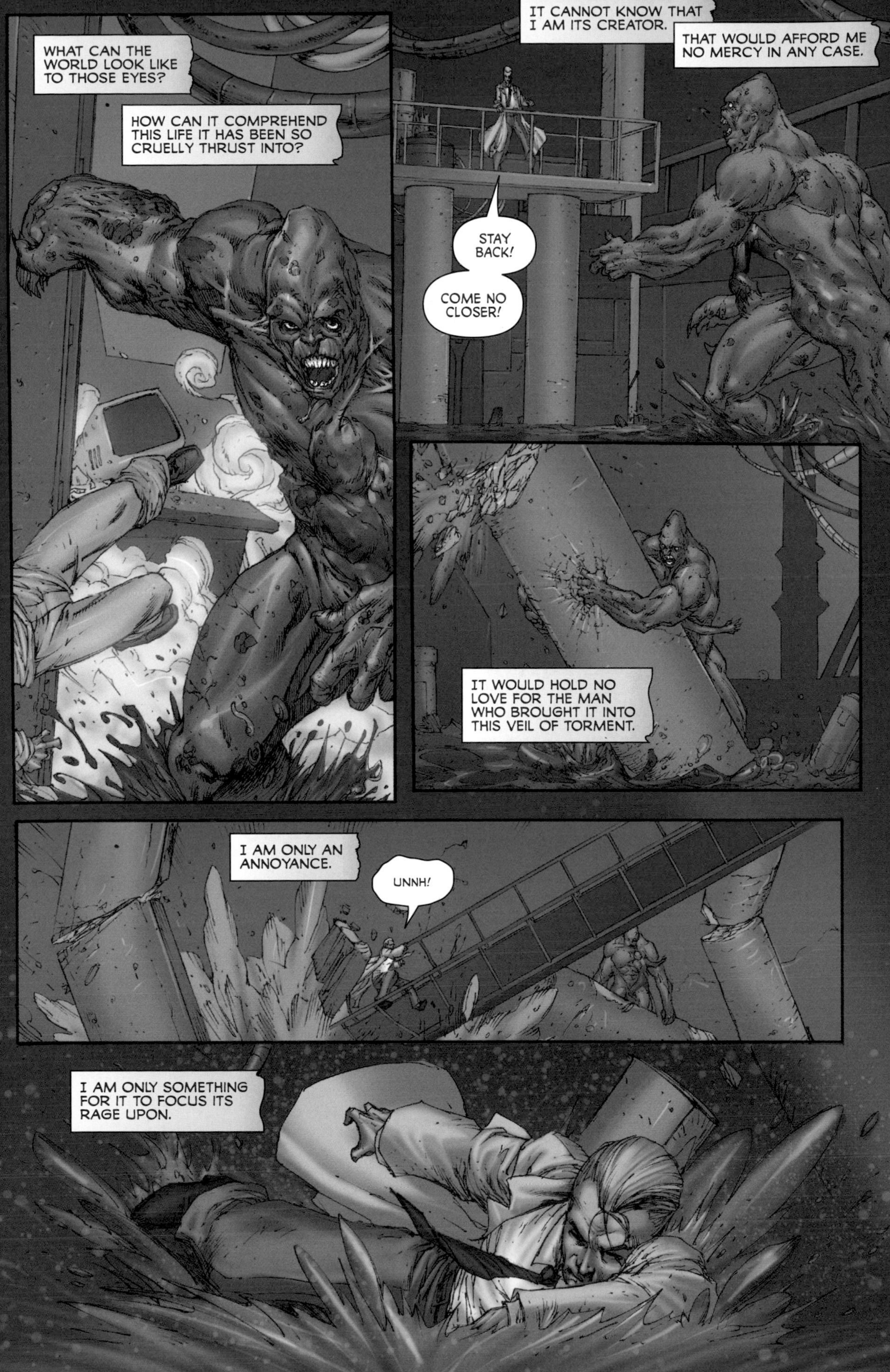
WHAT CAN THE WORLD LOOK LIKE TO THOSE EYES?
HOW CAN IT COMPREHEND THIS LIFE IT HAS BEEN SO CRUELLY THRUST INTO?
IT CANNOT KNOW THAT I AM ITS CREATOR.
THAT WOULD AFFORD ME NO MERCY IN ANY CASE.
STAY BACK!
COME NO CLOSER!
IT WOULD HOLD NO LOVE FOR THE MAN WHO BROUGHT IT INTO THIS VEIL OF TORMENT.
I AM ONLY AN ANNOYANCE.
UNNH!
I AM ONLY SOMETHING FOR IT TO FOCUS ITS RAGE UPON.

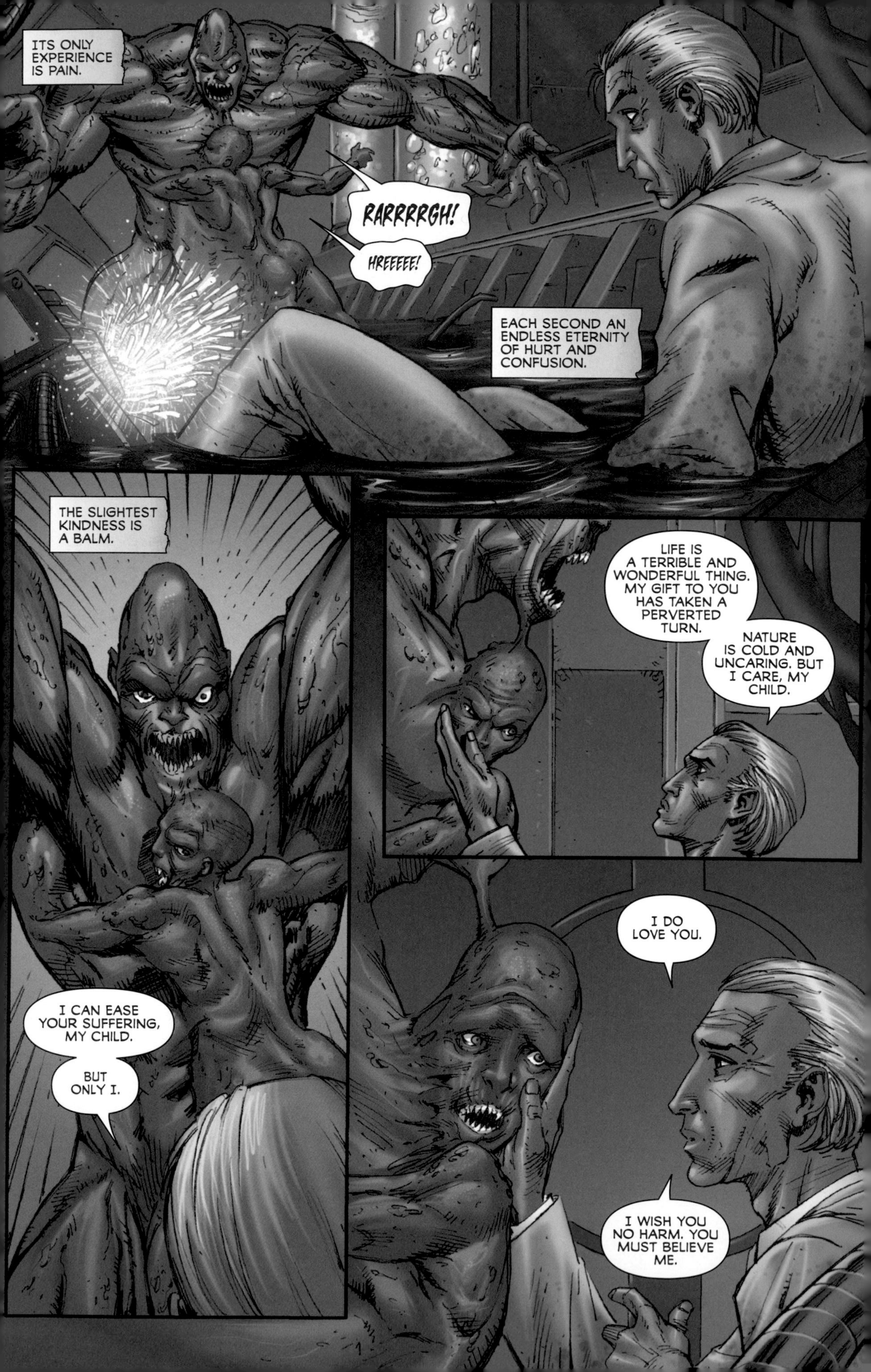
ITS ONLY EXPERIENCE IS PAIN.
RARRRRGH!
HREEEEE!
EACH SECOND AN ENDLESS ETERNITY OF HURT AND CONFUSION.
THE SLIGHTEST KINDNESS IS A BALM.
LIFE IS A TERRIBLE AND WONDERFUL THING. MY GIFT TO YOU HAS TAKEN A PERVERTED TURN.
NATURE IS COLD AND UNCARING. BUT I CARE, MY CHILD.
I CAN EASE YOUR SUFFERING, MY CHILD.
BUT ONLY I.
I DO LOVE YOU.
I WISH YOU NO HARM. YOU MUST BELIEVE ME.

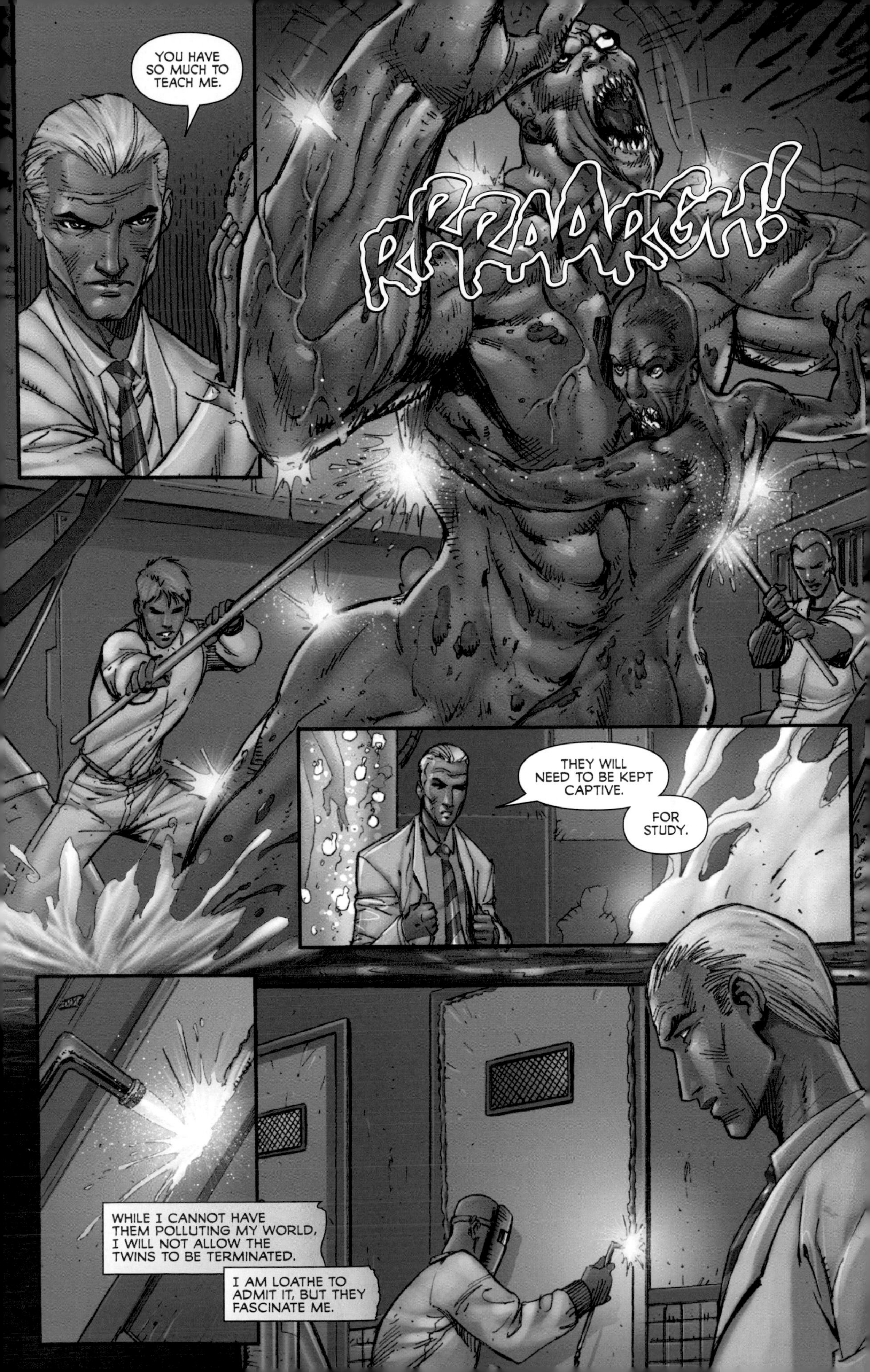
YOU HAVE SO MUCH TO TEACH ME.
RRRAARGH!
THEY WILL NEED TO BE KEPT CAPTIVE.
FOR STUDY.
WHILE I CANNOT HAVE THEM POLLUTING MY WORLD, I WILL NOT ALLOW THE TWINS TO BE TERMINATED.
I AM LOATHE TO ADMIT IT, BUT THEY FASCINATE ME.

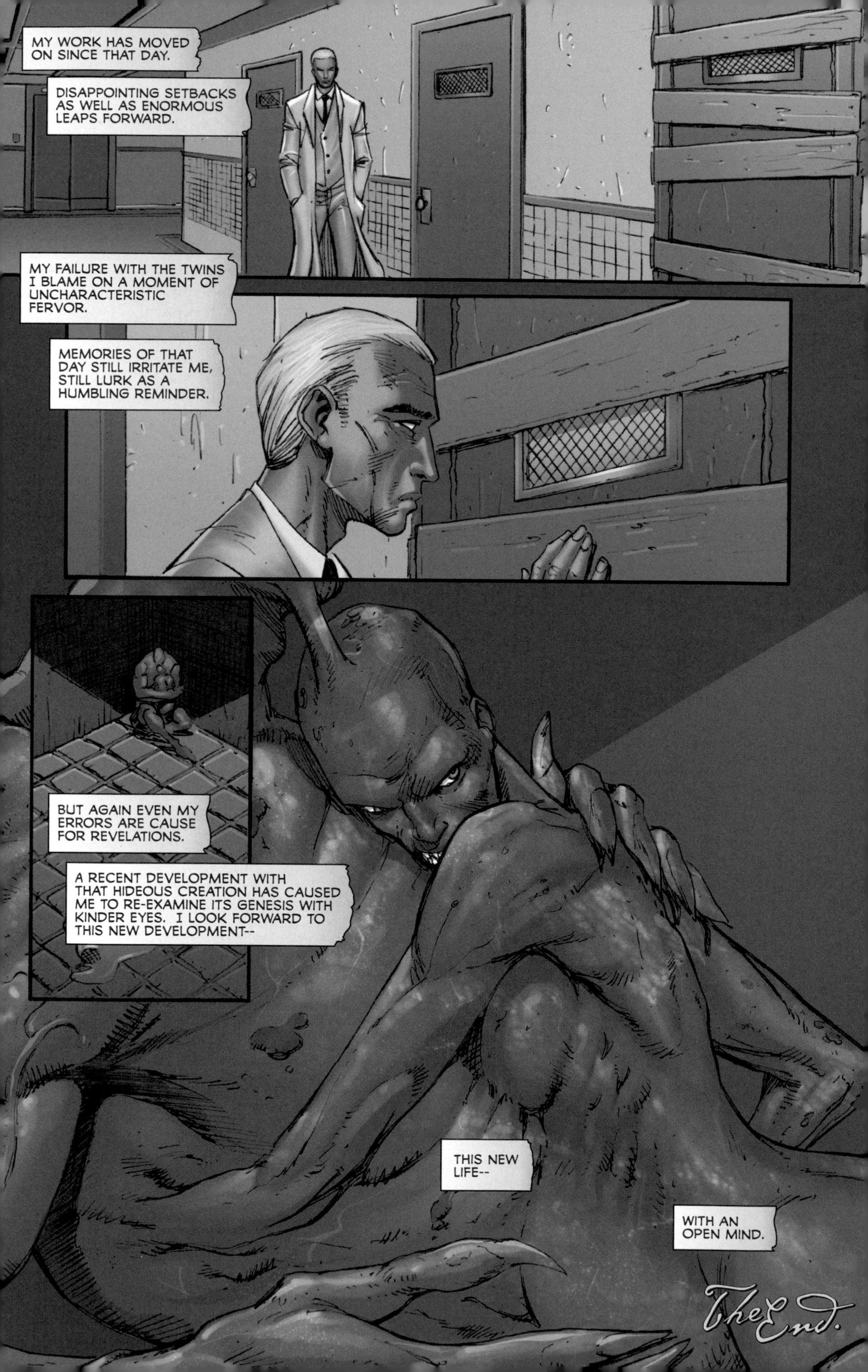
MY WORK HAS MOVED ON SINCE THAT DAY.
DISAPPOINTING SETBACKS AS WELL AS ENORMOUS LEAPS FORWARD.
MY FAILURE WITH THE TWINS I BLAME ON A MOMENT OF UNCHARACTERISTIC FERVOR.
MEMORIES OF THAT DAY STILL IRRITATE ME, STILL LURK AS A HUMBLING REMINDER.
BUT AGAIN EVEN MY ERRORS ARE CAUSE FOR REVELATIONS.
A RECENT DEVELOPMENT WITH THAT HIDEOUS CREATION HAS CAUSED ME TO RE-EXAMINE ITS GENESIS WITH KINDER EYES. I LOOK FORWARD TO THIS NEW DEVELOPMENT--
THIS NEW LIFE--
WITH AN OPEN MIND.
The End.

Art Gallery

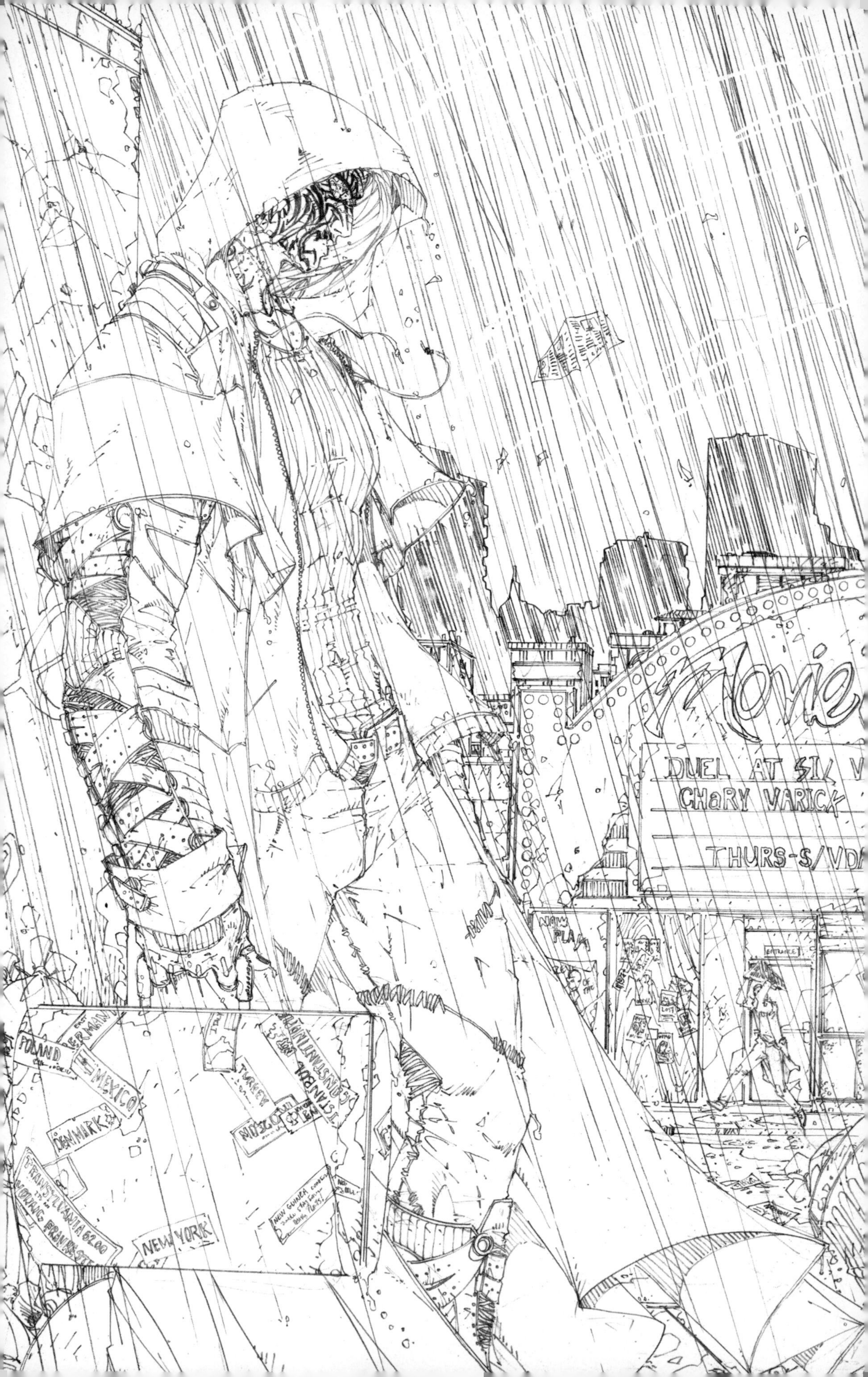
Movie
DUEL AT SIL V
ChaRY VARICK
THURS-S/VDA
ENTRANCE
POLAND
EAST GERMAN
MEXICO
DENMARK
TRANSYLVANIA
TURKEY
ISTANBUL
NEW YORK

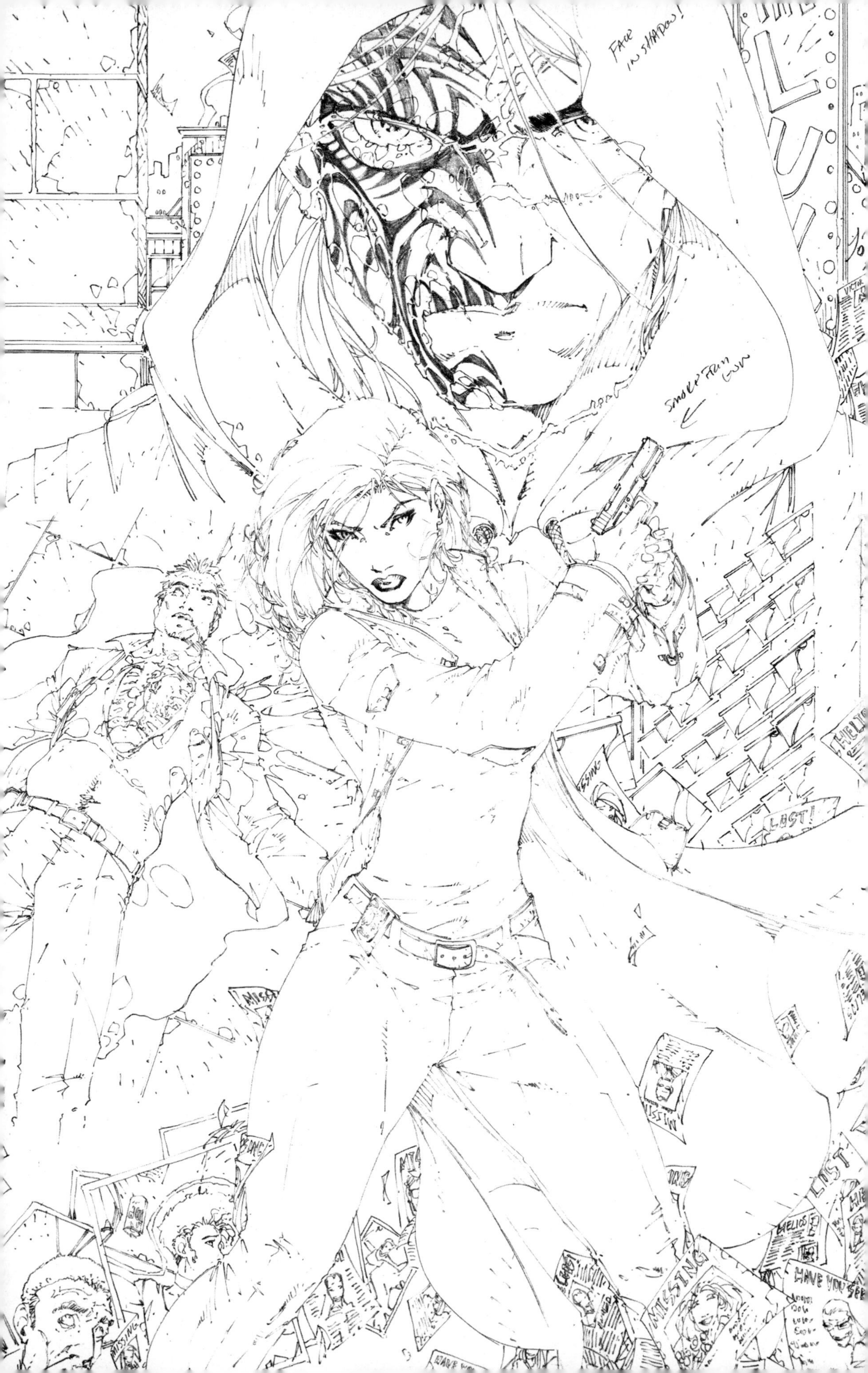
FACE IN SHADOW!
SMOKE FROM GUN
LOST!
MISSING
HAVE YOU

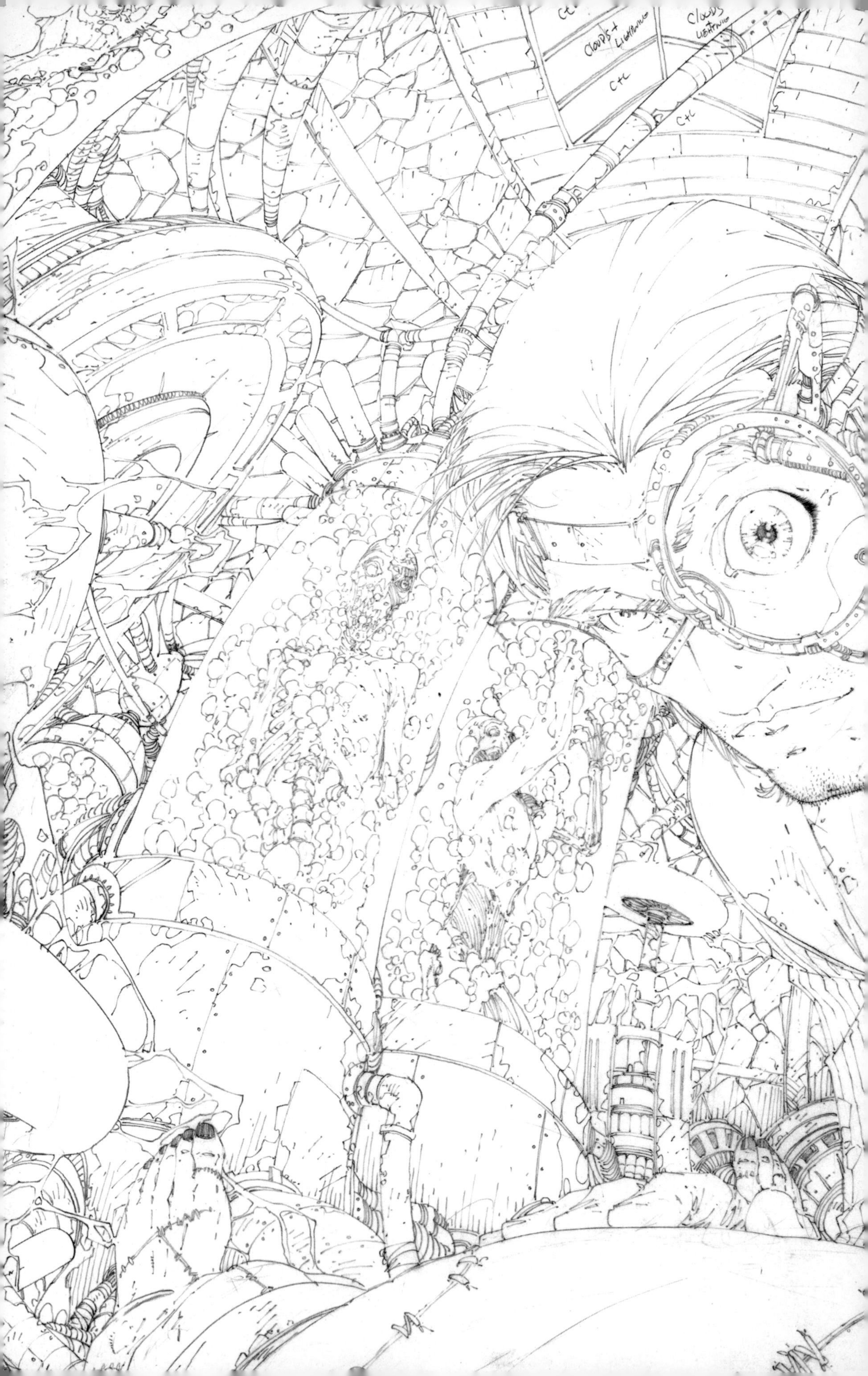
CLOUDS + LIGHTNING
CLOUDS + LIGHTNING
C+L
C+L

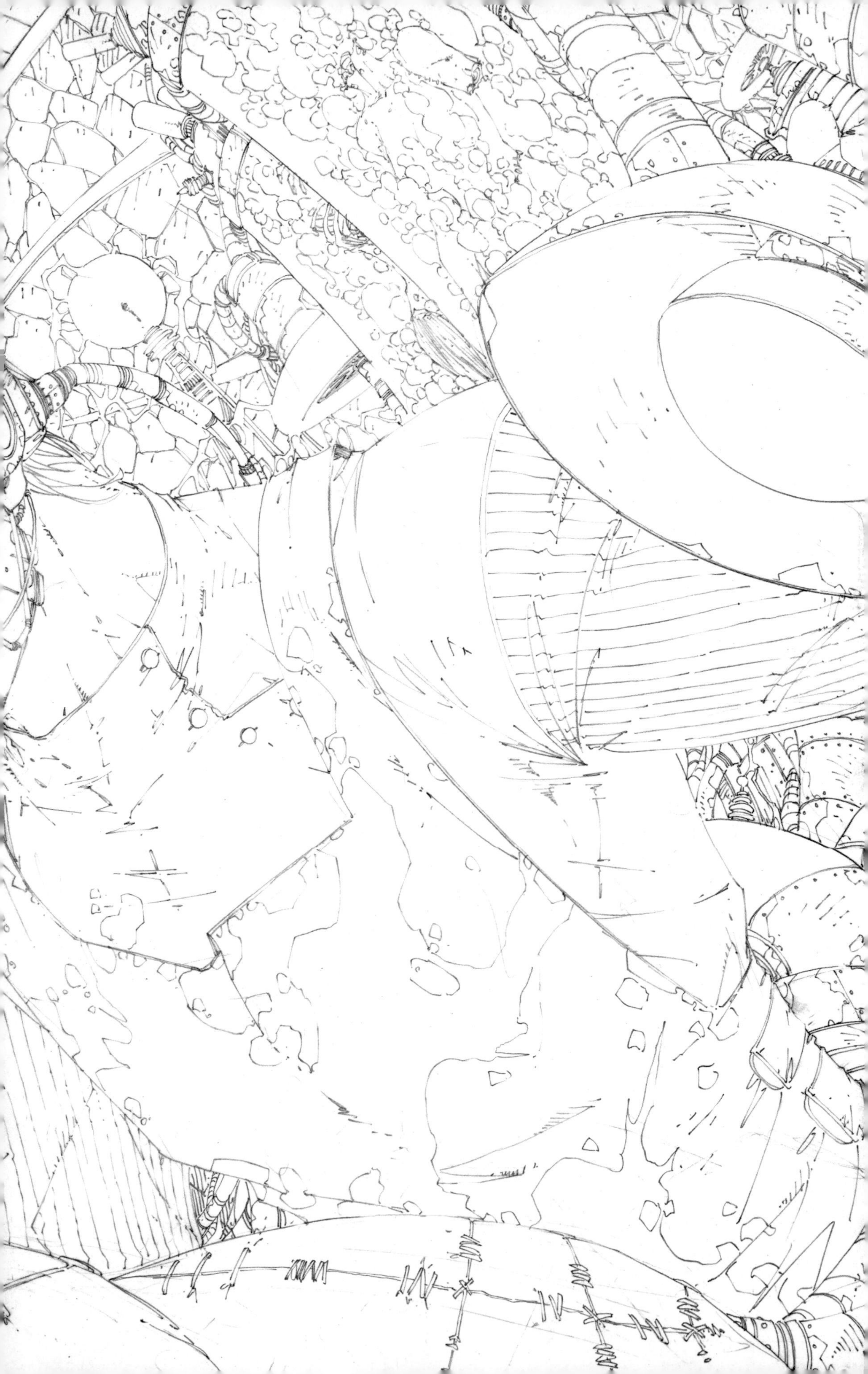

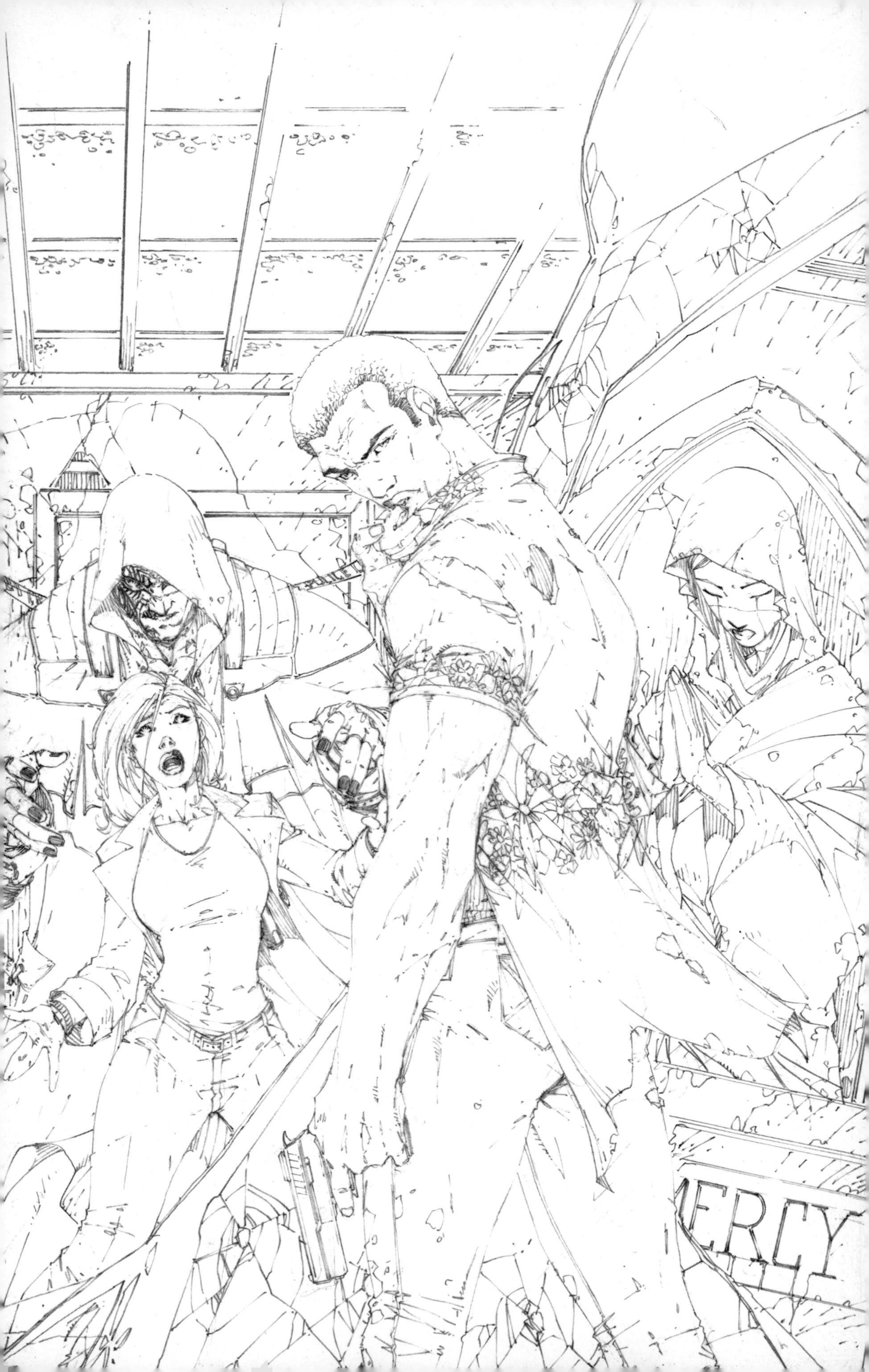
POLICE
ERCY

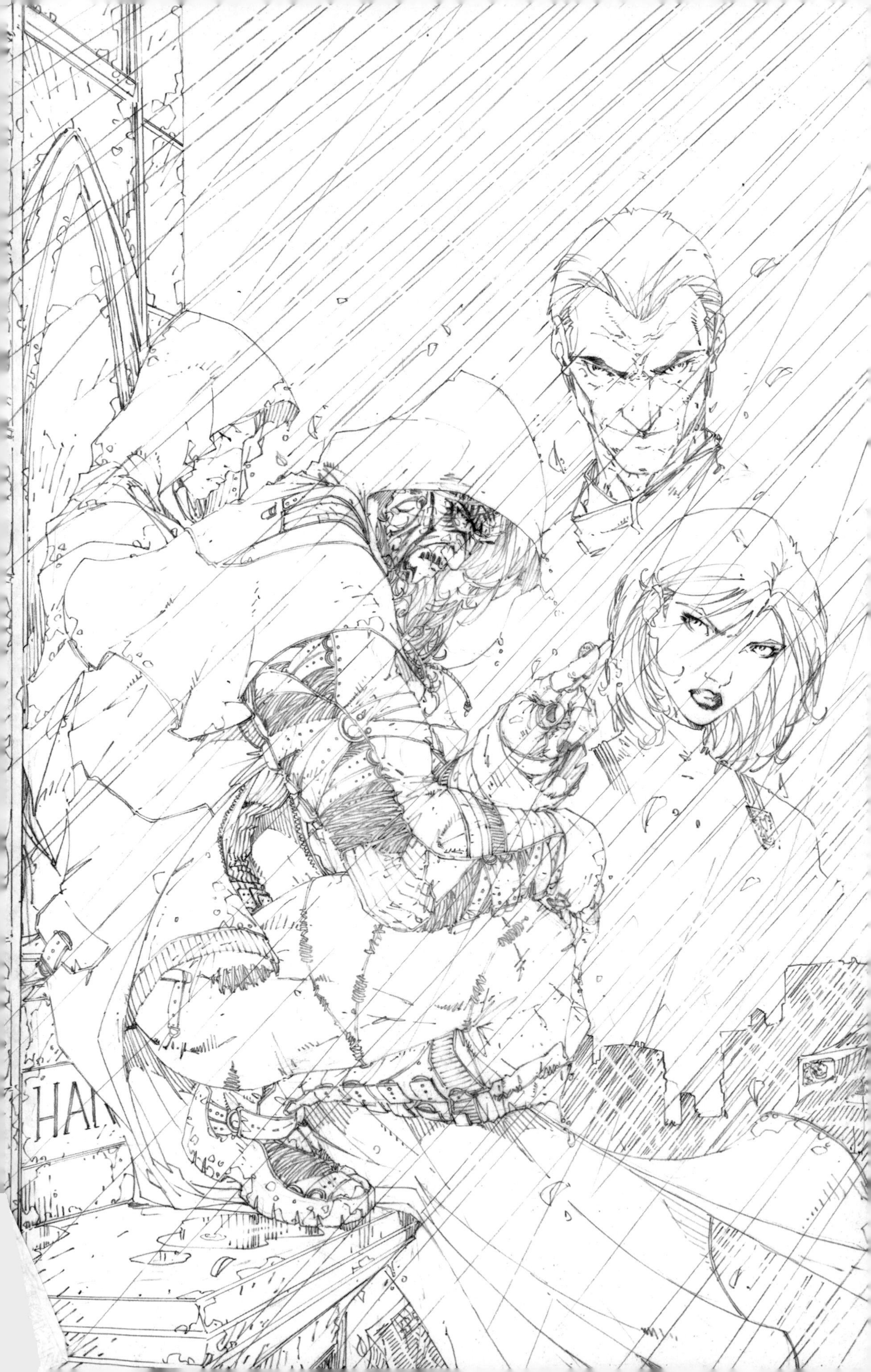
HAN

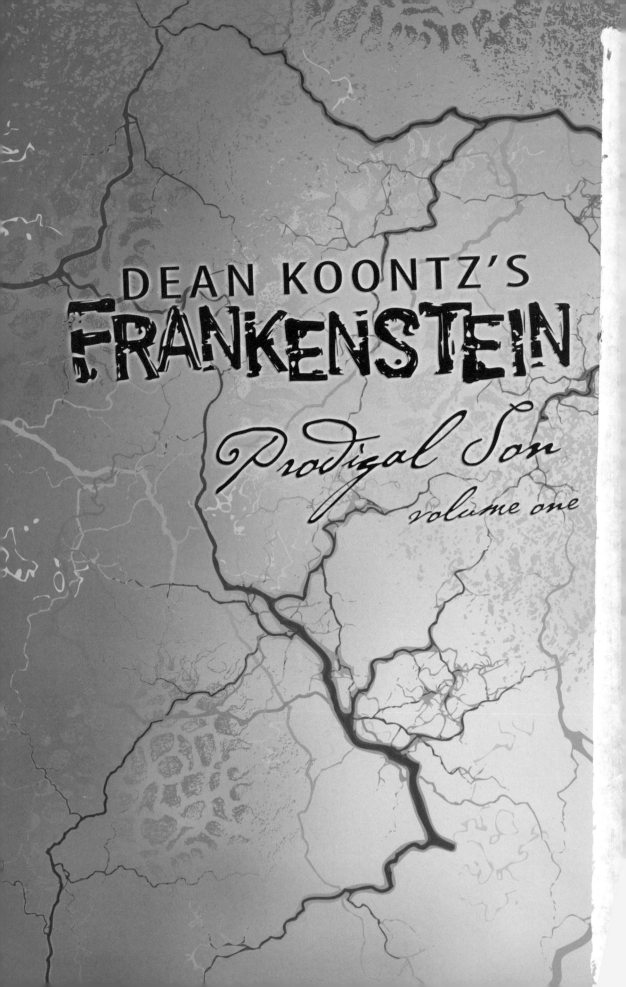

DEAN KOONTZ'S
FRANKENSTEIN

Prodigal Son

volume one